RELIGIOUS RESURGENCE

RELIGIOUS RESURGENCE

Contemporary Cases
in Islam, Christianity, and Judaism

Edited by RICHARD T. ANTOUN
and MARY ELAINE HEGLAND

SYRACUSE UNIVERSITY PRESS

The paper used in this publication meets the minimum requirements of American National Standard for Information Sciences—Permanence of Paper for Printed Library Materials, ANSI Z39.48-1984. ∞™

Library of Congress Cataloging-in-Publication Data

Religious resurgence.

    Includes bibliographies and index.
    1. Religion—History—20th century.   2. Religions—History—20th century.   I. Antoun, Richard T.
II. Hegland, Mary Elaine.
BL98.R43   1987   291   87-10225
ISBN 0-8156-2409-3 (alk. paper)

Manufactured in the United States of America

CONTENTS

PREFACE

The Iranian Revolution of 1978/1979 took the Western world by surprise, and forced the general public (as well as experts and scholars) into a reevaluation of their assumptions concerning the role of religion in the modern world. At the time of the formation of the Islamic Republic in Iran, the new interest in religion was largely limited to Islam; today, however, the thoughtful observer of current events and trends can find ample evidence to suspect a fresh resurgence of religion in other faiths as well. The main purpose of this volume is to examine the Islamic resurgence in comparative perspective. Through consideration of particular cases of resurgence in Judaism and Christianity as well as in Islam, we hope to answer the question whether similar social, economic, political, and ideological factors are involved in the resurgence of religion in various faiths and to see if similar processes and implications can be discerned.

The editors of this volume have prepared it to be useful to the student and the general reader inquiring into this intriguing current phenomenon, as well as to the specialist. Several different perspectives for viewing the resurgence are suggested, and questions are raised that the interested person can pursue further through reading, discussion, and research. The cross-religious, cross-national, and cross-disciplinary approach encourages comparison and contrast. Chapters examining the revival from international, national, and non-elite, local-level perspectives lead to a realization of the complex motives involved in joining religious movements, and of the importance of particular group affiliations.

In the first section of the volume, "Religious Resurgence: The Evidence," manifestations and characterizations of the religious resurgence are examined. How do we know that such a resurgence or revival is in fact taking place? Is there indeed a religious resurgence, or merely a modification in our perception of the role of religion in today's world? Is the phenomenon observed essentially political or economic, or is it an assertion of identity? Is the "resurgence" taking place only within certain religious groups? What are the diverse forms of the resurgence?

Throughout the section on "The Continuing Tradition: Enabling Factors for Change," we wish to emphasize the ideological, social, cultural, and political aspects of continuity in the resurgence of religion, even in the case of revolution. What are the ideological tools in the religious traditions? What modifications of interpretation and implication are being evolved? What traditional patterns of social interaction, authority, and charismatic leadership are available for the spread of religious movements? Are the political alignments organized in relation to differing interpretations of religion similar to the alignments organized earlier around other ideologies and terminologies? If so, why the change now in frameworks for conflict and competition?

Such enabling factors of change have long been present. What are the social, economic, and political factors giving impetus to religious resurgence at this point in history? The section on "Catalysts of the Current Resurgence" addresses this question. The current reassertion of religion is a highly complex phenomenon, and it would not be possible in this volume to discuss the many factors involved in each of the hundreds of examples of religious resurgence throughout the world. Nevertheless, can any general explanations be suggested? Are any similar historical, cultural, political, or demographic circumstances involved? Is resurgence partially the result of the failure of Western, secular models? Are the middle and lower classes becoming disillusioned with the ideology of nationalism and cynical about its contribution to their interests, presenting therefore a religious nationalism that more effectively symbolizes their concerns?

Religious systems of thought do not remain stagnant but are modified and changed in emphasis over time, as pointed out in the section on "Religious Resurgence and Political Systems." The ideological components of religious resurgence are often transformed ideologies—the result of religious theoreticians responding to changing historical conditions, other ideological influences, and the changing needs and ideas of adherents. The modifications in religious ideology can be studied in interaction with political processes. The Western public has, if anything, been overexposed to the political implications of the Islamic resurgence. But a resurgence in other faiths, such as Judaism and Christianity, is also taking place, in interaction with political processes. This section looks at village-level, national, and international movements of dissent by persons and groups attempting to defend economic, political, and cultural interests, and at the interrelationships between these political movements and religious ideology and ritual.

The final section, or "Overview," is a comparative treatment of ideological change in the three faiths in relation to historical events and conditions. The concluding discussion evaluates several explanatory frameworks for the resurgence, and points to some common catalysts and processes.

An effort is made in this volume to take into account the views of the participants in the resurgence. To this end, several of the authors are representatives of the three faiths considered. Others come from a religious background other than the one they are examining, and thus may be more sensitive to the meaning of religion in people's lives. Several of the chapters are based on anthropological fieldwork; the authors lived among the participants in religious resurgence, with the opportunity to observe at first hand over a long period of time the relevance of that resurgence in everyday life, the strength of commitment of adherents, and how the resurgence works out in terms of social reality. An attempt is made to view the resurgence in historical context, rather than as a development unconnected with other aspects of reality.

The chapters in this volume were originally prepared for two related conferences sponsored by the Program in Southwest Asian and North African Studies of the State University of New York at Binghamton. The first, "Conversations in the Disciplines: Islamic Resurgence in the Modern World," was held at SUNY/Binghamton on 13 and 14 March 1981. The second, "Conversations in the Disciplines: Religious Resurgence in Comparative Perspective: Selected Cases from Christianity, Islam and Judaism," took place on 27 and 28 January 1983. The authors wish to thank the State University of New York Research Foundation and the Southwest Asia and North Africa Program of the State University of New York for their financial support of these conferences and their administrative support in the editing of the ensuing volume. In addition, Mary Hegland would like to acknowledge her gratitude to the SWANA Program of SUNY/Binghamton and the Educational Foundation of the American Association of University Women for fellowship funding enabling her to work on this volume, and to Richard Antoun, Erika Friedl, and Henry Munson, Jr., for constructive comments on the introduction and conclusion. To the regret of the editors, no chapter on Liberation Theology was available for inclusion in the volume, although the conclusion briefly compares this religious movement with the liberation interpretation of Shia Islam.

All of the chapters except those by Ayoub and Dekmejian (which are theoretical and historical contributions) have been updated for this publication. In addition, several chapters have been almost entirely rewritten to better serve the needs of the intended audience. The chapters by Gaffney and Nagata reflect fresh information and insight gained in the field—in Egypt and Malaysia, respectively—at the end of the summer of 1986. In preparing conference results for publication, only those papers which fit into the cohesive framework of the book were selected, and an attempt was made to avoid duplication of material. Chapters were shortened, and detailed or complicated digressions were eliminated to facilitate ease of reading for the undergraduate and rapid grasp of main thrust for the more advanced reader. Since the chapters have been prepared with the nonspecialist as to area and language uppermost in mind, diacritical marks have not been used and foreign words are not italicized after first usage.

A major historical transformation seems to be occurring. The resurgence of religion is surely one of the symptoms or manifestations of this change, as well as one of the factors bringing about this change. Religion is an important political resource in today's world of changing balances of power, and as such is the subject of fierce struggle and debates. The editors hope that further work of a comparative and interdisciplinary nature will be conducted on the current resurgence of religion, and on how it relates to historical trends and general forces and problems. As anthropologists, the editors confess their desire that additional fieldwork utilizing the technique of participant observation be part of any future research efforts. Such fieldwork should include individuals who are *not* major political or religious figures; more light may then be shed on the surrounding circumstances of resurgence and on the attitudes, motivations, and participation of ordinary people. The religious resurgence seen from this perspective sometimes looks quite different.

Richard T. Antoun
Mary Elaine Hegland

CONTRIBUTORS

Richard T. Antoun received his B.A. in history from Williams College, his M.A. in international relations from Johns Hopkins University, and his Ph.D. in anthropology and Middle Eastern studies from Harvard University. Professor of anthropology at the State University of New York at Binghamton, he has published two books on Jordan (*Arab Village, Low-Key Politics*) as well as coedited the volume *Rural Politics and Social Change in the Middle East*. His interests include peasant societies in the Middle East, particularly Jordan, Iran, Egypt, and Lebanon; local-level politics; and comparative religion and symbolism. He is currently working on a book on the Islamic sermon and the Muslim preacher. He has just returned from five months of fieldwork in Jordan, where he studied rural social and economic change—particularly in the areas of international migration and the pursuit of higher education abroad.

Mahmoud M. Ayoub received his B.A. in philosophy from the American University of Beirut, his M.A. in religious thought from the University of Pennsylvania, and his Ph.D. in history of religion from Harvard. Research associate at the Centre for Religious Studies at the University of Toronto, Dr. Ayoub also lectures regularly at the Belamont Greek Orthodox Seminary in Koura, Lebanon, and the Centre for Islamic Studies and Muslim-Christian Relations, Selly Oak Colleges, Birmingham, England. Dr. Ayoub is active in dialogue among Muslims, Christians, and Jews, and has published many articles on Islam and Christianity. He is presently engaged in work for a projected ten volumes on *The Qur'an and its Interpreters,* the first of which has already been published. Dr. Ayoub is also completing a book on *Ja'far al-Sadiq, His Life and Time,* and another entitled *Towards an Islamic Christology: Images of Jesus in Islam.*

Eric Davis began his study of the Middle East in the Southwest Asia/North Africa Studies Program at the State University of New York at Binghamton, before going on to earn M.A. and Ph.D. degrees in political science at the University of Chicago. Dr. Davis, an associate professor at Rutgers University, has published works on economic nationalism, the political economy of oil, and religious radicalism in the Middle East. His study, *Challenging Colonialism: Bank Misr and Egyptian Industrialization, 1920–1941* (Princeton University Press, 1983), was recently translated into Arabic by the Institute of Arab Research (Beirut, 1985). He is currently engaged in a study of state formation, oil wealth, and the Iraqi working class from 1920–80, as well as coediting a volume of essays on the impact of oil wealth on state formation and social change in the modern Middle East.

R. Hrair Dekmejian is professor of political science and chairman of the department of political science at the University of Southern California. He holds a doctorate from Columbia University and is the author of many articles and three books on the Middle East: *Egypt under Nasser* (1971), *Patterns of Political Leadership* (1975), and *Islam in Revolution* (1985). His current research interests include comparative studies of leadership in messianic movements, the impact of multinational companies on third world societies, and politics in the Gulf countries.

Patrick D. Gaffney studied literature and philosophy at Notre Dame, going on to complete a professional degree in theology at the University of Utrecht in Holland. At the University of Chicago, he specialized in the culture and society of the Middle East, receiving his M.A. and Ph.D. from that institution's department of anthropology. Assistant professor in the department of anthropology at the University of Notre Dame, Dr. Gaffney has translated two books from Dutch to English as well as published several articles. He recently conducted a field study on local Islamic associations in Egypt, concentrating on the role of ritual specialists, such as preachers and other religious authorities. At present, Dr. Gaffney is working on a larger study of the religious and political dimensions of Islamic ritual, rhetoric, and social organizations. His interests include the modern history and ideological developments of the Islamic world, as well as the relationship of official institutions such as religious bureaucracies and training facilities to various types of mosques and Muslim voluntary societies.

Mary Elaine Hegland received her B.A. in sociology and psychology from Augustana College in South Dakota, M.A. in anthropology from New York University, and her Ph.D. in anthropology from SUNY/Binghamton. Her field research in an Iranian village focused on transformations in religious ideology and the role of ritual in political life in interaction with changing economic organization and political centralization throughout the last several decades. Dr. Hegland has published articles on the role of women in religion and in the Iranian revolution and on transformations in religious ideology and ritual related to the Iranian revolution. She is presently teaching anthropology at Franklin and Marshall College.

Judith Nagata earned her B.A. Hons at the University of London and her M.A. and Ph.D. in anthropology at the University of Illinois. She has done fieldwork, mainly related to ethnicity and religion, in Latin America, in Southeast Asia, and in North America among Amish Mennonites in the rural United States and Greek immigrants in urban Canada. Editor of *Pluralism in Malaysia: Myth or Reality* (1975), Dr. Nagata has also published extensively in academic journals and is the author of two books on Malaysia: *Malaysian Mosaic: Perspectives from a Poly-Ethnic Society* (1979) and *The Reflowering of Malaysia Islam: Modern Religious Radicals and Their Roots* (1984). Dr. Nagata is professor of anthropology at York University, Toronto. She is currently engaged in a project with South East Asian immigrants in Toronto assessing the role of religious and ritual communities versus ethnic associations in the adaptation process.

David J. Schnall is professor in the faculty of business and public administration of Long Island University and at the Wurzweiler School of Social Work of Yeshiva University. He holds a Ph.D. in political science from Fordham University, and has taught at Fordham and at the City University of New York. Dr. Schnall is the author of four books and more than forty articles, reviews, and essays on various aspects of American public policy and Middle East affairs. *Beyond the Green Line: Israeli Settlements West of the Jordan* (1984), Dr. Schnall's latest book, focuses on the people—Jews and Arabs—in conflict over West Bank settlement. His volume, *The Jewish Agenda,* will appear in early 1987.

Ninian Smart took a degree in classics and philosophy at Oxford University, going on to graduate work in philosophy of religion and comparative religion. Professor of religious studies at the University of California at Santa Barbara, Dr. Smart still spends some time each year at Lancaster University, where he founded England's first department of religious studies. Among Dr. Smart's significant books are *Reasons and Faiths, The Religious Experience of Mankind, The Science of Religion and the Sociology of Knowledge, Doctrine and Argument in Indian Philosophy,* and *Worldviews: Cross-cultural Explorations of Human Beliefs.* With Peter H. Merkl, Dr. Smart edited *Religion and Politics in the Modern World* (1983). He has published in the fields of philosophy of religion, history of religions, and politics and religion, and is currently working on a reappraisal of the relationship between South Asian religions and nationalism.

John O. Voll is professor of history at the University of New Hampshire, where he teaches Middle Eastern and world history. Receiving his Ph.D. degree from Harvard University in history and Middle Eastern studies, Dr. Voll has written extensively on modern Islamic history, with special attention to the history of the modern Sudan and the development of fundamentalism in the Islamic world in general. Author of *Islam: Continuity and Change in the Modern World, Historical Dictionary of the Sudan,* and numerous articles, Dr. Voll is currently working on a study of the development of Islamic revivalism in the eighteenth century.

Robert Wuthnow is professor of sociology at Princeton University. A specialist on religion in the United States, Dr. Wuthnow is the author of *The Consciousness Reformation* and *Experimentation in American Religion,* coauthor of *Adolescent Prejudice* and *Cultural Analysis,* and editor of *The Religious Dimension* and *The New Christian Right.* His most recent book, *Meaning and Moral Order: Explorations in Cultural Analysis,* will be available in 1987. Dr. Wuthnow is currently writing a book on American religion since World War II.

RELIGIOUS RESURGENCE

Introduction

MARY ELAINE HEGLAND

For many Westerners, the Iranian revolution of 1978–79 brought sudden realization of the on-going importance of religion in today's world. Most people had assumed secularization to be the result of modernization, Western influence, industrialization, and education. As Westerners saw Iran making great strides in development and modernization, they assumed that Iranians would become increasingly secular in outlook and would begin to restrict any remaining religious beliefs to their personal lives. Indeed, the religious establishments in Iran and other Islamic countries, as well as religious activities and religious terminologies generally, had been less prominent in preceding years; Islam was not a focus of interest for the media or for researchers. Even close observers of Iran, then, were not prepared for a revolution organized in large part by religious figures and apparently prompted, for most Iranians, by religious motivation.

The Iranian revolution is now several years old, and—after the initial shock—many Americans have drastically adjusted their views of reality. The consensus is that Islam does remain as a force in the temporal world. Islam is now a focus of almost obsessive interest on the part of both experts and scholars and the general public.[1] A resurgence of Islamic activity has been noted not only in Iran but also in Egypt, Pakistan, Syria, Algeria, Turkey, Saudi Arabia, Kuwait, Iraq, and Lebanon, among the Palestianians, in various African countries, in Malaysia and Indonesia—that is, in virtually all states with a sizable Muslim population, and even in the Soviet Union and the United States.

Somewhat more reluctantly, a resurgence in religious activity and a new prominence of religious beliefs and religious figures has been recognized in the West as well. In addition to the fundamentalist activity and pronouncements of the National Conference of Catholic Bishops in the United States and the formation of new religious groups (many of them influenced by Eastern religions), a resurgence in religion has been apparent in Central America, where priests have become government officials (Nicaragua) and where liberation theology provides the most effective ideological weapon against repres-

1

sive regimes. Indications of an increasing allegiance to Christianity and respect for religious figures and beliefs are also to be seen in Poland, in many African countries, and elsewhere—even in China.

Although Israelis maintain an adherence to Zionism—a secular ideology rooted in Jewish messianism—many, if not most, Jews, particularly among the Ashkenazim, who came from Europe, have become largely secularized with respect to beliefs about the afterworld. A sizable group of Jews are now organizing their worldly activities according to religious beliefs, while others are responding more actively to religious symbols and groups. In third world countries, a pattern of increased loyalty to religion and to fellow believers is visible and receiving the attention of media and scholars. An example is the determination of Indian Sikhs to protect both their interests and their temples, with the resulting Sikh-Hindu conflict. The involvement of religious figures, groups, and ideology has been noted as a factor in the recent change of governments in Haiti and the Philippines, and in the South African conflict.

We are now faced with the challenge of explaining this apparent aberration —an increase in religiosity—given the assumption that modernization brings secularization in its wake. In grappling for an explanation, most analysts appear to have been influenced by the dominant Western ideology concerning social movements. This ideology views stability and equilibrium as the normal state for a society. "Radical political, social, or religious movements are usually seen as results of or reactions to fundamental social disruption and the extreme personal disorientation associated with radical change."[2] Such movements are thought to be the result of deprivation, social disorganization, or psychological maladjustment.[3] Such an approach implies pathology and regression in religious movements, such as those seen in recent years in the Middle East, and a lack of personal resources and adaptive skills on the part of participants. This approach to religious movements has been used to explain the resurgence of Islam. Resurgence is a response to dislocation, anomie, and confusion which is set off in turn by major changes, such as the move of large numbers of people from rural to urban settings; the shock of Western contact for traditional people; and the distress of defeat by Western economic, political, military, and cultural forces.

Because they can't cope with the new and frightening requirements of modernization, the threats to their interests and traditional ways of life, and the breakdown of traditional social structure (this explanation continues), Muslims have sought comfort and protection through a defensive return to their religious practices and beliefs, or even through aggressively attacking intruders or those who threaten their old way of life, under the banner of Islam.[4] In keeping with this theoretical approach, commonly found in explanations offered for the resurgence of interest in religion, are such words and phrases as "alienation," "anomie," "crisis," "dislocation," "deprivation," "impersonal urban settings," "tension," "disorientation," "breakdown," "defeat," "confusion," "uprootedness," "shock," "uncertainty," "confusion," "suffering," and "disaffection"—in the face of all of which Islam offers "solace, safety, and security."

We wish to suggest an alternative to the approach that movements are a defensive and nonconstructive reaction to drastic change. Movements might better be seen as both "cause and effect of change," and as adaptive mechanisms through which "change is shaped and directed" (Gerlach and Hine, p. xiv). With this interpretation, movements can be viewed as creative, innovative, and active responses to change and to the perceived needs of society, groups, and individuals. Movement participants seek not only to respond to change but also to bring about change through their own activity—to form a society better able to provide for human needs as well as address their own interests. Movement leaders and participants are seen, not as refugees retreating from frightening new circumstances, but as courageous, confident, and able people who actively seek to influence their lives and social environment according to their own ideals and aims, their conduct motivated by hope, optimism, and determination rather than by despair and defeat.

A goal of the editors of this volume is to question which of these interpretations might be more productive and more accurate, and provide the more complete explanation for the resurgence of religion in today's world. By examining cases of the apparent resurgence of Christianity and Judaism as well as Islam, we wish to question whether any one approach is applicable to the resurgence in all three faiths. Another major aim is to consider if similar circumstances are involved or if any similar processes can be ascertained in the resurgence of the three faiths. Why is a religious resurgence, visible virtually worldwide, taking place at this particular point in history? The articles in the first section, "Religious Resurgence: the Evidence," evaluate the evidence for religious resurgence and the potential of a religious resurgence to bring about political and social change.

The Current Religious Resurgence: A Reality?

After examining several indices of American religious trends, such as sales of religious books, number of nonprofit religious associations, church membership, religious contributions, number of clergy, number of degrees granted in religion or theology, and personal religious involvement, sociologist Robert Wuthnow concludes that little evidence can be found to substantiate claims for a resurgence of Christianity in general in the United States. Wuthnow did find evidence of growth in fundamentalist or evangelical groups, in terms of membership, number of educational institutions, and such resources as donations and purchase of television time. Evangelicals are more likely to be politically active compared with the general population, and more often than not they are right of center politically. Wuthnow compares the influence of fundamentalists with that of other religiously inspired groups and nonreligious political interest groups, and finds little reason for concern about "a fundamentalist, totalitarian monolith seizing power in the U.S."

The fieldwork of Patrick Gaffney, an anthropologist, in Minya, Egypt, shows us the actual diversity of religious activity contained under the rubric of "religious revival." One shaykh of a local mosque magnified the role of ritual and rhetoric in his use of Islam to condemn actions and policies of his own and other governments, and in his efforts to encourage dissent. The shaykh of another mosque, however, expended most of his energy in organizing and administering the social services offered by his mosque and in cooperating with government officials to procure resources and services through the mosque. Gaffney finds the activity of the latter shaykh to be more effective in bringing about change. He concludes that the emotions aroused by the rituals and rhetoric of the first shaykh, if not urging adherents into foolhardy efforts tending toward revolution, end only in the aimless dissipation of energy and the isolation of those followers who are intent on exploiting the respect accorded to religion in order to further their own political claims.

The Continuing Tradition: Enabling Factors for Change

Certain aspects of religious heritage and of traditional social structure have lent themselves to the movements of religious resurgence in recent years. Proponents of change, leaders of movements, even revolutionaries do not generally propose a society completely divorced from past history and the accumulation of ideas. Rather, some aspects of existing theology, mythology, or ideology are brought forward to rationalize the desired changes. The use of familiar aspects of a culture provides a commonly understood terminology and has the advantage of appealing to formerly inculcated emotions and attitudes. Movement leaders or ideologues will generally either change the emphasis in the traditional ideologies or modify them to make them more appropriate to the new set of circumstances.[5]

Mahmoud Ayoub traces the history of the concept of martyrdom in Christianity and Islam, finding several points of comparison. Early Christians looked upon martyrdom as imitating Christ's witnessing and stoic suffering, in the hope of receiving remission of their sins and attaining salvation. Muslims considered martyrdom the act of striving against evil, not only on the battlefield but in one's self and society, although true martyrs were those who had been killed "in the way of God." The blood of martyrs of both faiths was believed to wash away their sins and prepare them for entry into paradise. For Shia Muslims, martyrdom and suffering take a central position in their beliefs, as they contemplate the self-sacrifice of Husain, who—through his death at Kerbala—provided a source of redemption and healing. Although arguing that stoic suffering is characteristic of the Christian ideal of martyrdom and death while activist striving in the way of God and against evil characterizes the Muslim ideal of martyrdom, Ayoub does perceive some variation in these patterns. He notes the emphasis on imitating the suffering of Husain during Moharram by Shia Muslims, and the submissive and silent deaths of some Muslim martyrs. Finally, Ayoub points to the development of liberation theology in Christianity, which advocates political activism in the face of poverty and injustice, as an indication of greater convergence between the two ideals of martyrdom.

R. Hrair Dekmejian's development of an analytical framework to examine the role of charismatic leadership in the cases of the Mahdi (Muhammad Ahmad) and the Messiah (Shabbatai Sevi) reminds us of the centrality of leaders in resurgence movements. "In the absence of a leader with charismatic potential," Dekmejian argues, "the process of charismatic development cannot be initiated regardless of the intensity of crisis"; both "a leader with charismatic potential" and "circumstances of turmoil" are necessary for the "development of charisma and a charismatic movement." In Dekmejian's view, due to the "overwhelming centrality of leadership, religious and ideological movements may be fruitfully studied as extensions of the leader's personality as it reacts with the social milieu of his time."

Dekmejian's chapter provides a history of the concept of charisma, and synthesizes the psychological approach of Erik Erikson and the sociological approach of Max Weber to provide a comprehensive analytical framework that takes into account the influence of social, economic, cultural, and political as well as psychological factors. Dekmejian's chapter does much to emphasize the interaction between person and history in charismatic movements and is a corrective against neglect of either social forces or leaders in such movements.

Religious ideology, as in the concept of martyrdom, and ritual have been enabling factors of change provided by the continuing tradition in countries experiencing religious resurgence. Cultural tradition lends itself to the development of charismatic leaders, and charismatic leaders in turn form part of religious traditions. As Nagata's article demonstrates, aspects of traditional social structure and authority systems can also provide means by which change—in this case, the Islamic resurgence—is brought about. In her research in Malaysia, Judith Nagata found three factors attracting recruits to religious resurgence: the appropriateness of the content of the *dakwah* ("renewed commitment to the faith") movement to the contemporary life of Malaysian Muslims; the traditional forms of personal relations; and social pressure. The indigenous Malays were attempting to mobilize in order to gain an economic advantage previously held in the hands of the Chinese and Indian traders and businessmen. The various branches of the Islamic movement were welcome means of organizing to this end and asserting Malay identity. The *dakwah* movement also appealed to those Malays wishing to assert a national identity and culture against the "intellectual and cultural assault of the West." In addition to the appeal of the "message," however, the medium, or the social matrix, was important in the transmission of *dakwah* ideas. Horizontal networks and small cliques of "equal-status, same-generation peers," a traditionally prevalent form of social interaction in Malay society, provided the means both to convey information about the *dakwah* movement and to pressure for increased commitment to the movement. Malay students who traveled abroad for education brought back ideas about resurgent Islam that were then radiated through networks of peers. Face-to-face social groups, especially the tight *dakwah* groups formed on campuses, were effective in maintaining conformity to *dakwah* requirements. The traditional respect for the teacher, or *guru,* in Malaysian society ensured that the message spread by *dakwah* members—especially those returning with a much-admired western education—would be well received by their subordinates in the areas of civil service, the military, and law enforcement (or by villagers in their areas of administration). Religious resurgence in Malaysia, as elsewhere, is being propagated mainly by small, intimate, face-to-face groups, and not by appeals using the mass media (newspapers, radio, television), as is often suggested.

Catalysts of Resurgence

The articles in the second section of this volume present aspects of the continuing tradition, which in a transformed mode lend themselves to the dissemination of an ideology of religious resurgence and to the encouragement of commitment to various religious movements. Yet why did these specific transformations take place at the present time? And why did believers respond to the call to intensify their religious commitment at this point in history? The articles in the third section place religious resurgence in a historical, political, and economic context to address the question of why religious resurgence is taking place during the last quarter of the twentieth century. The articles suggest that the resurgence is due in large part to the response to changes in the balance of power, both among nations and, within nations, among groups and classes. All of these articles give some reason to believe that it is "enabled" people, rather than "deprived" persons suffering from anomie due to drastic social dislocation, who have joined religious movements.

John Voll places the contemporary resurgence of Islam in a historical perspective of the changing relationship between western and Muslim societies. In the eyes of many present-day Muslims, the West has failed not only spiritually but materially. Growing disillusionment with the western ideologies of capitalism and communism has been followed by perception of failure in the areas of military, political, and economic systems, and finally material and economic advancement and power. One of the mainstays of westernization, the idea of "development," has also met with growing cynicism as to its actual effects upon society. This concept of the "failure of the West" has freed Muslims from the need to address the modern West and allowed them to enter into a dialogue with other Muslims[6] based more exclusively on the Islamic tradition. It has freed Muslims from the western beliefs that secularism is a prerequisite of modernization and that modernity is necessarily western, thereby strengthening the legitimacy and appeal of a fundamentalist Islam that has remained relatively untainted of the charge of catering to western modernity.

The West is perceived as failing, not only in Muslim societies, but elsewhere as well. The perceived declining power of the West and its ideologies has opened the way for the rise of alternative ideologies promoted by peoples gaining in terms of relative power and influence. The political scientist, Eric Davis, points to the decline of secular, populist nationalism during the late 1970s and the rise of radical interpretations of religion, not only in the Middle East but in other third world sectors as well, suggesting a common reaction to economic factors and incorporation into the world market. Fluctuations in that world market would then be felt most severely by the lower and middle classes. Davis recognizes the greater ability of the middle classes to express discontent, given their education, urban concentration, and access to instrumental institutions. In Egypt, he observes rural, lower middle class migrants to the urban areas gaining influence not only by sheer force of numbers but through education, challenging their exclusion by the ruling elite and their ideologies though religious nationalist organizations. Likewise, large numbers of Jews from Arab countries, also upwardly mobile, and other middle class and lower middle class Israelis chose to express their hostility to the dominant Ashkenazis through participation in religious nationalist organizations. In both Egypt and Israel, then, the strength of religious nationalist organizations is partially a result of the failure of the elite to take account of the growing strength of new classes and groups in the political process, as well as from failures and weaknesses of competing, previously dominant ideologies. The middle and lower middle classes in both countries, according to Davis, are becoming increasingly cynical about the intentions of elites who tout the ideology of secular nationalism. Hoping to receive better consideration elsewhere, the groups are turning rather to the ideology of religious nationalism.

Both articles, then, suggest a religious resurgence on the part of those who are *gaining* in relative power and influence. The articles emphasize the change in relations between Muslim countries and the West in explaining the Islamic resurgence, and stress the need for further discussion of internal structural changes and the relative size and influence of social class groupings. Many indicators suggest that demographic changes, migration, new educational and work opportunities, exposure to urban environments and contacts, and access to new ideologies and information have empowered groups with new resources, enabling them to join movements organized around religious themes. Fundamentalists in the United States shared such new opportunities; many, according to Wuthnow's study, were recent migrants to northern urban areas from the southern Bible belt who were enjoying new educational and material advantages.

Implications for Ideology and Political Systems

In a number of situations in today's world, the influence of religion on the political process is becoming more apparent. Religious symbols can become "vehicles of social protest" when no alternatives are permitted, for they can disguise a political message.[7] Governments willing to repress other forms of organization are often reluctant to interfere with or prohibit "religious" activities—for example, the Friday congregational prayers and mass meetings at cemeteries in Iran in 1978–79 to mourn—and protest—the killing of "martyrs."

Political appeals in the form of transformed religious ideologies can unite adherents from a wide spectrum of political and religious views and can pull together into one effort a variety of aims. Religious symbols can provide "solidarity without consensus."[8] For example, even before the Iranian Revolution, Mangol Bayat pointed out that Ali Shariati could "appeal to two different kinds of follower: those whose impulse is primarily religious and who believe that they should react against the irreligious materialistic tendencies that are overcoming society; and those who are politically-minded and want to undertake a revolution."[9]

Schnall's article describes the interaction between religious ideology and political process and structure. More specifically, he provides an example of a religious movement developing an appeal to both religious and secular Israelis. Schnall traces the development and ideology of the Israeli Gush Emunim movement, from its inception as a dissident group in 1974, critical of the Labor government for its lack of commitment to settlement, to a legitimate and respected force in Israeli politics with a significant impact on Zionist ideology and government policy. In contrast to radical Islam and Catholic liberation theology, Schnall argues, Gush Emunim does not disagree with the basic goals of Zionism or of the Israeli government; rather, it is dissatisfied with the slow pace of the process of settlement in the occupied territories, and with the level of funding and resources appropriated to this effort. Gush Emunim is similar to the other two religious movements—transformed Shiism and liberation theology—in that it is rooted in religious tradition and at the same time action-oriented, with redemption based on activity in this world—in the case of the Gush Emunim, through settling land. The movement has served to combine religious aims with this-worldly concerns of settlement and military strategy.

In contrast to the other two religious movements, Gush Emunim does not emphasize theology and does not center on a messiah who might serve as a model for religious behavior within the political system; instead, it stresses political activity. The main thrust of the movement is Jewish nationalism, and its main policy emphasis focuses on accruing land for the nation state, to which end members work with secularists. The Gush have been successful in attracting both new immigrants, especially Americans, and funding for settlements. To secular Jews, the Gush presented West Bank settlements as an opportunity for an improved quality of life. Due to Gush instigation, the Begin government ultimately subsidized settlement programs, giving thousands of Israelis the option of cheap, relatively spacious housing.[10] The Gush have been successful in that they are accepted in government posts and their programs have now been taken over and funded by the state,[11] probably because their functions are highly valued (if politically sensitive). Whereas the advocates of liberation theology and transformed Shiism aim at bringing about a complete political and social transformation, the Gush Emunim—and American fundamentalists—accept the legitimacy of existing governments, seeking only to pressure those governments into implementing their ideals and goals through government policy. When the government does not implement their goals, Schnall notes, the Gush are willing to engage in acts of civil disobedience.

In the first section of her chapter, based on fieldwork in Iran during the revolutionary period, Hegland contends that, at least for villagers residing in the research site, the "Islamic Revolution" was related to political struggle against the central government and its village representatives. Any intensification in religious activity, sentiment, or terminology was related to the escalation of political resistance. Shia Islam provided the idiom and symbolic complex used in expressing, organizing, and promoting the political struggle against the shah and his regime, policies, and representatives at the local level. At the same time, as discussed in the second section of the essay, from their Shiite beliefs Iranians found the confidence and self-identity to resist the political influence of the United States with its support for the Pahlavi regime. At several different levels, then, Shiite Islam became the banner under which political underdogs struggled against the politically powerful, in an attempt to both gain freedom from political repression and serve their own political and economic interests.

Overview

In his chapter on "Three Forms of Religious Convergence," Ninian Smart examines fundamentalism in the Muslim, Christian, and Jewish faiths. We should not sharply differentiate between religion and secular ideologies, Smart advises, but rather aim to analyze worldviews that "are often a syncretic blend of themes drawn both from traditional religion and modern 'secular' sources." In the case of present-day fundamentalism, Smart argues, in none of these three cases is the worldview a movement backwards to earlier traditions; rather, all three forms of fundamentalism represent a merging of a religious worldview with the modern concept of nationalism. All three forms of fundamentalism, Smart cautions, are largely concerned with matters of identity and pride, and as such are more likely to lead to strife than to dialogue.

Drawing on the contributions to this volume as well as other materials, the concluding chapter discusses several of the issues raised in this introduction. Questions addressed include the following: Are religious movements defensive reactions to dislocation or attempts at influencing the course of change? Do they signal the reemergence of traditional or conservative forces or the emergence of newly developing social forces? Can any similar conditions or processes be seen behind the various movements of religious resurgence? What is the connection between religious resurgence and politics? How might the current religious resurgence fit into long-term historical trends?

Notes

1. Among the recent sources on Islam are the following: Said Amir Arjomand, ed., *From Nationalism to Revolutionary Islam* (Albany: State University of New York Press, 1984); Juan R. Cole and Nikki R. Keddie, eds., *Shi'ism and Social Protest* (New Haven and London: Yale University Press, 1986); John J. Donohue and John L. Esposito, eds., *Islam in Transition; Muslim Perspectives* (New York, Oxford: Oxford University Press, 1982); John L. Esposito, ed., *Voices of Resurgent Islam* (New York, Oxford: Oxford University Press, 1983); John L. Esposito, *Islam and Politics* (Syracuse: Syracuse University Press, 1984); Yvonne Yazbeck Haddad, *Contemporary Islam and the Challenge of History* (Albany: State University of New York Press, 1982); Nikki R. Keddie, *Religion and Politics in Iran: Shi'ism from Quietism to Revolution* (New Haven and London: Yale University Press, 1983); Edward Mortimer, *Faith and Power: The Politics of Islam* (New York: Random House, 1982); and John O. Voll, *Islam, Continuity and Change in the Modern World* (Boulder, Colo.: Westview Press, 1982).

2. Luther P. Gerlach and Virginia H. Hine, *People, Power, Change: Movements of Social Transformation* (Indianapolis: Bobbs-Merrill, 1979), p. xiii.

3. See David Aberle, "A Note on Relative Deprivation Theory as Applied to Millenarian and Other Cult Movements," in William A. Lessa and Evon Z. Vogt, eds., *Reader in Comparative Religion* (New York: Harper and Row, 1965), pp. 537–40.

4. There are, of course, even among non-Muslim westerners exceptions to this view of the pathology of adherence to belief in Islam. Alan Taylor comments on the Middle Eastern masses "who are deeply moved by Islamic symbolism and by the sense of hope and encouragement it gives them." Alan R. Taylor, "The Political Psychology of Islamic Resurgence in the Middle East," *American Arab Affairs* 4 (Spring 1983): 120–31. Likewise, Robert Dillon notes that "the Iranian religious heritage . . . provided resources to rekindle Iranian courage, sincerity, and brotherhood where despotism had previously compelled the protective adoption of caution, individualism, and dissimulation," although cautioning that "it has also raised the spectre of religious intolerance" (Robert Dillon, "Laying Bare the Background," *MERIP Reports* no. 88 [June 1980]: 27–28).

5. As Abner Cohen points out, "Symbols are continually interpreted and reinterpreted. . . . In the new situation the old symbolic forms may perform new functions. . . . Old symbols are rearranged to serve new purposes under new political conditions." Abner Cohen, *Two-Dimensional Man: An Essay on the Anthropology of Power and Symbolism in Complex Society* (Berkeley: University of California Press, 1976), pp. 37, 39.

6. Harvey Cox also notes a change in audience for some Christian theologians: "The new generation of postmodern theologians, many of them Latin American, African, and Asian, refused to agree that their labors should be addressed primarily to the 'cultured despisers' of religion. Instead, they began to forge a theology in conversation with the disinherited and the culturally dominated sectors of the society." Harvey Cox, *Religion in the Secular City: Toward a Postmodern Theology* (New York: Simon and Schuster, 1984), p. 179.

7. Gustav Thaiss, "Religious Symbolism and Social Change: The Drama of Husein" (Ph.D. diss., Washington University, 1973), p. 442.

8. David I. Kertzer, "The Role of Ritual in Political Change," in Myron J. Aronoff, ed., *Political Anthropology, Volume II: Culture and Political Change* (New Brunswick, N.J.: Transaction Books, 1983), p. 63.

9. Mangol Bayat-Philipp, "Shi'ism in Contemporary Iranian Politics: The Case of Ali Shari'ati," in Elie Kedourie and Sylvia G. Haim, eds., *Towards a Modern Iran: Studies in Thought, Politics and Society* (London: Frank Cass, 1980), p. 166.

10. For further discussion of the advantages of West Bank housing for Israelis, see Peter Demant, "Israeli Settlement Policy Today," *MERIP Reports* 13, no. 116 (July–August 1983).

11. See Adit Zertal, "Faith and Financing," in "The Shahak Papers," trans. Israel Shahak repr. from *Ha aretz* (exerpts), *MERIP Reports* no. 103 (February 1982): 20, 21.

I

RELIGIOUS RESURGENCE

The Evidence

I

Indices of Religious Resurgence
in the United States

ROBERT WUTHNOW

The question of religious resurgence in the American context arises most directly from discussions of contemporary politics in which a religiously monolithic, archconservative mass movement is assumed to have arisen during the latter half of the 1970s, forging an alliance with secular, ultraright politicians to usher in a new era of Republican hegemony in the federal government and establish a strong organizational base from which to launch an attack on civil liberties, freedom of thought, and cultural pluralism. This view, as advanced in the popular press and by alarmed interests on the political left, is easily recognized as a caricature of more complex events. However, social scientists and others in the intellectual community have been sufficiently distressed by the spectre of the reassertion of unwelcome values to initiate research and debate on a wide variety of fronts in order to ascertain how well organized the new political currents may be and what they may portend for the future. The character of current trends in American religion has come under scrutiny, since religious leaders have played a highly visible role in recent political forays. At a less proximate distance, the question of religious resurgence also arises from long-standing orientations within the social sciences, particularly the sociology of religion.

These orientations posit secularization as a prevailing and increasingly prominent trend in the cultures of modern societies, among which the United States is assumed to be a leading example. Should there in fact be a serious episode of religious resurgence in the making, the problem which inevitably arises from the standpoint of this orientation is how to reconcile the persistence, even growth, of traditional religion with the obvious fact of an otherwise highly modernized society. Whether the current phenomenon represents a fundamental contradiction to assumptions of secularization, whether it is short-lived and explainable within the constraints of secularization theory, or whether it is simply an artifact of the popular press, having little basis in fact, are questions that prompt consideration of the nature and extent of religious resurgence. Finally, reflection on the religious characteristics of the

American people has been prompted by comparative considerations arising from the apparent resurgence of religious forces as significant political factors in many parts of the world—the Middle East, Iran, India, Vietnam, Indonesia, Central America, and North Ireland, to name a few. On purely intellectual terms, the nearly simultaneous occurrence of these events on a wide scale invites systematic comparative analysis, including consideration of those events closest at hand. On a more substantive, practical level, these events raise questions about the structuring of international political arrangements, cultural alliances, and economic stability, in relation to which the religious posture of the United States, as well as those of other countries, becomes a factor of clear importance.

Having established the value of clarifying the existence, nature, and extent of religious resurgence in the United States, I must note that the task of accomplishing this aim is more complex than might be supposed. The reasons are two-fold. First, religion in America is in fact far from monolithic: Roman Catholics, Jews, liberal Protestants, and evangelicals coexist, and within each further diversity is apparent by denomination, age group, and region, such that one segment (or several) could conceivably experience a resurgence of activity at the same time that another was in decline. Second, conditions constituting "resurgence" within American religion or in various of its component elements are themselves subject to varying interpretations. A veritable explosion of individual commitment may have no significance at the level of organized religious activity, and an outburst of organized religious activity may have little to do with the kind of political reorientation that commentators have identified.

The first of these problems points to the need for a consideration not only of global indices of religious resurgence in the society as a whole but also of differentiated estimates of the patterns of religious commitment within subgroups of the American population. A variety of indicators is available from which to ascertain trends at both levels. The second concern—different conceptions of resurgence—indicates the importance of considering the actual and potential capacities of different religious groups for mobilizing their constituencies to influence behavior in realms other than religion, particularly the political. Finally, any assessment of religious resurgence in America must also weigh the scope of this resurgence against other developments and movements that may be reshaping the basic institutions of the society.

Global Indices of American Religious Trends

I have charted seven indicators of the overall strength of American religion as an institution over time. Two of these indicators—religious books and nonprofit religious associations — span a full century from 1880 to 1979. Three of the others — church membership, religious contributions, and clergy in the labor force — cover almost all of the twentieth century. The remaining two — church attendance and construction of religious buildings — cover approximately the last half century. It should be noted that these are standard time-series measures frequently referred to in the statistical literature on churches as well as in sociological studies.[1] The exception is the nonprofit religious associations measure, which was developed for present purposes by coding the eight hundred national nonprofit membership organizations listed under *religion* in the 1983 *Encyclopedia of Associations* by date of founding, and then standardizing these figures by dividing them by the total number of nonprofit associations founded in each period. (Because the *Encyclopedia of Associations* lists over 15,000 organizations, the latter figures were estimated from a one-in-fifty random sample.) The resulting numbers were then tabulated according to date to represent the proportion of all religious nonprofit associations existing at various periods. The source used necessarily underrepresents organizations presently defunct; it does not entirely exclude them, however, judging from the fact that a number of defunct or nearly defunct organizations were identified. The other indicators were also standardized in order to take into account changes in population, the labor force, the business cycle, and so forth. Church membership and attendance are expressed as proportions of the total population. Attendance refers to those who reported attending a church or synagogue during the week previous to the interview.[2] The religious books category represents the proportion of all new published books classified as *religious* according to the Universal Decimal Classification system.[3] Contributions include all contributions for religious purposes as a proportion of personal income. Religious construction includes construction of new religious buildings at dollar value as a proportion of all new private-sector construction at dollar value. The category of clergy, finally, is the proportion of the total labor force listed as clergy or religious workers.

On balance, these indices give little support to the notion of a religious resurgence. Church membership actually declined as a proportion of total population during the 1970s, after a period of steady growth for nearly a century. Church attendance remained constant, though at a low level compared to the 1950s. Religious books showed a slight increase during the latter half of the 1970s, but overall remained at nearly the lowest level in history. Nonprofit religious associations also declined in the 1970s relative to other organizations. Contributions dropped dramatically, as did new construction. Only clergy as a proportion of the labor force experienced a noticeable increase, but even this increase did not depart significantly from the overall pattern of stability of this measure.

If religious resurgence is not a striking feature in these indices, neither is the idea of dramatic secularization. Church membership has risen, rather than fallen, over the long term. Clergy, church attendance, and religious organizations have shown remarkable stability over the past half century or longer, but church construction has fluctuated too widely to permit any conclusions about definite tendency. Only religious books and religious contributions have shown steady downward trends, and these trends may be less symptomatic of the vitality of religion than of the tremendous expansion in incomes, education, and information occurring in the larger society over the course of the past century. Thus, the evidence from long-term indices yields little in definitive support for either the idea of religious resurgence in the recent past or the idea of religious decline over a longer period. The various indices chart different patterns, leading perhaps most clearly to the conclusion that American religion is sufficiently multifaceted to defy simple description on the basis of global indices.

A weakness of long-term indices, of course, is that they may fail to capture early signs of religious resurgence in the very recent past. This is an especially important concern here, since the discussion of religious resurgence sometimes suggests that significant change came about only as recently as 1979 or 1980. To check out this possibility, I have examined annual statistics on six of the indices of institutional religion for the period 1970 to 1980. (Annual figures on clergy are not available.) This is a particularly interesting period, since a variety of previous research has suggested that American religion hit a low point in institutional strength about the time of the antiwar movement and counterculture of the early 70s. It should be possible to discern any signs of resurgence at the end of the decade quite clearly in relation to this earlier period. But again, the data lend little support to the idea of resurgence. Church membership has remained virtually static, declining slightly (from 62 percent to 61 percent) over the course of the past decade. Gallup polls, it might be noted, project church membership at somewhat higher levels, but the trends are much the same; according to the latest data, 68 percent of the public claimed to be church members in 1984, the same as in 1978, and down by 3 percentage points since 1976.[4] Church attendance fell from 42 percent in 1970 to 40 percent in 1971, where it remained through 1975. In 1976, it jumped to 42 percent (evoking widespread speculation about a religious revival!), but since 1976 it has fallen again, reaching 40 percent in 1979 and 1980, 41 percent in 1981, and 40 percent again in 1983 and 1984.

Religious organizations declined from 7.5 percent of all nonprofit organizations in 1970 to 5.4 percent in 1980, while religious books have shown a somewhat more erratic pattern. After a five-year low in the early 1970s, they rose from 4.5 percent of all new books published in 1975 to 5.3 percent in 1978. Since then, however, the proportion has fallen, reaching 4.8 percent in 1980. Construction activity lends some support to the idea of resurgence, since the proportion of all new construction expenditures devoted to religious buildings has risen steadily since 1977. Even with this increase, however, construction has not fully recovered from the negative effects of the recessions of 1973 and 1976. Contributions, finally, have shown virtually no variation since 1970.

Before turning to other types of indices (which may be more reflective of individual religious commitment), several other indicators regarding institutional religion, which are less systematic but which contribute to the assessment of recent trends, are worth summarizing. Sales of religious books (as opposed to copyrights granted for new books) is one type of data on which detailed records exist for several years in the recent past — and these figures indeed give some evidence of religious resurgence. According to a recent compilation published in *Publishers Weekly,* purchase of religious books rose from .15 books per capita in 1970 to .32 in 1975 and then to .38 in 1980.[5] In other words, about three in eight people, on the average, purchased a religious book in 1980, compared with about one person in eight in 1970. As a proportion of all books purchased, religious books rose from 5.4 percent in 1970 to 8.5 percent in 1975, but then slipped slightly to 7.8 percent in 1980. *Receipts* for religious books present a somewhat less supportive picture, rising from 4.5 percent of all receipts in 1972 to 4.9 percent in 1977 and then falling to an all-time low of 4.3 percent in 1980; however, receipts may be a less useful measure than unit consumption.[6] Detailed breakdowns for 1972 and 1977 also suggest a significant change in the *composition* of religious book sales. Bibles declined from 31 percent of the total to 19 percent, while "other" religious books and pamphlets increased from 61 percent to 71 percent. It is difficult, of course, to know whether this shift reflects a secularizing tendency (away from biblical religion), or whether it suggests a growing penetration of religious books into other realms of life. A detailed content analysis of religious books from evangelical publishers, for example, showed a significant level of concern with psychological and family-oriented issues.[7]

What is perhaps most noteworthy about the trends in religious book sales is simply the fact that a greater proportion of the public appears to be including religious books in its literary diet. One of the reasons for this tendency may be, as will be demonstrated later, the fact that education levels among the more religiously conservative sectors of society (those most likely to be interested in religious books) have risen dramatically over the past two decades.

The field of education is another source for claims of religious resurgence. Of all earned degrees conferred at the bachelor's level in 1972, degrees in religion or theology comprised only 3.9 percent. By 1975, this figure had climbed to 4.8 percent and in 1980 it stood at 6.2 percent.[8] This growth is perhaps all the more surprising because of the shift in recent years toward such economically oriented specialization as engineering and business administration. At the masters level, a somewhat different pattern is evident: degrees in religion and theology *declined* from 1.5 percent of the total in 1970 to 1.1 percent in 1975, and then rose slightly to 1.3 percent in 1980. At the doctorate level, degrees in theology in 1970 were at a low of 1.4 percent (falling from 2.8 percent in 1960), but then rose to 2.6 percent in 1975 and to 4.2 percent in 1980. The increase at the doctorate level appears to be due primarily to the fact that doctoral work on the whole remained constant during the 1970s, whereas doctoral studies in theology rose steadily, partly as a result of new programs that permit clergy to obtain doctorates without interrupting their pastoral careers. Overall, these figures suggest that religion has at least maintained itself at the professional level, despite the significant rise in higher education. Whether this level of activity compensates for changes in other areas, however, is a different matter. For example, the 5,300 clergy and religious workers who received advanced degrees in 1980 are equivalent to only about a third of the number who earned degrees in medicine, a seventh of the number earning law degrees, and one-seventeenth of the number earning degrees in engineering. By other indications, the availability of clergy may have actually experienced a decline. For example, the number of Roman Catholic sisters declined from 153,000 in 1971 to 122,000 in 1981, while the number of Catholic priests managed only to hold its own at 58,000 over this period.[9]

A final measure, while of less significance than the foregoing, nevertheless illuminates yet another aspect of institutional religion: the amount of funding given to religion by private foundations. This figure represented 6.4 percent of all foundation donations in 1970, and 6.8 percent in 1971. In 1980, however, it was only 2.1 percent.[10] In absolute terms, donations from foundations remained virtually constant during this period (not counting depreciation in value due to inflation). As a result, the absolute value of foundation funding for religious purposes fell roughly by two-thirds between 1971 and 1981.

It is also worth noting that inflation and economic conditions have seriously eroded the institutional resources of American religion in other ways as well. While religious contributions have remained roughly constant relative to personal income since 1970, the uses to which these funds have necessarily been put have altered considerably. A study of fifty randomly selected churches sponsored by the National Council of Churches, showed that expenditures for utilities rose from 7.4 cents of every dollar in 1970 to 10.9 cents in 1979. In comparison, pastors' salaries and expenses fell from 34 cents of each dollar to 28 cents. The study concluded that churches were not only faced with cutbacks in the types of programs they could sponsor, but were likely over the long run to experience a decline in qualified professional leadership as well.[11] (The latter prediction depends greatly on options in other segments of the labor force.)

Turning next to indices of *personal* religious involvement, we find first of all that evidence dates only to the early 1950s. It becomes considerably more difficult to sort out long-term trends from short-term fluctuations. The problem is also compounded by an absence of comparable data for more than two or three widely separated points in time. Nevertheless, some patterns do emerge. In comparison with the early to middle 1950s, virtually all measures of personal religious devotion were down by the late 1970s, and in most cases these declines were already in evidence early in the decade. Persons polled in national surveys were less confident that religion could solve the world's problems, were less likely to say religion was personally important to them, thought religion was declining in influence, and were less likely to pray.[12] According to recent Gallup figures, they were also less sure that the Bible was literally God's word.[13] By 1986, several of these trends appeared to be continuing, but there were also some mixed patterns. There was a slight increase in the percentage of persons who felt religion could solve the world's problems and in those who said religion was very important in their personal lives. There was also a significant rise since 1970 in the number who thought religion's influence was increasing, although this number was not as high in 1986 as it had been in 1976. Thus, the only real support for the resurgence claim was that people had begun to *think* that religion was on the upswing, at least up until 1976. The bulk of the evidence suggested either that religious attitudes and behavior were subject to long-term secularizing influences, or, in such special cases as belief in heaven (or a comparable Gallup item on belief in hell), that religious belief was relatively stable.

These conclusions appear to be supported by other attitudinal data of a more limited sort. Gallup questions on religious preference showed that slightly more (9 percent) volunteered "no religion" as their preference in 1985 than had in 1972 (5 percent) and that this figure was about the same as in 1977 (8 percent). Sampling error is considerable on percentages this small, but the data give no evidence of a recent upsurge in religious commitment. On a different measure — confidence in organized religion — Gallup figures also point toward stability, rather than resurgence: 66 percent of those questioned said they had a lot of confidence in the churches or organized religion in 1973, compared with 68 percent in 1975, 64 percent in 1977, 65 percent in 1979, and 66 percent in 1980.[14] Over a somewhat longer period, Gallup polls revealed two significant sources of decline that may have important consequences in the future. The proportion of adults receiving religious training dropped from 91 percent in 1965 to 83 percent in 1978, and the proportion who wanted their children to receive religious instruction declined from 96 percent to 87 percent over the same period.[15] (On the latter question, 1981 figures showed a further decline to 83 percent.)[16] The only significant departure from these patterns—indeed, about the only indicator that could be regarded as evidence of religious resurgence across the board—was a Gallup statistic from data collected late in 1981 showing that 26 percent of the public had received some kind of religious instruction outside of worship services, within the last two years—up from 17 percent only three years previously.[17] Curiously, there was no similar increase in the proportions involved in Bible study groups (19 percent in both years), or in more specialized religious activities such as speaking in tongues (4 percent) or the charismatic movement (3 percent).

In sum, the evidence from global indices of religious strength yields almost no support for the idea that there has been a recent resurgence of religious commitment in America. Belief and practice, giving, new organizations, new book titles, and construction are all at record or near-record lows. Other measures, such as clergy in the labor force and confidence in religious organizations, are virtually unchanged from a decade ago, while only a few scattered indices, such as religious book sales, advanced degrees in theology, and participation in religious instruction, suggest any appreciable increase in the strength of organized religion.

In the face of such an overwhelming lack of supportive evidence, we might well ask what could be the source of the current impression that religion is on the upswing. One possibility is that global indices fail to capture significant movements *within* religion, movements that may alter the qualitative character of American religion or its relation to the rest of society without being reflected in gross statistics. This is a possibility to be considered in some detail momentarily. To set the stage for that discussion, however, another possibility needs to be entertained—namely, that much of the discussion of religious resurgence has been generated by the press. We can, for example, consider the number of articles on *Religion and Politics* indexed in *Readers' Guide* each year since 1977. Here, the pattern is indeed one of "resurgence" —a dramatic awakening of interest in the political role of religion. Nevertheless, even this form of resurgence may be relatively short-lived.

Indices within Subgroups

The possibility of a resurgence of religious interest *within* religion that is not reflected in overall religious statistics can best be examined by comparing indices within specific subgroups of the American population. Age groups and denominational groups are the two most likely candidates for such comparisons.

Age groups have received considerable attention in the literature on religion, since young people not only often serve as bellwethers of emerging trends, but as they mature, their views become the majority religious opinions. Young people's views are also particularly subject to the confluence of larger social trends that may indirectly shape religious orientations—education, regional migration, professionalization, and voluntary responses to current events, such as the counterculture of the early 1970s or the nuclear freeze movement in the 1980s. In the early 1970s, it was shown that young people had become considerably less involved in organized religion than older people, due to the differentiating effects of the counterculture, drugs, the antiwar movement, student unrest, and new sexual norms, as well as changes within the churches, such as the Vatican II reforms. The question at issue presently, therefore, is whether this pattern still holds or whether, on the contrary, young people have experienced a religious rebirth.

It seems clear that there has been no significant religious awakening among younger Americans.[18] In church attendance, the gap between young and old emerging by the middle 1970s is still as apparent as it was then. More specifically, people under 30 and people over 50 were equally likely to attend church in the base year 1958; in a typical week that year, 48 percent of each group attended. By 1970, 44 percent of the older group still attended, but the figure for the younger group had fallen to 32 percent. In 1975, the older group had risen to 46 percent, but the younger group had fallen further to 30 percent. And by the 1980s, the older group had risen by 1 percent and the younger group by 2 percent, leaving the gap still at a dramatic fifteen percentage points. We should also note that young people continue to be less convinced than older people about the capacity of religion to answer "today's problems." Compared with 1957, when young people were actually more likely to believe religion could answer problems, 1974 figures showed an eleven-point gap in this response. By 1980, this gap had risen to fifteen points, as older people's confidence in religion rose while younger people's remained almost constant.

Further evidence that there has been no recent revival among youth comes from the results of Gallup polls of teenagers conducted in 1977 and again in 1981. In the former year, 42 percent said their religious beliefs were very important. Four years later, the figure was still the same. Nor were any differences recorded in church attendance, in church membership, or in the belief that religion had been an important influence on one's life.[19] If there is any religious resurgence taking place, in short, it does not seem to be happening among young people.

How about differences in denominational groups? Conventional wisdom associates the visible intrusion of religion into the public sphere primarily with fundamentalist Protestantism (that is, those churches espousing biblical inerrancy). Earlier studies have pointed both to growth in these denominations and to stagnation or decline in the ranks of liberal Protestantism and Roman Catholicism. With respect to the Catholic church, evidence does indeed demonstrate more serious declines than in Protestantism as a whole. We have already noted the decline in the number of women in Catholic orders and the absence of growth in numbers of priests. Church-attendance figures also bear witness of decline. Taking 1958 as a base year again, Catholics experienced a decline of twenty-two percentage points in church attendance by 1978, compared with a decline of only 4 percent for Protestants. Since 1978, Catholic church attendance has dropped by 1 percentage point, as it has among Protestants.[20] The patterns for questions about the importance of religion in one's personal life confirm these differences: Catholics were twenty percentage points less likely to regard religion as a very important aspect of their life in 1980 than they were in 1965. By comparison, Protestant figures declined only thirteen points.[21]

Within Protestantism, membership data also support the claim that fundamentalist or evangelical groups (usually affiliates of the National Association of Evangelicals) have grown, in comparison with liberal denominations. (The figures available are from data reported in the *New York Times*.)[22] Although these figures cover only a few of the many evangelical or sectarian groups, they illustrate the rapid growth experienced even by some of the largest of these denominations, including the Southern Baptist Convention which, at more than 13 million members, is the largest of all Protestant denominations. By comparison, of the mainline denominations only the American Baptists have experienced similar growth. All of the more liberal groups, such as the United Presbyterian Church, the United Church of Christ, and the Episcopal church, have experienced net declines in membership.

Evangelical denominations have grown not only in membership, but in resources and organizational structure. A common stereotype holds evangelical denominations to be small, isolated splinter groups incapable of sustaining a stable internal structure, let alone of engaging in cooperation with other groups. This stereotype is to some extent valid, since there have been literally dozens of schisms and splinter groups within certain families of fundamentalists — Pentecostal and Holiness groups being perhaps the most conspicuous example. Nevertheless, this characterization does not apply to many evangelical groups, as attested by the Southern Baptist Convention, a large denomination remarkably free of internal divisions or sectarian offshoots over the past half-century. In addition, the following evangelical denominations all count members in figures of half a million or more: Assemblies of God, Churches of Christ, Church of God in Christ, Jehovah's Witnesses, and Seventh-Day Adventists.[23]

Internally, evangelical denominations as a rule also command two key resources in greater quantity *per member* than most liberal denominations: churches and clergy. Evangelical denominations generally have somewhere between five and ten churches per 1,000 members, depending on overall size and theological orientation, compared with between two and four churches per 1,000 members in liberal denominations.[24] Thus, the typical evangelical worships with 100 to 200 other people — a number he or she can more easily get to know and share common values with — while the typical liberal Protestant worships with 250 to 500 other poeple. Moreover, the clergy/lay ratio is also higher among evangelical groups, approximately ten to fifteen pastors per 1,000 members, compared with only three to six pastors per 1,000 members in liberal denominations.[25]

Evangelicals also appear to give more generously to their churches than do liberal Protestants. There is no precise data on this point, but a 1981 Gallup poll asked members of various denominations what percentage of their incomes they gave to their churches.[26] Southern Baptists were the only evangelical denomination large enough for figures to be reported separately, but the differences were pronounced: 37 percent said they gave a tenth or more of their incomes, compared with 28 percent among other Baptists, 15 percent of Lutherans, 12 percent of Methodists, and 8 percent of Roman Catholics. And because they give more, evangelicals have been able to support more churches and clergy per capita and a variety of other activities as well. Mission work is one significant example. According to one comprehensive study, more than 35,000 missionaries were sponsored by American and Canadian mission boards in 1976. Of these, only 3,000 were sponsored by denominations belonging to the National Council of Churches (in other words, liberal denominations), and another 2,200 were sponsored by denominational affiliates of the National Council of Churches. Thus, the remaining 30,000 were largely sponsored by evangelical groups, the largest of which were Southern Baptist and Wycliffe Bible Translators.[27]

Christian schools provide another significant example. By the late 1970s there were 5,870 Protestant-supported Christian schools in the United States, with 66,080 teachers and 1,068,000 pupils. These figures represented about a third of all nonpublic schools in that year and about one fifth of all pupils in nonpublic schools. More impressive, however, was the *trend* discernible in these figures: between 1971 and 1978, there was a 47 percent increase in the number of Christian schools, a 113 percent increase in teachers, and a 95 percent increase in pupils.[28]

Religious broadcasting is another important activity in which evangelicals have become heavily involved. Prior to the middle 1970s, broadcast time was provided by local networks at no expense as a public service, and the most popular religious programs were largely local, with a few exceptions such as Billy Graham, Oral Roberts, and Bishop Fulton Sheen. With changes in FCC regulations, religious television shifted to a for-pay basis, and by 1979 over 90 percent of all religious television was commercial—most of it controlled by evangelicals. Between 1970 and 1980, expenditures for religious programming mushroomed from $50 million to more than $600 million annually, and the revenues taken in annually by some of the TV preachers reached staggering proportions: Oral Roberts, $60 million; Pat Robertson, $58 million; Jim Bakker, $51 million; and Jerry Falwell, $50 million (according to 1979 figures reported in the *Los Angeles Times*, 25 February 1980). Five years later, all four preachers were taking in revenues in excess of $100 million annually. Over all, 50 percent of the public in a recent survey claimed to have watched a religious television program in the past twelve months, ranging from 64 percent in the South to 42 percent in the Northeast, and from 62 percent among churchgoers to 43 percent among nonchurchgoers. Moreover, evangelicals were about twice as likely as the public at large to say they had watched two or more hours of religious television a week. Nor does this viewing, as sometimes alleged, appear to take the place of actual involvement in local churches: 27 percent of viewers said viewing had increased their local involvement, while only 7 percent said that their involvement had decreased. Analysis of data collected in 1984 also disputes the fear that religious television viewing was eroding church attendance.[29]

Evangelicals enjoy considerable resources, and it appears that there has been a genuine upsurge in some of these resources over the past few years, particularly in the areas of schools and religious broadcasting. At the same time, stereotypes of evangelicals as marginal, disadvantaged groups also continue to have a strong basis in fact. Evangelicals, defined by Gallup as those who believe literally in the Bible, claim to be "born again," and proselytize, are more likely than the general public to be nonwhite, old, poorly educated, and from rural areas in the South.[30] In the short term, their ranks have probably been swollen by demographic expansion in older cohorts and by Sun Belt migration. Over the long run, however, predictions based on dominant social trends would suggest a diminution of strength as larger segments of the population become college-educated; as younger, less evangelical cohorts mature; and as nonevangelical families from the Northeast and Midwest migrate to the South, carrying more liberal convictions with them. It is important to remember, nevertheless, that evangelicals have in the past shown greater capacity to withstand the secularizing influences of the larger culture than was generally thought possible. Since 1960, too, education and income levels have risen dramatically among evangelicals, to the point that many of them are indistinguishable from liberal Protestants on these grounds.[31] They have also accommodated to modernity by focusing more intently on family issues and subjective problems, and by developing more refined arguments in defense of their interpretations of the Bible.[32]

Overall, therefore, it is possible to sustain arguments for religious resurgence if those arguments are specified to mean *evangelical* resurgence. While other segments of the population, particularly Roman Catholics and the young, have diminished in religious commitment, evangelical groups have grown in membership; have retained their appeal to older persons, blacks, rural citizens, and Southerners at the same time that they have experienced an overall upgrading in terms of education and income levels; and have sponsored more mission programs, more schools, and more religious broadcasting in recent years than ever before.

Religion and Politics

If there has indeed been an upsurge of evangelical activity, then, the question remains: What impact has this upsurge had on society, particularly in the political realm? Specifically, have evangelicals mobilized politically, and if so, what direction has their political activity taken?

All the evidence suggests that evangelicals have indeed become politically mobilized. A decade ago, most observers had concluded that evangelicals were simply too other-worldly, pietistic, and individualistic to become enmeshed in the messy business of politics. More than a dozen empirical studies, conducted over a twenty-year span among church members and the general public, among clergy and laity, and in different parts of the country, seemed to confirm this conclusion.[33] But after 1976, the pattern shifted. Between 1976 and 1981 no fewer than ten studies, seven of which involved national samples, showed that evangelicals were *more* politically involved than other religious groups. Compared with persons of similar social and geographic status, they were more likely to register to vote (and to vote), and were more likely than liberal Protestants or Roman Catholics to favor their churches' speaking out on political, moral, and social issues. In addition, they supported the rights of such groups as the Moral Majority to become involved in political activities, and their pastors did in fact speak out on such issues as abortion, pornography, and the equal rights amendment. Such leading evangelical publications as *Christianity Today* reversed earlier policies that condemned political involvement, and the number of articles dealing with political issues suddenly tripled. The National Association of Evangelicals, representing approximately 3.5 million evangelicals in 38,000 local churches from 75 denominations, put a full-time lobbyist on its payroll and began publishing a monthly newsletter on political affairs. Television evangelists began taking stands on political issues, and viewer studies showed that substantial portions of their viewers watched primarily to keep informed on political issues.[34] Perhaps most significantly, such groups as the Moral Majority, Christian Voice, and Religious Roundtable—all with evangelical leadership and strong financial backing from the evangelical community—emerged into the political limelight.

Nor were these isolated or exceptional undertakings. The number of culturally defensive religious interest groups (that is, groups promoting religious fundamentalism and traditional morality) had been growing steadily since the late 1950s and reached a peak only in the late 1970s. These movements, all of which were organized on a national scale, included efforts within denominations to restore fundamentalist theology and traditional morality to prominence, as well as extradenominational organizations aimed at reforming the entire society. In addition, press accounts have identified literally hundreds of local groups with similar objectives.

Disagreement continues concerning both the actual impact and the political potential of this mobilization. Apart from questions about the role of evangelicals in the 1980 and 1984 elections, for example, doubts continue to be expressed as to the capacity of evangelicals to cooperate with one another or about their inclination to participate in other community organizations from which their power base might be expanded. Nevertheless, recent studies, conducted largely between 1980 and 1984, continue to document the political mobilization that has come to characterize evangelicals. Gallup data show that evangelicals are more likely to be registered to vote than nonevangelicals; that a majority would be more likely to vote for a candidate if he or she were an evangelical; that conservatively religious Christians are just as likely as anyone else to hold memberships in local community or civic organizations other than churches; and that they are *more* likely to be involved in social service and charitable activities.[35] Analysis of data from the 1980 and 1984 national election surveys also shows that evangelicals were more likely than nonevangelicals to have voted, even though the pattern had been exactly the opposite in previous elections.[36] Further analysis of new voters showed that Southern evangelicals in particular had experienced a significant "political rebirth." Specifically, almost half of the Southern evangelicals who had not voted in previous elections *did* vote in 1980, compared with only a third of their evangelical counterparts in the North and a sixth of Southern nonevangelicals.[37]

Disagreement also prevails over the reasons behind this mobilization. A variety of evidence points to the fact that Jimmy Carter's identification with evangelicalism and the subsequent media exposure that other evangelical celebrities received may have given evangelicals a sense of political "entitlement." Other evidence suggests that the fusion of moral issues with politics as a result of Watergate, the 1973 Supreme Court decision on abortion, and intensified media coverage of matters of moral and ethical concern may have convinced evangelicals of the importance of expressing their views on moral issues in politics — issues on which they had been united for some time.[38] Yet another argument holds that the sheer accumulation of evangelical resources, together with their rising social status and the declining voice of liberal Protestants, may have encouraged evangelicals to assume a more visible role as spokespersons for the American civil religion.[39] Still another possibility, suggested by the growth in Republican support in the South generally and the propensity of Southern evangelicals to support Republican candidates, is that evangelicals may have simply been mobilized by the bandwagon effect of the Republicans' successes in the 1980 primaries, polls, and national election. (The Moral Majority itself claimed credit for much of the new registration of evangelical voters, but this claim has been widely disputed, since evangelical support for the Moral Majority in 1980 did not seem to be strong. If anything, the Moral Majority capitalized on a preexisting network of evangelical organizations, rather than vice versa.)[40]

The resurgence of evangelical activity, both religiously and politically, has raised the spectre in many quarters of a fundamentalist, totalitarian monolith seizing power in the United States, or at least acting as the vehicle for a radically conservative shift in the direction of American politics. This view appears to be partially supported by recent research, at least in the matter of attitudes. A variety of surveys show evangelicals to be disproportionately right of center politically; against the equal rights amendment; in favor of banning abortions, increasing nuclear weapons, and promoting prayer in the schools; and concerned with limiting pornography and homosexuality.[41]

The spectre of an archconservative monolith quickly turns out to be illusory, however, when the internal *diversity* of evangelicals is considered. Nationally, only a third are self-styled conservatives; the majority are moderates or liberals. A majority actually *supported* the Equal Rights Amendment, and on most issues, such as nuclear power, gun control, and the death penalty, evangelicals are indistinguishable from non-evangelicals.[42] Even in the most conservative districts, anywhere from 30 percent to 60 percent of evangelicals take liberal positions on questions concerning the role of women, ERA, homosexuality, the death penalty, and abortion.[43] Indeed, about the only issue on which evangelicals are unified is voluntary prayer in the schools, and even on this issue the more specific questions about how best to implement this idea show a wide range of opinion.

In short, evangelicals have become interested in politics, after several decades of political self-exile, and their numbers are not insignificant—both the Gallup and University of Michigan studies suggest that about one person in five falls in this category. But their impact on the political scene scarcely threatens to significantly alter the character of American politics. The sheer diversity of political views within their own ranks mitigates the likelihood of their becoming a unified political force.

The Wider Context

Nevertheless, it cannot be denied that a number of major religiously inspired political action groups, such as the Moral Majority, have come into existence over the past several years; that they have overtly sought to influence the legislative process (with some success); and that they have played a highly symbolic role in recent discussions of American politics. If they succeed in pressing for legislation on moral issues, or if they manage—despite their relatively small numbers—to initiate reforms on civil liberties, on the rights of minority groups, on defense spending, or on the relations between government and religious practice, they could have important social consequences, whether they speak for a large "majority" or only a tiny minority. One of the main targets of their attacks—prohibition of school prayer—was, after all, originally brought about by a group of atheists representing a much tinier fraction of the American public than is represented by the religious Right.

To put the resurgence of the religious Right in perspective, two comparisons of a broader nature must be considered. The first is the general role of religion in the United States compared with its role in other countries. Although the United States is industrially and educationally the most "advanced" country in the world, it stands as an important exception to theories that equate industrialization with secularity. To be sure, there have been signs of secularization in recent decades, as some of the previous evidence has indicated. But in comparison with other industrial societies, the United States demonstrates a very strong degree of religious involvement. According to Gallup polls conducted in 1981, 61 percent of the American public stated that "following God's will" was very important as a personal value; the comparable figure in Great Britain was 35 percent. Similarly, for 40 percent of the U.S. sample, "taking part in church-related activity" was very important, compared with only 15 percent in Great Britain.[44] Another study, involving seven industrial socie-ties, showed that the U.S. population had the highest level of confidence in the churches or organized religion of all other countries except the Irish Re-public, exceeding Italy, France, Spain, Great Britain, and West Germany, among other states.[45] Still another study, this one conducted in 1979, showed that 76 percent of the American public believed "there exists one and only one absolute God," compared with 66 percent in Canada, 63 percent in Italy, 57 percent in Great Britain, 52 percent in West Germany, 51 percent in Australia, and 44 percent in France. Differences were even more pronounced concerning the response to the statement "people's daily life should be governed by religious commandments": U.S., 68 percent; Italy, 48 percent; Australia, 45 percent; West Germany, 40 percent; France, 40 percent; Great Britain, 34 percent; and Canada, 32 percent.[46]

What all this means is that it should not be surprising to find religious values as the source of social action movements or as expressions of public sentiment in the political sphere. The Moral Majority represents simply one of a long series of religiously inspired involvements in the public sphere in recent decades, including the Religious Taskforce of the Nuclear Freeze Com-mittee, the Nestle Boycott, the United Nations resolutions on human rights and religious tolerance (backed strongly by the World Conference on Reli-gion and Peace), the continuing efforts of Jewish and various evangelical groups to lobby for defense and aid for Israel, the heavy involvement of campus ministries in antiwar activities during the Vietnam years, the civil rights move-ment during the previous decade, and the anticommunist activities of the decade before that. It should be evident even from this brief enumeration that the pluralism which characterizes American religion shines through when religion becomes the source of political activity. Indeed, this pluralism has contributed greatly to the multiplicity of causes and issues that have arisen in the public sphere.

The other consideration to be kept in mind in any evaluative treatment of the religious Right is its relative strength in comparison with other political interest groups in the United States. As of 30 June 1982, there were 3,149 political action committees in the United States, up by 132 percent from 1977, and these PACs were estimated to have spent over $80 million by the end of the 1982 elections. Of these, company-sponsored PACs were by far the larg-est category (1,415), and a 1982 survey of leading executives found that 71 percent were pleased with the results their PACs were obtaining.[47] By com-parison, there were only two *Christian* PACs at the national level: Christian Voice Moral Government Fund (CVMGF) and Christian Voters' Victory Fund (CVVF). (One other, Moral Majority PAC, came into existence in 1979 but was terminated a year later, after raising only $22,089. Another, Christian Coalition for Legislative Action, had also been terminated.) In comparison with business PACs, then, which spent close to $9 million as of mid-1982, CVMGF spent a meager $251,501 (accruing large debts in the process), while CVVF spent only $4,500.[48] In short, fundamentalist PACs were a mere drop in the bucket alongside the efforts of business PACs.

The same can be said of culturally defensive nonprofit associations. Although the formation of such groups sharply increased in the late 1970s, the total number of such groups in 1982 was, as previously seen, only 44, compared with more than 800 religious associations, over 1,000 public affairs groups, and more than 3,000 scientific and educational organizations.

As for Jerry Falwell and the Moral Majority specifically, after more than two years of vigorous press coverage 45 percent of the American public was still unaware of its existence in late 1981, and of those familiar with it negative sentiment outweighed positive feelings by a ratio of more than two to one.[49] (Only 5 percent of those polled said they might be willing to join.) Views of Falwell himself were somewhat more favorable (35 percent), but nearly as many were unfavorable (29 percent) and a large minority had no opinion at all (35 percent).

Seen in a wider context, then, there is reason to expect religious groups to become involved in the public life of the nation, but also evidence that the recent involvement of the religious Right has been a minor presence in the larger political scene. Much of the hue and cry about fundamentalist resurgence, American ayatollahs, threats to the American way, and the like were apparently premature, or else so successful as to nip those threats in the bud. At the same time, there are important lessons to be learned. One is that familiarity with long-term patterns is essential to any evaluation of short-term developments in American religion. Another is that American religion has proven repeatedly to be more adaptable, and consequently less predictable, than many of its observers have been willing to concede. The sudden political rebirth of American evangelicals after years of quiescence is but the latest example. Still another lesson is that the national press has come to play a major role not only in the making of political and religious movements, but in setting the agenda for scholarly discussion as well. Finally, the relative lack of evidence found here for anything tantamount to a resurgence of religion in American life more generally implies neither that religion is inconsequential for the society nor that the efforts of those who have devoted themselves to moral, social, and political reform on the basis of religious convictions have been entirely in vain. That these issues have been adopted for discussion on such a wide variety of platforms is itself testimony to the success of these efforts.

Notes

1. N. J. Demerath III, "Trends and Anti-trends in Religious Change," in E. B. Sheldon and W. E. Moore, eds., *Indicators of Social Change: Concepts and Measurements* (New York: Russell Sage, 1968), pp. 349–448; Robert Wuthnow, "Recent Patterns of Secularization," *American Sociological Review*, 41 (1976): 850–67; and Daniel Rigney, Richard Machalek, and Jerry D. Goodman, "Is Secularization a Discontinuous Process?" *Journal for the Scientific Study of Religion* 17, no. 4 (1978): 381–88.

2. George Gallup, Jr., *Religion in America* (Princeton: Princeton Religion Research Center, 1982).

3. For validation of this measurement, see Robert Wuthnow, "A Longitudinal, Cross-National Indicator of Cultural Religious Commitment," *Journal for the Scientific Study of Religion*, 16 (1977): 87–99.

4. Gallup, *Religion in America* (1985).

5. John P. Dessauer, "Book-Buying Patterns in the '70s Showed Real Gains — Mostly Through Retailers," *Publishers Weekly*, 221 (2 April 1982): 37–39.

6. *Statistical Abstract of the United States, 1981* (Washington, D.C.: U.S. Department of Commerce, Bureau of the Census, 1981).

7. James Davison Hunter, *American Evangelicalism: Conservative Religion and the Quandary of Modernity* (New Brunswick, N.J.: Rutgers University Press, 1983).

8. *Statistical Abstract.*

9. Constant H. Jacquet, Jr., ed., *Yearbook of American and Canadian Churches* (Nashville: Abingdon Press, 1982).

10. *Statistical Abstract.*

11. Loyde H. Hartley, "Inflation and Recession Hit the Local Church Budgets," in Constant H. Jacquet, Jr., ed., *Yearbook of American and Canadian Churches* (Nashville: Abingdon Press, 1981), pp. 256–65.

12. Gallup *Religion in America* (1982), (1981).

13. Ibid. (1982).

14. Ibid. (1981).

15. Ibid.

16. Ibid. (1982).

17. Ibid.

18. Ibid., (1981), (1982).

19. Ibid. (1982).

20. Ibid. (1985).

21. Ibid. (1981).

22. Kenneth Briggs, "Church Growth Lags Far Behind that of U.S.," *New York Times*, 24 September 1982.

23. Jacquet, *Yearbook.*

24. Calculated from figures in ibid.

25. Calculated from ibid.

26. Gallup (1982).

27. Richie W. Hogg, "The Role of American Protestantism in World Mission," in R. Pierce Beaver, ed., *American Missions in Bicentennial Perspective* (South Pasadena, Calif.: William Carey Library, 1977), pp. 354–502, and Phillip E. Hammond, "In Search of a Protestant Twentieth Century: American Religion and Power Since 1900," *Review of Religious Research* 24, no. 3 (1983).

28. *Statistical Abstract*, p. 148.

29. Gallup (1982), pp. 65–66, and Annenberg/Gallup Research Team, *Religion and Television* (Philadelphia: University of Pennsylvania Press, 1984).

30. Figures computed from data reported in Gallup (1981).

31. John Stephen Hendricks, "Religious and Political Fundamentalism: The Links Between Alienation and Ideology" (Ph.D. diss., University of Michigan, 1977).

32. Hunter, *American Evangelicalism.*

33. Robert Wuthnow, "The Political Rebirth of American Evangelicals," in Robert Liebman and Robert Wuthnow, eds., *The New Christian Right* (New York: Aldine, 1983).

34. Ibid.

35. Gallup (1981), (1982).

36. Corwin Smidt, "'Born Again' Politics: The Political Attitudes and Behavior of Evangelical Christians in the South" (Paper delivered at the Citadel Symposium on Southern Politics, Charleston, S.C., 1982), and Robert Wuthnow, *The Restructuring of American Religion: Society and Faith Since World War II,* forthcoming.

37. Smidt, "'Born Again'"

38. Wuthnow, "Political Rebirth."

39. Hammond, *In Search.*

40. Robert Liebman, "Mobilizing the Moral Majority," in Robert Liebman and Robert Wuthnow, eds., *The New Christian Right* (New York: Aldine, 1983).

41. Gallup (1981), (1982).

42. Ibid. (1982).

43. Jill Auerbach and John D. Hutcheson, Jr., "Issue Constraint and the Religious New Right" (Paper delivered at the Citadel Symposium on Southern Politics, Charleston, S.C., 1982).

44. Gallup (1982).

45. Ibid.

46. "Cross-National Religious Values and Lifestyles," *World Opinion Update,* 5 (1981): 64–65.

47. "How Business Is Getting Through to Washington," *Business Week* (4 October 1982): 16.

48. Margaret Ann Latus, "Mobilizing Christians for Political Action: Campaigning with God on Your Side" (Paper delivered at the annual meetings of the Society for the Scientific Study of Religion, Providence, R.I., 1982).

49. Gallup (1982).

2

The Local Preacher and Islamic Resurgence in Upper Egypt

An Anthropological Perspective

Patrick D. Gaffney

Explicit and sometimes forceful assertions of religion have deeply marked the recent history of many Middle Eastern states. In cases as different as Saudi Arabia, Pakistan, and Iran, to cite only a few Islamic examples, conflicts involving the role of religion in public affairs have overturned governments as well as established them, and have stirred up mass responses on a scale unmatched by any secular ideology. In Egypt, it was only during the presidency of Anwar Sadat (1970–81) that an intensified expression of Islam rose to command a foremost place amid the country's national and international concerns. Very rapidly (and to the surprise of many observers), religious symbols and related political claims began to emerge as a preeminent banner of mass mobilization at a time when the nation under Sadat's leadership was undergoing sweeping changes in its political priorities and its economic orientation.

In some ways, this widespread wave of Islamic expression had the air of a "revival" in that it drew largely upon a body of thought that had been advanced by conservatives and traditionalists in the earlier decades of this century.[1] Many of these ideas were strongly apologetic and anti-Western in character. To a large extent, they had their origin in the era when European colonialism posed a threat to traditional self-understanding and challenged Muslim intellectuals to respond to questions about the nature of Islam, its reform, and its proper application in the modern world. But the vitality of these discussions had largely degenerated into academic repetition and pamphleteering. Throughout this century, these scholastic Islamic pronouncements on the pressing issues of the day lost their spark of relevance, and in their place such other ideological currents as nationalism, liberalism, Arabism, and socialism came to predominate. Also, increasingly—and especially following the 1952 revolution that brought Nasser to power—the formal institutions of Islam were progressively brought under the direct jurisdiction and management of a state strongly influenced by the Eastern bloc. The Egyptian government took its responsibility to include the ideological guidance as well as the material welfare of the nation.[2]

Numerous cumulative measures taken during the Nasser regime (1952–70) enabled the state, ruling through a one-party system, to achieve supremacy over all of the nation's significant institutions. Included among these were the *ulama* (Islamic scholars), who once constituted an indigenous elite that operated as a diffuse corps with a virtual monopoly in the fields of religion, law, education, and the administration of religious endowments, but who now found themselves "denied not only political influence but even autonomy in religion itself."[3] These steps, which brought mosques, schools, courts, and extensive property under an expanding centralized bureaucracy, were finally, in 1961, directed at the Azhar, Cairo's great mosque-university, founded in the tenth century. The government effectively "nationalized" and fundamentally restructured this center of learning, devotion, and political ferment, which had evolved into a bastion of obstructionism and withdrawal on the part of Islamic traditionalists.[4]

Also, from 1954 onward, in a number of successive purges, Nasser moved decisively to suppress the Muslim Brothers. This society, founded in 1928 by the compelling orator Hassan al-Banna (1906–49) as a religiously inspired association engaged in active social reform, had gained a wide following, especially among the urban lower middle class. In the 1940s, it grew increasingly militant and began to unveil aggressive political ambitions, notably through the activities of secret cells whose members had few scruples about the resort to violence and even assassination.[5] Nasser not only disbanded the society and prohibited its publications, but imprisoned thousands of its members and put to death several of its leaders who stood convicted of plotting to overthrow the government.

The popular triumph of Nasserism in conjunction with the state's tight control over the freedoms of expression and of assembly seemed to drown out or dispel from Egypt all ideological currents that bid to undermine a unity loyal to the revolution and its nationalist and socialist goals. But in 1967, the foundations of Nasser's charisma were suddenly and traumatically shaken as a result of Israel's overwhelming victory in the Six Day War. It was the perceived moral implications of this military defeat and the accompanying psychological impact on national self-confidence that prompted the initial impetus for a religious revival, not only among those who had earlier opposed Nasser in the name of Islam but in official circles as well. As one noted analyst put it: "The defeat of 1967 was viewed by the Brethern as that divine revenge they had long awaited. The regime was shaken. Religion was used by the regime for a certain kind of 'religious rearmament.' It was said that the defeat was predestined. No precaution would have prevented it. It came as a result of disbelief and the abandonment of God. Therefore returning to faith was the road to victory."[6] Signs of this new religious awareness arose in all quarters of public and private life. In some cases, the emphasis was on the virtues of patience and perseverance, while elsewhere the stress was on consolidation and reform.

Later, after Nasser's death, a more worldly and articulate reaction stirred the nation to reflect on the dark side of the man. Acknowledging his own complicity, one of Egypt's and the Arab world's most respected writers, Tawfiq al-Hakim, called it "a strange case of anaesthetization." In his celebrated book, *The Return of Consciousness*, al-Hakim reexamined the spell that Nasser had held over Egypt. He called for a reassessment of the revolution's leader who, despite his achievements, wracked untold damage through poor planning, social repression, and costly and ill-fated gestures of military bravura: "The truth is that until that time [Nasser] had inundated us with magic and dreams in such a way that we didn't know how he inundated us. Perhaps as they said it was his personal magic when he spoke to the masses, or perhaps it was the dream in which we had begun to live because of those hopes and promises. Whatever the fact, those glowing images of the accomplishments of the revolution made out of us instruments of the broad propaganda apparatus with its drums, its horns, its odes, its songs and its films."[7]

On the university campuses, starting in the early 1970s, Islamic groups began to replace Nasserist ones. The mass media reflected the trend with substantial increases in the radio broadcast of religious programming and in the publication of religion-related articles in the press. Many intellectuals who had shown no earlier inclinations toward piety now turned their attention to the words and deeds of the Prophet, while an unprecedented profusion of pious statements and gestures emanated from those in the highest positions of government. Anwar Sadat was officially presented as the "believer" president, and in photographs, interviews, speeches, and public appearances displayed a conspicuous attachment to religion. Nor was this spiritual awakening restricted to Muslims, for it was also profoundly felt among Egypt's native Christian population, the Copts. In fact, due to certain developments in their own modern history, the Coptic community had begun to experience a strong interior revitalization even before this, although it was heightened and politicized by the strong sectarian aspects of the Islamic resurgence.[8]

A significant vindication and reenforcement of this popular religious sentiment came with Egypt's military successes over Israel in the October, or Yom Kippur, War of 1973. On the battlefield, this conflict (which Egyptians referred to as "The Crossing") ended in an internationally mediated truce without great territorial gains, but in terms of Egypt's national consciousness, the event took on almost mythic proportions, signaling a restoration of pride and confidence that was widely declared to be the affirmation of divine favor.[9] Sadat's later peace initiative—launched by his dramatic visit to Jerusalem in 1977, and the subsequent Camp David process—abounded with religious symbols.[10]

The ideological basis upon which the contemporary Islamic resurgence is built has been the subject of a great number of detailed studies.[11] The principle aim of the movement is the familiar aspiration to establish an "Islamic order" in all parts of the society, including the replacement of Western-style civil and criminal codes with the "application of Islamic law." The intellectual substance of these arguments draws largely from ideas promulgated by Mawlana Abul Ala Mawdudi, who shaped the Islamic right in Pakistan, and Hassan al-Banna, who first formulated the program of the Muslim Brothers. But in the half-century since these two and others had forged a basic politico-theological synthesis, the experience of practical frustrations and frequent imprisonments led many proponents to radicalize these views. This radical and absolutist trend of which Sayyid Qutb (1906–66) is recognized as the principal author insisted that Islam divides the world into a sharp dichotomy consisting of the Party of God and the Party of Satan. Furthermore, Qutb argued, those who were not committed to the struggle for the establishment of the Islamic order were acting in disobedience to revelation and must be opposed. He thereby asserts a divine justification, indeed a divine imperative, for revolution—and more specifically, for the taking up of arms against fellow Muslims in order to achieve the goal of an Islamic state.[12]

The highly polarized categories of Qutb's theories prompted the formation of a number of Islamic associations that sought to maintain a distinct identity. They separated themselves by their doctrinal convictions and their moral judgments, and through the display of symbols that defined their purpose as different from merely "popular," or "establishment," Islam. The use of explicit items of personal dress or demeanor, such as veils among women and beards and white skullcaps among men, spread widely and took on great significance.[13] At the same time, not surprisingly, a broad sector of Egypt's population lent diffuse and passive support to the movement, opposing the new course of the dominant power structure. This class, which had benefitted only marginally from the economic and political gains of Nasser's regime, felt a growing uncertainty about any meaningful participation in the promised prosperity under Sadat. Here, what amounted to "the effort of a disaffected stratum to substitute its own ideology and development model for what Islamic militants perceived as the bankrupt ideologies of Western liberalism and secular socialism" resulted in a contest to discredit Sadat's legitimacy, a contest carried out in terms of a dispute over the authentic interpretation of Islam.[14]

Because of this extraordinary condensation of religious and political references into Islamic symbols, appeals to the public conscience played a central part in the strategy of both the Islamicists and those institutions representing the established order. But in the domain of information and opinion formation, the state had a formidable advantage. Although in the opening years of his presidency Sadat had greatly relaxed many of the tight censorship measures inherited from Nasser, he later sought to impose new regulations such as the so-called law of shame of 1979. This article of legislation gave the government virtually arbitrary powers to penalize anyone acting in a way judged to be contrary to "the genuine traditions of the society of the Egyptian family." Sadat proposed the law to a docile Parliament and then submitted it to a referendum in which, according to official reports, approximately 99 percent of the voters registered their approval.[15]

However, the pattern of growing authoritarianism under Sadat went beyond efforts to muzzle negative criticism and restrict inflammatory or disparaging commentary; it extended to a control over what events were allowed to be reported as news in the print and broadcast media. Throughout the late 1970s, tensions mounted steadily in upper Egypt. Intimidation, open provocation, and violence sparked by extremist Islamic groups were rapidly escalating. Consequently, anxieties came to preoccupy the communities involved — yet nothing was reported in the Egyptian media. University campuses in Minya and Assiut could be paralyzed by demonstrations and rallies, with the local police and even the army required to maintain order, but not an inkling of these events appeared in the official press. Of course, rumors spread wildly, especially in the Coptic community, whose institutions were often the targets of attack. Informed articles were also appearing in leading European newspapers, but officially in Egypt no problem existed.[16]

This artificial silence was broken only in April of 1979, though with stunning effect, when Sadat himself came to Assiut and delivered an address to the faculties of several upper Egyptian universities. In forceful terms, heavy with religious innuendo, he upbraided the Islamic activists as misguided and unpatriotic, and threatened them with severe countermeasures. This long speech was printed verbatim in the semiofficial daily newspaper *al-Ahram* and was rebroadcast several times on radio and television, but it did not lead to subsequent press coverage of on-going disruptive events of a politico-religious nature. When Islamic student extremists acted in defiance shortly afterwards, for the first time several were arrested. Mass outbursts on the part of student sympathizers followed, incurring heavy police intervention and more detainments—but once again, none of these confrontations was alluded to in the Egyptian press. Clearly, Sadat's government meant to deprive Islamic groups at the national and international news-reporting levels of the publicity their efforts sought (and to a large extent achieved locally).

Under the presidency of Mubarak, which began in 1981, a tactic of selective exposure has often been used instead of calculated disregard. Lengthy reports complete with photos and comments appear in response to certain ideologically motivated assaults, such as the fire-bombing of video parlors that occurred in the summer of 1986; however, the intended effect is to stigmatize the deeds as purely criminal.

Still another and potentially more volatile channel of communication (and therefore also an opportunity for propaganda) is the pulpit of the mosque. As has happened many times previously in Islamic history, the preacher has come into contention in contemporary Egypt because of the ambiguous character of his function, which implies both political and religious authority. Through various administrative procedures and selective subsidies the state exercises extensive control over preaching, despite protestations about the freedom of expression arising from both the Islamic tradition and the respect for religious rights within a democratic society. Of course, one of the most effective ways to control the mosque pulpit is to restrict access to it by law. The Egyptian government has not entirely succeeded in this extreme policy, but narrow regulations define the requisite credentials of an approved preacher. Of course, in cases where the preacher has all the formal qualifications to carry out his office, and where he may have a distinct personal following as well, a ban on his preaching could cause him to be treated as a martyr and provoke disruptive accusations of encroachment on the rights of religious freedom. Therefore, except in cases of declared emergency, a preacher who subtly opposes the government may be allowed to continue, with only indirect measures taken to limit his influence.

One celebrated instance of this is the dissident blind preacher of Cairo, Shaykh Abdul-Hamid Kishk. Although he is undoubtedly the best-known preacher in Egypt, his sermons have never been permitted to be aired on the broadcast media, which carry numerous programs that include preaching. While Shaykh Kishk regularly attracted thousands to the small mosque to which he had been officially assigned, with listeners spilling over into the streets, he was not permitted to leave the city or to speak elsewhere. Nevertheless, cassette recordings of his sermons enjoyed mass distribution and were listened to devotedly everywhere. He did not represent a particular political faction, but rather lent his voice to a more generalized dissatisfaction with the moral fiber of the nation, laying the blame pointedly on those charged with public responsibility. His popularity did not stem from the brilliance or refinement of his ideas, but rather from an appreciation of his virtuosity as a stylist and his daringly specific denunciations of corruption and immorality.[17] In September of 1981, Shaykh Kishk was apprehended along with more than a thousand others. He was released from custody shortly thereafter, but he is still barred from preaching. Interestingly, however—and an indication of the special political potency of preaching—this prohibition does not extend to publishing. In fact, Shaykh Kishk has written a column in Egypt's most widely available Islamic weekly since the beginning of the Mubarak administration. The paper, which appeals to a mass audience, is published by the National Democratic Party, which is not only currently in power but has controlled the political life of the country since Sadat founded it in 1978 to replace the Arab Socialist Union.

Traditionally, Islamic preaching takes place in a definite context, culturally defined as sacred—that is, separated by recognized symbolic boundaries from the world of ordinary experience. Also, as is typical of sacred oratory, it is embedded in an authoritative tradition that prescribes the customary rules of its performance, the absence of which reduces or deprives the speech of its special significance. The rhetoric of a sermon has specific requirements for formalization that include such things as the proper time and place as well as the text's structure, content, and linguistic style. It is partly because of this relatively restricted range of expression that traditionally defines the sermon as holy that it tends toward "archaism" and "ambiguity" and is, "from the point of view of the creativity potential of language, impoverished."[18] But this composite quality of formalization also serves to explain the difficulties many Islamic activists have felt about the mosque pulpit as an adequate base for their designs. Years ago, the inherent limits of this medium convinced some, including Hassan al-Banna, that "the Mosque alone did not suffice," and attempts were made to proclaim "guidance" from more popular settings as well.[19] However, among later Islamic radicals it was not an expansion of the arena for public speaking that was sought so much as an altogether new and urgent mode of communicating: action, not talk, was needed. Hence, armed strikes against symbolic targets were undertaken. The underlying motive behind this violence was not to engage in a confrontation so much as to gain attention. This desire for publicity is revealed, for instance, in the terms used by members of the Islamic groups responsible for such actions as the armed assault on the National Military Academy in 1974, and the 1977 abduction and murder of Shaykh Hussein al-Dhahabi, formerly Egypt's minister of religious endowments. When interviewed in prison, these extremists referred to these operations using an Arabic term that means, literally, an "outrage for God"—or, as Saad Eddin Ibrahim renders it, "propaganda by deed."[20] Nevertheless, even though most Islamic radicals have moved beyond the constraints of the mosque pulpit, the influence of their ideas and behavior on many of those who *do* preach is unmistakable. And because ritual preaching remains the common regular occasion for the public articulation of Islamic religio-political symbols, whatever understanding the wider Egyptian society has about the Islamic resurgence derives chiefly from the voices of particular preachers who have come to be identified with a rededication to religion and the better world it promises.

The approach taken here to the examination of two local preachers draws on the theoretical perspectives of contemporary anthropology to ritual, symbolism, and verbal performances.[21] It also enjoys the advantages (and concedes the limitations) of the classical anthropological research methodology — that is, an extended period of intensive personal observation and interaction known as *ethnographic fieldwork*. This technique concentrates on a microcosm, and — while it does not assume that the events and personalities encountered in that one setting are replicas of all those in parallel circumstances elsewhere — it does proceed on the premise that these particulars occur within a socio-cultural macrocosm that essentially shares the same structural forms and conceptual presuppositions.

The term *preacher* as used here with reference to Islam also merits clarification, for the term can invite confusion if it is understood to correspond to patterns of church authority in the Christian tradition. Sunni Islam staunchly denies the existence of an "official clergy," despite its long history of distinctive specialists. Thus, the term *preacher* in this context does not specify an occupational category or an inalienable ecclesiastic status, but rather particular actors who are distinguished by their habitual exercise of the function of ritual preaching. Unavoidably, this social role also carries with it a potential for status prerogatives. It also connotes the possibility of considerable influence upon the wider society, although as a ritual role such implicit authority does not have its basis in achievement or ascription in the ordinary sociological sense. Nor can the status it confers be aptly classified in the complementary paradigm of "secularity" and "religiosity" founded in the so-called metaphysics of dualism that classical social science formalism sets out as its characteristic frame of analysis.[22] Instead, ritual imparts a "liminal" rather than a "structural" authority to the one who disposes over it. The force of the "ritual process" stands apart from the power inherent in the hierarchical and segmental relationships that define and maintain the juro-political and socio-economical structure of society. Ritual therefore facilitates a modality of social solidarity — called "communitas" by Victor Turner — that temporarily lightens the gravity of this-worldly experience: "Rules that abolish minutiae of structural differentiation in, for example, the domains of kinship, economics, and political structure liberate the human structural propensity and give it free reign in the cultural realm of myth, ritual and symbol."[23]

Ritual requires a separation from the "incumbencies of social positions and statuses" because on that basis it suspends the ordinary cognitive and conventional restraints that constitute the world of common sense. Only then can there occur what "is perhaps the principle function of the rite, that of allowing intellectually 'impossible' things to happen."[24] Ultimately, however, this ritual realm of the ideal and the "impossible" has meaning only in its relationship to the real world of inescapably limited possibilities. Although a ritual may exhibit playful reversals or exalt in flights of fantasy, it finally resolves with the reestablishment of that essential structure without which no human society can survive. The social function of ritual, therefore, with its generative and transformative potency, resides in the need to integrate fragmented and isolating roles into the satisfying involvement in a cohesive societal unity — to change coercion into cooperation and to translate belief into morality.

The effect of ritual can be both as a catalyst and as a stabilizer. From one perspective, ritual performs a function of reflection, since it derives meaning from a logic of exaggeration and opposition against the prevailing pressures of nature, power, wealth, obligation, and affection. Ritual sanctions the public interpretation of ideals and provides the occasion for a collective commitment to a divinely revealed vision of the "really real," hidden beneath the appearances of this passing world of day-to-day reality. Ritual therefore variously reflects this imperfect world, with its institutions of competition and production, but ritual also strives to shape them on the basis of equity and justice.[25]

Often, in crisis circumstances, when extreme tensions are disrupting the relative equilibrium of a social structure, this dynamic and creative dimension of ritual supersedes its more static and affirming aspect. Hence, the familiar adage, heard frequently in today's Egypt, that people return to religion in troubled times, rightfully points to a connection between the Islamic resurgence and underlying social, political, and economic conflicts; however, it tends to focus on only one side of a more complex phenomenon. What this commonplace observation overlooks is the fact that this widespread escalation of ritual and religious enthusiasm includes not just a reaction to recent history, but a determination to steer it in another direction. Religion not only provides a haven of comfort to the weak and confused victims of structural change, it offers a source of inspiration for those who seek to reorder it according to other-worldly criteria.

The particular Islamic ritual concerned in this discussion is the Friday noon prayer service, whose unique and distinguishing feature is a sermon.

This weekly event is the single obligatory occasion for ritual preaching in the Islamic tradition, and the one who preaches does so in the name of the community. Historically and theologically, this has meant that he acts in the name of the legitimately reigning caliph, who presides as the Prophet's successor. But following a long era of decline in Muslim civilization and the erosion of even a nominal political unity within the Islamic imperium, such a theoretical relationship of the preacher to a religiously confirmed ruler has become problematic. Moreover, due to the long process of socio-political deterioration that characterizes much of Egyptian history since medieval times, the authority of the local preacher—especially outside the few large urban centers—has been progressively deflated.[26] One consequence of this more generalized and prolonged cultural atrophy was the virtual fossilization of the Islamic sermon. It was not until the beginning of this century that ritual preaching began to undergo a minor renaissance, spurred by the efforts of some of the same Islamic reformers who laid the foundations for the contemporary resurgence.[27]

Hence, it may well be that the range of variation among mosque preachers in present-day Egypt is greater than it has been for hundreds of years. So too the degree of influence a preacher exercises in his community also varies widely. A preacher's authority cannot be reduced solely to his technical skills as a orator, nor can a given preacher's actual influence be equated with the traditional indices of prestige that accompany his position in an official sense, such as his titles or the size or standing of the mosque he serves. Rather, in order to appreciate the impact of a preacher—and particularly one who represents the current Islamic resurgence—a composite of three factors may be considered. First, an examination of the biography of the preacher is vital, both in terms of local knowledge and his own self-presentation, especially within the ritual, for this supplies a general schema for his overall social identity. Then, reference to a common stock of understandings about the practice of preachers qualifies the relationship of any particular ritual specialist to the pattern of those who speak for the sacred. Finally, the conduct of a preacher in the comprehensive life of the community apart from his ritual role elucidates the extent to which he exemplifies a concrete realization of what he recommends by his words of structural contradiction.[28]

The research upon which the following discussion draws was carried out primarily in Minya, the capital city and minor metropolis of the governorate in upper Egypt of the same name. It was done during an eighteen-month period in 1978–79, with a return visit of shorter duration in 1985. Minya is a city of approximately 200,000 residents but for a large proportion of these, as is the case in other upper Egyptian cities, the distinction between a rural and an urban lifestyle is not always clear. The city has an odd shape in that it stretches for several kilometers in a thin strip along the western bank of the Nile. The city center, though now greatly dilapidated, shows its origins as the product of the Victorian colonial era when a European commercial and landholding enclave prospered alongside an emerging Egyptian *haute bourgeoisie,* whose crumbling mansions have after the revolution come to serve such new purposes as party headquarters or multifamily residences. On its northern and southern end, the city merges with preexisting and ever-growing rural villages. On the eastern side, the city's rapid expansion has recently leaped its natural boundary of the Ibrihammiya Canal, alongside which runs the Nile Valley's only highway and rail line. While older residents decry the city's decline from its past stature as a provincial outpost of urbane gentility, Minya nonetheless remains the hub of a populous rural hinterland as well as the locale of district branches of all government ministries. Also, not only does Minya serve as the center for the region's primary economic activity (agriculture), but it is also the regional point of concentration for agricultural processing, light industry, finance, commerce, transportation, medical services, entertainment, education, and religion. A university established in the city in 1976 has a student population of nearly 10,000.

Among the Muslims of Minya there are understood to be three basic types of religious institutions. One of them is represented by the Sufi brotherhoods, and it need not concern us in the present discussion, since it is relatively marginal except for certain extravagant displays on such holidays as the Prophet's birthday. The other two are conceptualized as types of mosques, although they include a great deal more than the physical buildings. The first of these, which stands as the normative, traditional form, is referred to in the colloquial language as a government mosque. These mosques are distinguished by the fact that they are operated under immediate state supervision through the ministry of religious endowments. But even more socially visible than this source of support is the identity of the preacher, or shaykh, as he is called. The preacher in a government mosque is always a graduate of the Azhar who has been assigned to a given mosque by means of the same bureaucratic procedure whereby all functionaries in all ministries receive their appointments. Similarly, he is paid on the same salary scale, graded to his education credentials, his seniority, and his job rating, as reported by inspectors and superiors. Such a preacher is highly visible in several respects. For instance, he wears at all times a distinctive uniform consisting of a dark, ankle-length coat and, on his head, a red *tarboosh* topped by a black silk tassel, around the base of which a white cloth band is wrapped. Also, the manner in which these professional shaykhs carry out their functions conforms to what is considered to be the classical model. This includes significant stylistic details about the way they lead the ritual prayer and, more important, the way they preach.

As preachers, they tend to be very formal, even stilted. Generally, their sermons are brief and compact, showing a strong conservativism with regard to both form and content. Nevertheless, some are regarded as masters of this learned oratorical genre and admired from an aesthetic viewpoint for this skill, while what they actually say in the preachment evokes less interest. To this extent, it is not what they say but who they are, as elucidated by this manner, that gives their performance its effectiveness.

These mosques spoken of as belonging to the government tend to be the older establishments that fell to the state after it nationalized the properties designated to provide funds for their upkeep—or they are mosques the ministry has lately appropriated in pursuit of its long-range plans for the eventual alignment of all religious institutions in some form of regulation.[29] Many of these mosques owe their origin to the popular devotion to a holy man (or woman), whose tomb at this site may continue to draw pious visitors and elicit contributions. These practices are regarded by Azhar-trained preachers and by those inspired by the Islamic resurgence as inexcusably heterodox. Yet within the government system they are tolerated, and in fact many of those employed at such mosques benefit substantially from the alms left at such shrines. Certain government mosques also serve a civic or cathedral function. Here, community ceremonies may be carried out, or high state dignitaries attend the Friday ritual prayers, often arriving with an official entourage and being grandly received with considerable deference. President Sadat, especially in his final years, often frequented government mosques in this manner, and it was a common thing to see a photograph on the front page of Saturday's newspaper showing him in the first row of the congregation among whom he had prayed the day before.

The final type of Muslim institution, and the one that will receive the most attention in this discussion, is the type of mosque known in colloquial Egyptian Arabic as a *popular mosque*. The etymology of this term lies in a now obsolete legal distinction between types of religious trust funds, but today the term designates a mosque that is not directly supervised by the ministry of religious endowments and in that sense is "free"—a term that is also sometimes used to describe such mosques. In theory, these mosques are supported by private contributions and staffed by volunteers, although in fact there are many indirect sources of state subsidies available and the ministry of religious endowments has the authority to intervene in their conduct of public ritual, (although it may not always exercise that right). In principle, such an institution is not primarily a mosque, but in the eyes of the government it constitutes a charitable foundation that may include a place of public prayer as an outgrowth of what is officially known as a "voluntary benevolent society."[30] The philanthropic motive is considered to be the essential one, and for this reason these associations are technically regulated by the ministry of social affairs even though in many cases religious ritual is the only real activity. Over the last decade and a half, the number of such societies has grown throughout Egypt from the hundreds to the thousands, and this fact also forms part of the pattern of the Islamic resurgence.[31]

In Minya, perhaps forty such voluntary benevolent societies have been founded for different stated purposes of social assistance. Many of them also have attached to them mosques of various sizes, which are used with varying degrees of frequency. Two such societies, however, stand out as both the most prominent and the largest. Another factor — and a pivotal one — that gives these two societies unusual distinction is the renown of their preachers. In both cases (and it is not at all the rule for most popular mosques), the preachers are regular and permanent — that is, they preside each week rather than partake in a sort of rotation. Although neither has any of the formal training considered necessary for a traditional professional preacher, each is not only the leader in ritual but also holds the office of president of the society's executive council. Consequently, each is officially charged with a dual role, and each projects his particular personality into all facets of his respective organizations. One obvious sign of this extraordinary influence is reflected in the way local Muslims refer to these mosques. They do not use the proper name of the society, as is done in most other cases, but the societies are spoken of in terms of the mosque and the mosque is known by the name of its preacher — that is, "the mosque of Shaykh X." Among all the preachers of Minya, these two most clearly embody what is felt to represent the new spirit of Islam.

The first of these two preachers is the elder, whom I shall call Shaykh Abu Bakr. Over seventy years of age, he is remarkably vigorous, at least in his role as a forceful and even bombastic orator. His whole message and manner invite the listener to regard him as a lifelong exponent of a stern and uncompromising Islam. In fact, not only is he a favorite of the local students (who regard themselves as the vanguard of Islamic consciousness), but many youthful admirers compare him to Ayatollah Khomaini, who in 1978–79, was the center of world attention. In his actual sermons, Shaykh Abu Bakr often includes autobiographical allusions, or relates judgmental opinions upon historical events of his lifetime (from the 1940s or 1950s, for instance), always implying a continuity of absolute fidelity to divine commands.

Upon careful investigation, however, one discovers that the image of Shaykh Abu Bakr as a religious revolutionary was only recently acquired (or rather, constructed). He began his career as a primary school teacher, trained in the provincial school system of more than a half-century ago where the Quran played a key part in the curriculum. In the 1940s, Shaykh Abu Bakr emerged from the relative obscurity of a rural upper Egyptian grade-school classroom to become a prominent spokesman for the regional unit of the syndicate of school teachers. Eventually, he brought the interests of this lower echelon of country teachers and similar functionaries to national forums, where he won a reputation for defending their cause against the growing tide of an education system modeled on a Westernized, secular curriculum. He was appreciated for his performances as a fiery and indefatigable speaker who could stir up the emotions of the masses with virulent assaults upon the power brokers and overlords of the day—the British and their cat's-paws among the Egyptian aristocracy.

After the revolution of 1952, Shaykh Abu Bakr became an ardent Nasserist. Many of the older generation still vividly recall his thunderous public addresses extolling the glories of Arab socialism and lashing out at imperialism and reactionary capitalism, those great demons seeking to undermine the progress of the nation. In fact, during that era, Shaykh Abu Bakr won the epithet of Orator of the Revolution, although today he projects no clue that he was once a very prominent mouthpiece for the party and the state. During these same years, not only did the shaykh frequently share a podium with state and party officials, but he was given the rare opportunity to travel abroad in the service of Nasser's propaganda campaigns. In his sermons, the shaykh occasionally alludes proudly to his "personal acquaintance" with the wider world, usually to certify a declaration of European perfidy or moral corruption; but, again, he never elaborates on the context of or reasons for such a trip.

The great bulk of Shaykh Abu Bakr's devoted congregation is made up of lower-class or lower middle-class young men, most of whom are one or two generations removed from a village background. Many are illiterate, while others have only enough education to have been able to find work as laborers, drivers, small artisans, and petty merchants. But this shaykh also attracts a type of zealous student and follower from that growing number of poorly paid and often geographically displaced young men who have minor posts in one of the many local government offices. The mosque complex is situated in the far southern end of the city, which has only fairly recently been built up but is already overcrowded and straining the available public works facilities. This location is important not only because the mosque naturally draws from the surrounding neighborhoods, but also because of its considerable distance from the university, which is at the far northern end of the city. Members of the Islamic student groups, therefore, who at first were among the most ardent supporters of Shaykh Abu Bakr, have gradually diminished among his regular listeners, partially because of the very long walk required to attend. However, another reason for this gradual decline in audience among student Islamicists is the increasing growth in the size and consolidation of their own organization, which has established independent bases for meeting and prayer closer to the university. Further, this incipient split had underlying ideological and political grounds as well: as the group identity of the Islamic student group became more pronounced (and as their reputation for civil agitation grew), their association with Shaykh Abu Bakr decreased. On the other hand, when police appeared in large numbers around the university to effectively prevent demonstrative meetings, an alternative for the Islamic student group was to attempt to stage their events from this other location.

The mosque in which Shaykh Abu Bakr preaches is very large by local standards, capable of holding approximately 1,500 people seated on the floor. Built only in 1969, it is officially called the "new mosque," for it replaced a much smaller structure nearby that has been adopted by the benevolent society operating the present mosque and the adjoining complex of social service facilities. This particular benevolent society is not altogether the product of local initiative, but is rather a branch of a national network of associations knows as the *Shar'ia* ("Islamic law") Society, with central headquarters in Cairo. The whole complex is enormous, covering an area of approximately a square city block, and includes a student residence for women, a children's day care center, a pharmacy, a playing field, an office building designed to house such facilities as a counselling center, meeting rooms, and study halls. In fact, though, as I observed, the welfare-related services at this mosque were in a very poor state of organization. While some of those connected with the benevolent society boast of their extensive offerings, in actuality the complex is all but abandoned except on those occasions when Shaykh Abu Bakr preaches, when the mosque is sometimes filled to capacity. It is as though the politically provocative Islam embodied in this shaykh since he has lately become the mosque's preacher has had the side effect of dissipating the interest and energy required to support the more mundane services. Also, Shaykh Abu Bakr himself is rarely at the mosque except in order to preach. When he receives visitors or occasionally presides at meetings, his manner is typically very aloof and his remarks often have an affected quality that seems to retain the pulpit tone and vaguely recreate the oratorical context in a way that hampers discussion.

Another significant feature of Shaykh Abu Bakr's self-presentation is his highly ceremonious dress, which is evidently designed to epitomize what is conceived by local Islamicists to be the literal imitation of the Prophet's apparel. Most important, of course, is the beard, which in this Shaykh's case is without moustache and cut in a peculiarly meticulous manner that is the ultimate in Islamic correctness. His outer garment is an ankle-length coat roughly of the same style as the traditional uniform worn by a professional, Azhar-trained preacher. However, this coat differs in its more expensive fabric, its lighter color, and in the exquisitely tailored cut—details that make it highly distinctive and, as one admirer put it, simply "more chic." Beneath this coat, the shaykh wears a similarly fashionable belted kaftan of white silk offset with dark, lengthwise pinstripes. (These latter elements do not have explicit precedent in the traditions of the Prophet's garb, but they were justified as fulfilling the divine love of "beauty.") On his head, Shaykh Abu Bakr wears a large felt *tarboosh* that is also highly distinctive—in fact, there is nothing quite like it anywhere else in the city. Beige in color instead of the dark red identified with the traditional shaykh, it lacks the silk tassel of the classical *tarboosh,* for Islamicists insist that the Prophet has forbidden such adornments to men. Around the bottom of the fez he wraps a white cloth band, again in the manner of the traditional Azhar uniform but differing in one conspicuous particular: the pointed end of the abbreviated turban dangles down several inches over the back of his neck, in a fashion said to mirror the way in which the Prophet wore his headpiece. To this basic ensemble, the shaykh also sometimes adds such striking accouterments as an ample woolen cloak that has almost a folkloric grandeur, and a stylish wooden staff about the length of a swagger stick.

In his sermons, too, Shaykh Abu Bakr has developed a marked manner of his own, which relies heavily on rough-hewn but flamboyant rhetorical devices that are clearly aimed at producing a pitch of excitement among his audience. His sermons are long, often going on for an hour or an hour and a half. (A government mosque preacher normally speaks for no more than fifteen or twenty minutes.) He follows the approximate structure of a traditional sermon, but he plays freely with it, often displacing the order and engaging in exaggerated introductions and elongated conclusions. Moreover, he uses the colloquial dialect, although generously charging it with classicisms, whereas an Azhar-trained preacher uses only formal Arabic in the pulpit. This linguistic factor is very important, not only because of the much greater directness of communciation and the added liberty of expression available in the everyday idiom, but because an uneducated or barely educated audience to a large extent cannot understand high Arabic (although hearing it, they feel a sincere respect for the cultural authority it connotes).

Shaykh Abu Bakr, like other preachers involved in the Islamic resurgence, attempts to make his sermons topical and, within certain limits, critical of what fails to correspond to the norms of an Islamic order. He therefore strives to comment on familiar political and social dynamics, which he recasts into a framework of religious imperatives. In 1978 and 1979, Islamic student groups at the University of Minya had succeeded in exacerbating implicit sectarian and social tensions both on the campus and, increasingly, in the city to the degree that serious clashes were breaking out that threatened to trigger dan-

gerous chain reactions of retaliation. Later, it was an outbreak of just this nature in Cairo, again precipitated by a local sectarian—that is, Christian-
Muslim—feud, that led to the series of escalating reprisals that Sadat had
moved to end by means of mass arrests and crackdowns a month prior to his
assassination.[32]

One particularly dramatic and disruptive display on the part of these Islamic groups occurred in March of 1979, on the very day that the Camp David
Accords were being signed in Washington by Carter, Begin, and Sadat. The
Islamicists opposed this settlement as a betrayal of the religious duty of *jihad*
and a sellout of "Islamic Palestine," and now to manifest their rejection of
the treaty they blocked the entry of students to the Minya university campus
—in effect, to close down the operation of the university. Other less ambitious
gestures of defiance occurred elsewhere, and a mood of emboldened confrontation arose in what was already a highly charged atmosphere. While this provocative one-day boycott ended without incident, it showed a new level of
disregard for public authority. Police and and other security forces did not
intervene at the time, but afterwards they responded by arresting two of the
leaders of the Islamic student group and by posting guards and agents around
the university. Apparently, the Islamic groups planned to continue their initiative on the following Friday, with a march and perhaps other displays of
protest that would originate at the mosque of Shaykh Abu Bakr after the
noon prayer. It was hoped, of course, that those who came to hear the sermon
could then be enlisted in the march, where the greater numbers would lend
force to whatever disruptions were planned by the ringleaders.

The police, however, preempted this scheme, preventing what would have
surely been an occasion for large-scale antigovernment rabble-rousing and could
have led to an explosion of mob frenzy. But the security forces not only saw
to it that no public protest occurred, they also made a contrary display of
their own might by dispatching a contingent of troops to the mosque in the
early morning hours and announcing that it would be closed for the day, thus
cancelling the Friday prayer. Such a closure is most extraordinary and had
to impress the community with the seriousness of the circumstances, although
judgments about the "right" of the state to make such a definitive move against
"Islam" were predictably divided along ideological lines. A week later, when
the mosque reopened and Shaykh Abu Bakr returned to his pulpit, he issued
a virulent condemnation of this move by the government and its agencies.
However, he never mentioned the actual facts of what had happened, nor
did he make any defense (or imply his innocence) of ulterior plans of a week
before. The following segment from this sermon of 4 April 1979, which I
managed to tape-record, illustrates certain typical patterns of his rhetorical
style in the fusion of religious and political symbols. Although this transla-

tion conveys the text of his preaching, it unavoidably loses the high voltage of Shaykh Abu Bakr's vocal mastery and his use of tempo, volume, and pitch, nor can it preserve the rhetorical force imparted by repetition and plays on Arabic morphology. This citation falls toward the beginning of his sermon, where he is lashing out at those who, in his words, are utterly "without religion, without goodness, without truth," and therefore the consummate enemies of God:

> Those who live their lives in this [godless] way are mounts for any rider, fair prey for any thief, and those who believe in the Day of Reckoning and responsibility before God, exalted be He, and then permit themselves to serve the hand of falsehood, whether it be that of a king, a president, a minister, the rich or the powerful, a father or a son, what will that bring them? For if there is someone who believes in the day of resurrection, in the rising and judgment, in the reward on earth or in heaven, and he permits someone, whoever it might be, to direct him to falsehood, to lies or evil, the Book of God, glorious and majestic, confirms a fact about them when it says: "Assuredly thou art calling them to a straight path; and surely they that believe not in the world to come are deviating from the path." (Sura 23:72–73).[33]
>
> Indeed I ask every one of you a question that you should put before your eyes at this instant: Do you want to please God? If you want to please God and you are a [government] employee or a worker, whatever happens to be your position, your place of work, whatever your job is, high or low: Do you have anything that can protect you from God? Is there anyone you can turn to for protection from God?
>
> If you want to please God, and indeed you believe that there can be no one to protect you from God, then why do you commit falsehood? Why do you do anything before you have determined whether it is truth or falsehood? This is the question that everyone must pose to himself day and night so long as you want to please God. Then why do you do what God does not want?
>
> If you truly believe that there is no one who can protect you from God, and this is affirmed by the prophets and angels, for the Prophet said to his sons, "I cannot protect you from God," and what is more, the noblest of all creatures, the pinnacle of creation, the one closest to God, exalted be he, that is Muhammad, said to his own daughter, "I cannot protect you from God." If the Prophet himself says this, then why do you obey the President in a matter that angers your Lord? Put the matter before you and go through with it so that no one will be able to divert you to a lie, or to falsehood, or to hypocrisy, or to evil, for this world is paltry, its pleasures are small and it lasts but a short time. Nor will its enjoyments help you.
>
> If you believe in the Day of Reckoning and you are in any position or in any job, then take heed! Take heed lest you commit forgery, falsehood or evil!
>
> Someone asks—I'm a government employee in such and such an agency, a

teacher, a supervisor, a judge, an engineer, a clerk, a head of a department, governor of a governorate, the chief of the secret police. What will you do about the policies of the government when they ask you to arrest someone without any reason whether it be false or true? This is the question I want to put to everyone on the face of the earth.

One of the most striking features of this citation (and of Shaykh Abu Bakr's sermon rhetoric generally) is his use of stark and absolute contrasts. He avoids refinements of judgments or qualifications of thought that might temper the exclusive character of his dichotomies. He constantly reiterates such extreme polarities as truth and falsehood, good and evil, honor and disgrace, Islam and godlessness, always painting with broad and definite strokes of either black or white, with nothing in between. What is more, he repeats these declaratives, sometimes in long litanies of contrary pairs. One intention behind this technique is obviously to vilify and stigmatize any person, action, or event the shaykh wants to insert into this archnegative column of the moral ledger. But interestingly, to accomplish this goal another set of assumptions is also implied—namely, that he, the preacher, speaks for the archpositive side.

This implicit claim on the right to represent what is good and holy appears in another form in the manner and frequency of the shaykh's resort to the text of the Quran. Clearly, he fully controls this sacred text, memorized as a child and then taught for a lifetime, and is capable of fitting into his speech those verses that he asserts are affirmations of whatever it is he has been elaborating. Sometimes, whole sermons are couched as commentaries on quranic verses, wherein he quotes enormous amounts of the book. Another of his favorite ploys is to set up what he calls comparisons between the Quran on the one hand and the Gospel and the Torah on the other. These discourses are often wild jumbles of misquotations from these scriptures of the "people of the book"—that is, Christians and Jews—with the object of the exercise always to show the utter truth of the former and the absolute falsehood of the latter two. In fact, such textual exercises serve merely as transparent attacks on the communties represented by these books, and the preacher frequently leaps precipitously from parodies of textual analysis to open insults directed against Jews and Christians. Not only does he use such code words as *Crusaders* and *Zionists,* which signal sectarian aggression, but at times he singles out leaders of the Coptic church by name and labels them as godless and treacherous. Related to this is another trope employed by Shaykh Abu Bakr that inevitably draws an enthusiastic response from his listeners. It involves the very rapid recitation of lengthy sections of the Quran in an accelerated tempo, as though a 45-r.p.m. record were being played at 78 r.p.m. Unless one already knows the text, it is impossible to hear and actually understand what is being said in such a rattling recitation, but the effect of this deluge of sacred words in itself evokes excitement.

The other implication of Shaykh Abu Bakr's habitual rhetorical dualism is the removal of his frame of reference from the actualities of any particular time and place into a lofty realm of uninhibited feeling and idealized abstraction. It is the ritual setting that enables him to achieve this elevation from the real world that adds a distant and ethereal quality to the apocalyptic urgency tied to the question, "Do you want to please God?" Ralph Nicholas has sharply described the societal dynamics embedded in this mode of cultural expression: "If a movement seeks a positive goal, a total social, political, and economic restructuring, it does so in the face of opposition from the powers that be. . . . Whatever the ultimate ground of authority in a culture, a general tendency in ideology is to draw an absolute antithesis between the prevailing secular authority and the authority on which the movement is based, between absolute evil and absolute good. Manichean imagery is a common feature of ideologies; it endows an ideology with absolute authority by demonizing its opposition."[34]

In the excerpt of the sermon above, it is noteworthy how the preacher selects his examples with an eye for implied political reference. He starts with the most diffuse category, that of government employees, but he is soon extrapolating to higher realms of decision making and policy setting. Instead of turning then to the local officials who actually carried out the police action, he builds up this momentum to a roaring jeremiad. At its climax, Shaykh Abu Bakr resorts to apostrophe, calling upon President Sadat personally to answer to God. Nor does the shaykh stop there, but names Egypt's prime minister and minister of defence as well. In this pointed choice of cabinet ministers singled out for rebuke, he suggests the evident priority of his preoccupations—that is, forceful confrontations that suggest political intentions. Thus, by a logic of association, he inflates the importance of what happens in Minya by fixing the responsibility for these local events upon the highest powers imaginable while omitting any mention of local officials. And this soaring to judgment does not stop with the heights of the nation, for the shaykh goes on to condemn by name the leaders of several Arab states, including Libya, Syria, and Iraq, for their alleged outrages against Islam. He continues with sweeping damnations of the superpowers, the United States and Russia. Then he finishes by adding Europe and listing its countries one by one in a rousing roll call, rebuking them all as monstrous perpetrators of godlessness upon the earth.

Behind this fantastic corralling of worldly powers for divine judgment is a ritual reversal by which this preacher exalts his congregation as the true and the righteous ones regardless of their exclusion from the decisive affairs of even their own community and nation. The political symbols seized by Shaykh Abu Bakr are the gross emblems of those unapproachable forces that are blamed for life's misery in an upper Egyptian slum. His conjuring up of distant evil forces on the one hand and the pride of local honor on the other only thinly masks an essential we-and-them vision that splits the world on many levels. Not only is it a question of "our" religion and "our" nation against the "others," but the preacher refers to the condemned in abstract and distant categories while the divinely favored are reducible to the concrete experience of that immediate congregation.

The amplification and intensification of the ritual itself is therefore the consequence of Shaykh Abu Bakr's leadership. Constructing his interpretation of reality on such heavily subjective premises, he evidently does bolster a collective feeling of power, but at the price of separating those who partake in the ritual from the world of structure and natural forces. Hence, the charitable services supposedly delivered by his benevolent society (which are theoretically the fruits of their inspiration) have virtually disappeared, and all that remains is the ritual. The mosque comes to resemble a theatre fairly unconnected to the real world outside, in which spirited rehearsals are conducted in anticipation of that Last Day when the most ardent hope for another and better world will be fulfilled.

The other voluntary benevolent society and associated popular mosque regarded as the second prominent exemplar of the Islamic resurgence in Minya is similar to the first in its formal structure, but quite different in orientation and character. Moreover, the particular qualities of Shaykh Ali, its preacher, offer the best image of what the institution represents as a whole. Compared with Shaykh Abu Bakr, he is a young man, approximately forty-five years of age. Although Shaykh Ali is also originally a school teacher, his training and career occurred within the framework of a modern secular educational system. Shaykh Ali had been very successful in the classroom, and in 1977 was appointed to one of the highest positions in the regional office of the ministry of education. There he continues to head the department of public relations, and as such enjoys extensive contacts both throughout the governorate and within the national bureaucracy that oversees teachers and schools. As a person he projects a casual and self-confident air, at ease with people of all classes — capable of being serious, and yet never without a simple, peaceful charm and a hardy sense of humor.

The father of Shaykh Ali was also a school teacher, as is his only brother, who serves as the assistant principal at Minya's most prestigious high school. It was the father who founded this benevolent society some fifteen years prior to his death in 1977. At that time Shaykh Ali was selected to succeed his father, who until then had served as the the head of the society and, on Fridays as the ritual preacher. Even before Shaykh Ali took over—or, in a manner of speaking, inherited—this double position, he had already been active for years as a preacher in a number of smaller popular mosques, most recently at the place for prayer located in the basement of the teachers' club. Shaykh's Ali's father had been widely respected in the local Muslim community as a kindly man of simple but firm religious convictions. In his youth he had joined the Muslim Brothers, and after the 1952 revolution had suffered the fate of many others who shared this affiliation. He was imprisoned on four separate occasions coinciding with the major crackdowns under Nasser. The fourth time, in the mid-1960s, Shaykh Ali was arrested with his father and imprisoned for about a month. Neither in his conversation nor in his preaching, however, does the shaykh refer to this experience in his past, although it clearly brings him a tacit prestige among many younger Islamicists, who tend to romanticize what they regard as persecution for the sake of religious ideals.

Shaykh Ali received his primary education in Minya's government schools of the post–World War II era, when the city had a thriving European population of several thousand—largely Greeks, but many French, British, and Americans as well. He also attended a traditional *kuttab* ("Quran school") after hours, and it was there that he learned to recite the Quran by heart. From all indications, however, this feat of childhood memorization did not prepossess Shaykh Ali's attitude toward his later intellectual formation with respect to religion. He says rather that he was an avid reader in his youth, and the book that made the most lasting impression upon him was Muhammad Husayn Haykal's *Life of Muhammad*. This famous work was widely praised at the time of its publication in 1935 as the first competent biography written by a Muslim according to the criteria of scientific historiography, and it is reckoned today as a classic of Islamic modernism.[35]

After graduating from a teacher-training high school in Minya, Shaykh Ali continued his secondary education at the British teachers' college in Assiut, the largest city in upper Egypt, some 150 kilometers to the south. In virtue of this training and his own dedication, Shaykh Ali speaks fluent English, a feat which is unusual even among language instructors in this part of Egypt. This language proficiency has clearly opened up broader horizons, making him something of a provincial intellectual who has in recent years been recruited to provide his services as a translator for distinguished visitors to the city. In 1985, his oldest son received his doctorate in English literature from the University of Edinburgh, and is now on the faculty of the University of Assiut.

Shaykh Ali dresses in a way that fully conforms to the standard custom of his age and his profession. Depending on the season, he wears a light or heavy two-piece suit with a shirt and tie. Following the practice of Egypt's secular elite of the last generation he wears no hat of any kind, not even when he prays or preaches (in spite of the fact that many orthodox Muslims consider a ritual head-covering to be very important). He has a full moustache but no beard, and has refused to grow one despite the pressure of Islamicists. He preaches in approximately the same clothes that would be worn to his job or to a public gathering, thereby expressing a deliberate and striking informality. With regard to ritual gestures, he also follows this same pattern of reducing the external symbolic tokens of his function to a minimum. For instance, quite contrary to custom, he often preaches from prepared notes. His posture is likewise extraordinary, for he does not mount the traditional pulpit but sits on the floor at the same level as and facing his audience.

The compound that makes up the facilities of Shaykh Ali's mosque is somewhat smaller and more compact that that of Shaykh Abu Bakr. The mosque itself is a plain and relatively small structure set apart from the real center of the society, which consists of a long one-story building divided into several sections. An annex built beside and above the mosque houses university students. Bordering the property on the south is a rough wooden shed that serves as a food cooperative for members of the society. Geographically, the complex, though quite recent, is located fairly near the city center, largely due to a quirk in the way Minya expanded westward across the Ibrahimiyya Canal. The site where the society's cluster of buildings now stands is on the bank of that waterway but is oddly enclosed on three sides. The canal is on one side, and—parallel to it—the railway line and highway are on the other. Bordering it on the north is one of the city's major bridges over the canal; the bridge is unusually high, to allow for the passage of boats. The highway at this point rises on a ramp that goes up to the level of this high bridge, creating a partial roof for what now serves as an open court neatly integrated into the whole complex. Before the benevolent society took an interest in the site, it had been used as a garbage dump. Today, the overall impression is of a compound snugly nestled into a sheltered oasis removed from the commotion of traffic, commerce, and neighborhood streets.

Another feature of Shaykh Ali's society is the sense of activity that hums throughout the compound, even apart from times of ritual prayer. As already mentioned, students—all male—occupy rooms here at a nominal cost. These dormitory facilities, though extremely simple, are much in demand, and the society has recently expanded this service by obtaining another building a few blocks away. There is also a medical clinic that provides primary care and checkups at a price well below that of private doctors. Besides these facilities, the society seems to be constantly adapting to the interests and needs of different groups and helping to provide space and the proper environment for various self-help programs. Examples include the obtaining of a few sewing machines and offering sessions to train women to make clothing, or a course of lessons in do-it-yourself repair of household appliances.

The congregation that attends this mosque on Fridays tends to be well-educated, and a large proportion have had some college training. Many of them are younger men, but there is also a healthy proportion of older heads of families, whose political awareness and cultural refinement probably surpass their economic capacities. These generally dissatisfied and underemployed people tend to be more heavily involved in the affairs of their families and neighborhoods than in their salaried work. They are not especially prone to ideological appeals, but are eager to understand the ideas that stir public opinion and to participate in the significant movements of the contemporary world.

The sermon style of Shaykh Ali, like that of others inspired by a vision of Islam applied to modern society, attempts to be relevant to the issues of the day; however, the rhetoric is characterized by subtlety, pragmatism, and a call for moral discrimination on the part of the individual. In his preaching Shaykh Ali rarely cites the Quran, and even when he does, the lines are usually from its most familiar passages. His normal sermon is constructed around episodes drawn from the life of the Prophet and his companions. Shaykh Ali has a cultivated way of playing at once both the story-teller and the commentator, often mixing the two together chronologically while he maintains the separate levels through a number of dramatic devices, such as the use of linguistic skills related to code-switching and diglossia. He supplements these technical rhetorical devices with a good bit of friendly response to the crowd. The latter maintains a respectful silence, but the shaykh reacts to their facial expressions and body language and comments upon these in a sort of dialectical fashion.

In content, Shaykh Ali's sermons can have a penetrating editorial tone, focusing on local events or on national or international happenings of the past week. Frequently, the key to understanding the unstated point behind an account in the Prophet's life (or that of one of his heroic contemporaries) is to have read the newspaper. For instance, in 1978, shortly after Palestinian terrorists had highjacked a plane to kidnap Yusef Sabai, former editor of *al-Ahram* and one of Sadat's inner circle, Egypt attempted and badly bungled an Entebbe-like rescue mission at a Cyprus airport. The hostage was killed along with a score or more Egyptian commandos, while the kidnappers were unharmed and eventually surrendered to Cypriot authorities. The following Friday, Shaykh Ali avoided any direct reference to this incident, but instead recited a series of episodes from the lives of the early caliphs and their triumphant army commanders. He emphasized their great solicitude for the lives of their men, and the detailed planning and weighing of contingencies before subjecting soldiers to danger that characterized their tactics. He also chose stories stressing this point, referring to sea battles between the Muslims and the Greeks around the islands of the eastern Mediterranean.

While Shaykh Ali can frequently be heard delivering critical innuendos regarding national policy or mores, such as Sadat's lavish life-style and perceived cronyism — points he makes by elaborating on the frugality, humility, and fairness of the second caliph, Umar ibn al-Khutab — he is also capable of leveling his gentle rebuffs at behavior on a local level. Many times, for instance, he preaches about the "youth" in the days of Muhammad, pointing out how responsible, well-mannered, and compassionate they were, often proving to be more cool-headed, moderate, and prudent than older members of the community at Medina. In ways that are ingeniously indirect yet quite explicit for those with ears to hear, he thus reprimands not only the thug element in the student Islamic groups but also other forms of youthful behavior which, though less politically charged, are still unacceptable to Islam.

Shaykh Ali's position within a government ministry is overlaid with relations that function on the basis of his duties and status in that bureaucracy; however, some features of this public identity clearly carry over into his role as a ritual leader. He is basically a realist who accepts the facts of modern institutions and differentiated authority. He strives to distinguish between the formal structure of a rationalized system of governing and the individual functionary, who makes moral choices within a limited range of moral categories. He tends to single out the domain of the individual as a moral rather than a political participant. By his daily decisions rather than by his performance or enthusiasm at religious ritual, a Muslim either cooperates or obstructs, promotes or retards, the improvement of society. Responsibility, however, is not equally divided, and Shaykh Ali often focuses on those who are in the public spotlight.

The following citation comes at the end of a long sermon preached on 15 December 1978 in which the issue of bureaucratic overregulation was raised. It is noteworthy, not only for its approach to the legendary inefficiency of public works in Egypt (summed up by the word modern Arabic has borrowed from the French and English: "routine"), but also because it is framed in a self-referencing anecdote on the part of Shaykh Ali. He reveals how his role as a representative of a "religious" and "charitable" society has its special rights outside of the necessary structure of obligation and courtesy. He also shows, variously, his self-perception as one who is *in* but not *of* the local elite:

> The ogre of routine, my brothers, and the system of procedures, will we ever see an end to the ogre of routine in our day? I was representing you at a meeting of the good and gracious people at the police headquarters and it all went very well. It was [the occasion] when the director of the Ministry of Agriculture in

Minya, that is, the land reform, was saying farewell to become the General Director of the regional agricultural office in Beni Suef. It's a fine thing. Undoubtedly it will come to a good end, for the man is good and righteous. Indeed, everyone was invited to be present at this farewell for our gracious brother, that is, to attend the celebration of our gracious brother, including the new governor of the Governorate of Minya, may God keep him from error. But we disagree with some of what was said before these two good sirs, for congratulating is a simple matter. Everyone bestows congratulations; all factions congratulate; all companies congratulate; and that is fine. A happy outcome results when the hearts of the good turn toward their brothers, for the Prophet says, prayers and blessings of God upon him: "Whoever performs for you some honorable service, reward him, and if you are not able to do so, wish him well when he departs."

Thus we spoke at the police headquarters on the benefits of increasing education. But it is necessary to move from congratulations to the efforts of everyone in every position, each striving in his own right to bring about good for the service of all citizens. The congratulations of organizations and groups and companies to one of our brothers is not sufficient, however much it is appropriate. Indeed it is also necessary to move on to the step that follows the giving of congratulations and that means putting your hands out and setting your mind to the project itself in order to serve citizens. For this truly adds both to those who congratulate and those who are congratulated.

We were present representing you, and to God, exalted and praised be He, to whom be power and honor, saying that where matters of agriculture are concerned, they should be regulated at the level of the town, for where matters of the governorate are in the hands of the people themselves and are regulated at the local level, that is best. We want to commend [these decisions] to the people of the outlying areas for these are the ones closest to the problems of the [rural] countryside. We want to support those who are near to those good people, that they might solve their own problems for they know them best. The ogre of routine! Islam fights against it, my brothers. Oh how I wish all of us today, in whatever position we have would set about doing something. Oh how I wish we would fight against routine.

In this passage the recognition and approval of differentiated roles is self-evident. It is, of course, an appeal for decentralization, but on the basis of redistributing responsibility in the interests of efficiency. Islam is not depicted as a societal model that stands in opposition to an established order, but rather as the demand that each individual assume the proper duties and opportunities of his position. The plea for empowering local communities to decide on matters involving their own needs and resources is the opposite of the one that lumps together moral and technical questions and then projects the responsibility for solving them (or the blame for failing to do so) onto the highest possible authority, such as President Sadat or—beyond him—the super-powers. Shaykh Ali does not locate the source of good and evil at the polar extremes of society's power structure, but rather places them and their tension within the mind and heart of each citizen, who must take a stand for or against the pervasive ogre of routine.

In conclusion, these brief case studies suggest two related tendencies in the Islamic resurgence of Egypt. Shaykh Ali represents an effort to underplay the potential of ritual and to direct its force toward a secular world in need of change. He strives to put Islam into action, starting with personal inspiration and individual responsibility. The final object is reform of society. He himself exemplifies this priority of placing ritual in service of a more successful professional accomplishment. Religion motivates the transformation of an arid bureaucracy into a human community. Religion renews the citizen; it is not a counterweight of permanent opposition to worldly power.

Shaykh Abu Bakr, on the other hand, exaggerates the exceptional and liminal properties of ritual. He exploits the subjective and emotional insecurities of his audience, and leads them to the threshold of a millenarian enthusiasm and away from an encounter with the changing circumstances of daily life. He encourages an escapist vision that makes of structural weakness a distorted justification for rejecting a genuine engagement with the particular elements that cause this oppression and exclusion. The inflated invocation of a one-sided divine retribution directs energy to the replication and expansion of ritual expressions, rather than toward planning and reform.

The preacher's task is double, since ritual and structure are correlatives that have meaning only in terms of their dynamic interplay. When he gives voice to the ideals and sentiments of religion he is capable not only of arousing feeling but also of directing thoughts toward a transforming vision of society. The Islamic resurgence cannot therefore be described merely in terms of an increase in gestures of divine fury or elaborate displays of ritual: no less important are the determined but tempered efforts of those Muslims who seek to adjust the meanings of their religious heritage to the uncertain forces encountered in the realities of modern life.

Notes

1. See, for instance, Hamilton A. R. Gibb, *Modern Trends in Islam* (Chicago: University of Chicago Press, 1947), and Wilfred Cantwell Smith, *Islam in Modern History* (Princeton: Princeton University Press, 1957).

2. Morroe Berger, *Islam in Egypt Today: Social and Political Aspects of Popular Religion* (Cambridge: Cambridge University Press, 1970).

3. Ibid., p. 128.

4. Daniel Crecelius, "Azhar in the Revolution," *Middle East Journal* 20, no. 1 (Winter 1966): 31–49, and A. Chris Eccel, *Egypt, Islam and Social Change: Al-Azhar in Conflict and Accommodation* (Berlin: Klaus Schwarz Verlag, 1984).

5. Olivier Carré and Gerard Michaud, *Les Fréres Musulmans (1928–1982)* (Paris: Archives Gallimard Julliard, 1983), and Richard P. Mitchell, *The Society of the Muslim Brothers* (London: Oxford University Press, 1969).

6. Hassan Hanafi, "The Relevance of the Islamic Alternative in Egypt," *Arab Studies Quarterly* 4, nos. 1, 2 (Spring 1982): 61.

7. Tawfiq Al-Hakim, *The Return of Consciousness* (New York: New York University Press, 1985), p. 28.

8. J. D. Pennington, "The Copts in Modern Egypt," *Middle East Studies* 10, no. 2 (Spring 1982): 158–79.

9. John Waterbury, "The Crossing," *Egypt: Burdens of the Past/Options for the Future* (Bloomington: Indiana University Press, 1978), pp. 13–44.

10. Norma Salem-Babikian, "The Sacred and the Profane: Sadat's Speech to the Knesset," *Middle East Journal* 34, no. 1 (Winter 1980): 13–24.

11. Yvonne Y. Haddad, *Contemporary Islam and the Challenge of History* (Albany: SUNY Press, 1982), and John L. Esposito, *Islam and Politics* (Syracuse, N.Y.: Syracuse University Press, 1984).

12. Yvonne Yazbeck Haddad, "The Qur'anic Justification for an Islamic Revolution: The View of Sayyid Qutb," *The Middle East Journal* 37, no. 1 (Winter 1983): 14–29.

13. Fadwa El-Guindi, "Veiling Infitah with Muslim Ethic: Egypt's Contemporary Islamic Movement," *Social Problems* 28, no. 4 (April 1981): 465–85, and John Alden Williams, "Veiling in Egypt as a Political and Social Phenomenon," in John L. Esposito, ed., *Islam and Development: Religion and Sociopolitical Change* (Syracuse, N.Y.: Syracuse University Press, 1982), pp. 71–86.

14. Eric Davis, "Ideology, Social Class and Islamic Radicalism in Modern Egypt," in Said A. Arjomand, ed., *From Nationalism to Revolutionary Islam* (Albany: SUNY Press, 1984), pp. 134–57.

15. Mohamed Heikal, *Autumn of Fury* (New York: Random House, 1983), pp. 109–11.

16. For example, an article appeared on 7 September 1978, in *Le Monde* (Paris) by their own correspondent with the headline: "Le Meurtre d'un Prêtre Copte Par des intégristes Musulmans Suscite une Vive Émotion Dans La Communauté Chrétienne."

17. J. J. G. Jansen, "The Voice of Kishk (b. 1933)," in *The Challenge of the Middle East* eds. Ibrahim A. El-Sheikh et al (Amsterdam: University of Amsterdam, 1982), pp. 57–66.

18. Maurice Bloch, *Political Language and Oratory in Traditional Society* (London: Academic Press, 1975), pp. 16–17.

19. Mitchell, *Muslim Brothers,* pp. 5ff.

20. Saad Eddin Ibrahim, "Anatomy of Egypt's Militant Islamic Groups: Methodological Note and Preliminary Findings," *International Journal of Middle Eastern Studies* 12, no. 4 (December 1980): 437.

21. The work of Mary Douglas on the relationship of social organization to symbolic codes, of Victor Turner on ritual, and of Stanley Tambiah on form and meaning in cultural expression has been seminal to this interpretation.

22. Irving L. Horowitz, "Religion, the State, and Politics," in Myron J. Aronoff, ed., *Political Anthropology: Religion and Politics* (New Brunswick, N.J.: Transaction Books, 1984), p. 8.

23. Victor Turner, *The Ritual Process: Structure and Anti-Structure* (Ithaca, N.Y.: Cornell University Press, 1969), p. 133.

24. Roger Grainger, *The Language of the Rite* (London: Darton, Longman & Todd, 1974), p. 22.

25. Cf. Clifford Geertz, "Religion as a Cultural System," in *The Interpretation of Cultures* (New York: Basic Books, 1973), pp. 87–125.

26. Gabriel Baer, "Waqf Reform," in *Studies in the Social History of Modern Egypt* (Chicago: University of Chicago Press, 1969), pp. 79–92; P. M. Holt, "The Pattern of Egyptian Political History from 1517 to 1798," in P. M. Holt, ed., *Political and Social Change in Modern Egypt* (London: Oxford University Press, 1969), pp. 79–90; and Afaf Lutfi Al-Sayyid Marsot, "The Ulama of Cairo in the Eighteenth and Nineteenth Centuries," in Nikki R. Keddie, ed., *Scholars, Saints and Sufis: Muslim Religious Institutions Since 1500* (Berkeley: University of California Press, 1972), pp. 149–66.

27. Patrick D. Gaffney, "The Revival of Islamic Preaching in Egypt," *The American Research Center in Egypt Newsletter* 132 (Winter 1986): 40–46.

28. This interpretive schema is indebted to an outstanding analysis of Islamic religious practitioners in northern Lebanon. Cf. Michael Gilsenan, "Lying, Honor, and Contradiction," in Bruce Kapferer, ed., *Transaction and Meaning: Directions in the Anthropology of Exchange and Symbolic Behavior* (Philadelphia: Institute for the Study of Human Issues, 1976), pp. 190–219.

29. Official estimates in 1984 place the total number of mosques in Egypt at roughly 40,000, of which approximately 3,000 are fully maintained by the ministry of religious endowments. Of the remaining, a relatively large percentage are either small or geographically redundant, and therefore do not normally have the Friday noon prayer (and hence, no sermon). The ministry has a budget and a schedule that foresee the ultimate incorporation of all of Egypt's mosques into the government's system, but given present circumstances this day would seem to lie far in the future. *Al-Ahram*, 11 November 1984, pp. 1, 6.

30. Berger, *Islam in Egypt*, 65.

31. Hamid Ansari, "Sectarian Conflict in Egypt and the Political Expediency of Religion," *The Middle East Journal* 38, no. 3 (Summer 1984): 407.

32. Gilles Kepel, *Le Prophète et Pharaon: Les Mouvements islamistes dans l'Egypte Contemporaine* (Paris: La Découverte, 1984), pp. 183–211.

33. While the translation of the sermon is my own, for quranic citations I defer to that of Arthur J. Arberry, *The Koran Interpreted* (New York: MacMillan, 1955). The Sura and verse identifications I have supplied.

34. Ralph W. Nicholas, "Social and Political Movements," in Bernard Siegel, ed., *Annual Review of Anthropology* (Palo Alto, Calif.: Annual Reviews, 1973).

35. An English translation of this work has appeared: Muhammad Husayn Haykal, *The Life of Muhammad*, trans. Ismail A. al-Faruqi (Indianapolis: North American Trust Publications, 1976). For a discussion of the book's significance, see Kenneth Cragg, *Counsels in Contemporary Islam* (Edinburgh: University of Edinburgh Press, 1965), pp. 91–93.

II

THE CONTINUING TRADITION
Enabling Factors for Change

3

Martyrdom in Christianity and Islam

MAHMOUD M. AYOUB

One of the most important marks of a person's faith or commitment to a religious ideology is his readiness to defend that faith with life itself if necessary. Examples of such heroic sacrifice or martyrdom abound in both ancient and contemporary society. In ancient times, the heroic indifference of such men as the Stoic philosopher, Epictetus, to torture and death in the affirmation of a noble ideal earned them the honor of martyrs; their example and ideal of total indifference to passions and worldly life provided a model for early Christian martyrs. In our own time, such men as Che Guaverra and his legendary comrade Tanya have been regarded as martyrs and even saints by some Catholic leftist priests. Martyrdom has been one of the most powerful instruments in the establishment and propagation of a faith or ideology, and hence of a new social order.

In this essay we shall examine the philosophy of martyrdom and the role of martyrs in Christianity and Islam. We shall first consider this phenomenon in each of the two traditions separately, and then briefly discuss similarities and differences of concept and attitude towards the martyr in the two communities. Our aim is essentially to appreciate the contribution which this phenomenon has made to the religio-political situation of today's world.

The term *martyr* as used in the New Testament means "witness." A martyr is a witness not to an idea but to an event, to the faith in the crucified and risen Christ. Thus the author of I John writes, ". . . that which we have seen with our eyes, which we have looked upon and touched with our hands . . . we proclaim also to you. . . ."[1] The first Christian martyr, Stephen, is reported to have seen the heavens open and the Son of God seated on the right hand of God.[2] Neither in the Old nor the New Testament, however, do we see any significant development of the concept beyond an almost juridical meaning of *witness*.

In biblical and post-biblical Judaism, martyrdom was considered to be an individual work of piety and resistance to evil. The cases of the woman and her seven sons in IV Maccabees (8:3ff) and the three young men in Daniel (ch. 3) have survived as powerful symbols in the liturgy and hagiography of the Church. The aim of martyrdom in Judaism was essentially to perfect the victim and edify the people. Since martyrdom, as a religious and moral concept, can best develop within an eschatological framework, it is significant that in Judaism this concept appears only in late Biblical and apocryphal writings in an eschatological context. The early Church fell heir to both Jewish eschatology and its moral implications.

In Acts 22:20, St. Paul acknowledges his role in the martyrdom of early Christians, "when the blood of Thy servant Stephen was shed."[3] The book of Revelation, the apocalypse of the early Church, presents a vivid image of the martyrs: "I saw the woman drunk with the blood . . . of the martyrs."[4]

During the apostolic age, the concept of martyrdom took on new meaning as the number of martyrs increased and their memory lived on. Yet the two elements of witnessing to one's faith and stoic indifference to pain continued to dominate the thinking of the early Church. Thus we read in I Clement 5:4–7 (written about A.D. 96):

> Peter, who because of unrighteous jealousy suffered not one or two but many trials, and having thus given his testimony went to the glorious place which was his due. Through jealousy and strife Paul showed the way to the prize of endurance; seven times he was in bonds, he was exiled, he was stoned, he was a herald both in the East and in the West, he gained the noble fame of his faith, he taught righteousness to all the world, and when he had reached the limits of the West he gave his testimony before the rulers, and thus passed from the world and was taken up into the Holy Place—the greatest example of endurance.[5]

One of the earliest and most eager martyrs of the Church was Ignatius, Bishop of Antioch, who died in A.D. 108. For Ignatius, the martyr was "he who imitated Christ in His sufferings."[6] He therefore used the term *disciple* rather than *witness*. His view was fully theological, and he insisted on bodily suffering as a proof that Christ, the crucified Son of God, was clothed in a real body. Ignatius wished his own body to be crushed between the teeth of wild beasts, to become a perfect loaf for Christ, whose own body is represented in the bread and wine of the Eucharist—regarded by Ignatius as "the medicine of immortality."[7]

In the account of the martyrdom of Polycarp, bishop of Smyrna, written about A.D. 155, witnessing faith to the humanity and suffering of the Son of God was fully developed as a concept.[8] In the Leonine letters of about A.D. 170 the term *martyr* signified persecution leading to the shedding of blood for Christ. Here, the example of Stephen, who saw (witnessed) the glorified Christ before his death, was used as a proof case. The letters vehemently protest the use of the epithet *martyrs* for confessors who endured persecution but did not seal their testimony with their blood.[9] In *The Shepherd* of Hermas, this imitator of Christ through martyrdom earns the martyr's salvation and a share in the glory of Christ. "Those who suffered for the name of the Son of God are glorious. All their sins have been taken away."[10] The martyrs are also pictured as sitting on thrones with crowns on their heads, with Christ engaged in judging the world.[11] Such glory belongs only to those who have suffered stripes, imprisonment, crucifixion, and wild beasts for Christ's name, insists the author of *The Shepherd*.

A rich and elaborate cultus evolved out of this great regard for martyrdom and the veneration accorded martyrs. We can discuss only the beginnings of this cultus, and some of its salient features. Apparently, the authorities responsible for the execution by burning of Polycarp sought to prevent the Christians from gathering his remains which, they feared, would be venerated more than Christ. The faithful protested this accusation vehemently, arguing that the veneration accorded to martyrs for their sacrifice is not the same as worship which belongs to God alone. The classic difference here stated and greatly elaborated in the Eastern Church is between honor or veneration and worship. The parishioners of the bishop did gather the bones of the saint for burial, considering them "to be more valuable than precious stones and finer than refined gold. . . . [They] laid them in a suitable place. There the Lord will permit us [they said] . . . to gather together in joy and gladness and to celebrate the day of his martyrdom as a birthday, in memory of those athletes who have gone before. . . ."[12] The "birthday of the martyr" as an annual memorial was a Christian adaptation of pagan custom that played a crucial role in the growth of the cult of martyrs.[13]

Others among the early Church fathers advocated great veneration for martyrs whom they considered to be the treasures of the Church. Martyrdom was considered to be a second baptism, the baptism of blood, granting the martyr immediate remission of sin and entry into Paradise. Martyrs who were imprisoned awaiting death, their families, and even the towns in which they resided were held in high honor. Those who remained steadfast through imprisonment and torture (although escaping death) gained positions among the elite of society. This honor gave them the privilege of episcopal office.[14]

From an early period, martyrs who were imprisoned were asked to pray for the health, well-being, and salvation of the pious. It was a natural development that such requests for prayers came to be renewed after the martyr's death. This controversial point no doubt led to an even greater tension between worship of the dead — a common practice in pre-Christian pagan society — and the veneration of martyrs. The cult of martyrs with its relics and shrines became the object of scorn to the Protestant Reformation; as a result the Catholic Church was forced to define its theology of martyrdom again and again. In the words of the Council of Trent, which met in part to answer the criticisms of the Reformation: "The holy bodies of holy martyrs, and of others now living with Christ—which bodies were the living members of Christ and the temple of the Holy Ghost (I Corinthians 3:16), and which are by Him to be raised unto eternal life, and to be glorified—are to be venerated by the faithful through which bodies many benefits are bestowed by God on men.[15]

While in Christianity a rich cultus arose around the shrines and relics of the martyrs, in Islam this phenomenon remained limited to Shi'i Islam, and even there took a different form and meaning. The "friend of God" or saint in Islam, whose shrine became a place of pilgrimage for the pious, was not required to be a martyr. In fact, the Prophet recommended that, whenever possible, martyrs should be buried at the spot where they fell in battle.[16] To my knowledge, there are no shrines in the Muslim world except those of the Shiah imams in Iraq and Iran, specifically erected as memorials for martyrs. Yet even here the imam's role is far greater than simply that of martyr.

The word *shahid* ("witness"), with its derivatives, occurs over fifty times in the Quran. In most of these references, the emphasis is on its linguistic meaning and usage as witness here on earth to the oneness of God, the apostleship of Muhammad, and the truth of the faith. Witnesses are not in a category by themselves but are classed with the prophets, the righteous, and the truthful—that is, with those who have found favor with God.[17]

The first question of concern to us is: Who is a martyr? The answer, as we shall see, is in the end legally determined. A man, we are told, said to the Prophet: "A man may fight in quest of booty. Another may fight for fame and still another for a show of status. Who among these would be fighting in the way of God?" The Prophet answered, "Whoever fights in order that the word of God be uppermost, would be fighting in the way of God."[18]

The famous traditionist, Ibn Hajar al-Asqalani, comments on this *hadith* ("Tradition of the Prophet"): "One may fight for one of five reasons: booty; a show of bravery; or a show before others; in defense of wealth, family, or land; and out of anger. Any one of these could in itself be praiseworthy or the opposite. So long as the main purpose remains that the 'word of God be uppermost' (which is here defined as defending the cause of Islam), it matters not what other reasons may exist as secondary causes."[19]

In yet another tradition, the Prophet was asked whether a man fighting for material rewards would also have a reward with God on the day of resurrection. The Prophet answered, "Nothing." He continued, "God would not accept a deed unless it is done sincerely for Him and that the doer seek by this only His (God's) face."[20]

At least in early Islam, the application of the term *martyr* was not limited to the person who is killed in the way of God on the battlefield. Martyrdom is an act of *jihad* (striving) in the way of God. *Jihad*, however, contrary to the common view held in the West, is not simply militance; more basic is the *jihad* against the evil in one's own soul and in society. It is this inner purity resulting from the *jihad* of the soul that creates the right intention of serving the cause of truth in whatever way possible. In addition to dying in defense of one's faith, property, or life, therefore, the act of falling off one's mount, dying of snakebite, or drowning is also regarded as martyrdom. Likewise, he who dies from a stray arrow or bullet, or from his house collapsing down upon him, is considered a martyr. Even those who die of the plague or a stomach ailment, or a woman who dies in childbirth, are considered martyrs. The famous traditionist, Ibn Abbas, is said to have declared: "A man dies in his bed in the way of God, yet he is a martyr."[21] Nevertheless, in spite of all this, the true martyr is he who is slain in the way of God.

Early traditionists may have used the term *martyr* very broadly and with caution because they feared the rise of a special cult of martyrs. Thus, in relationship to the authority of Abu Hurayrah, the Prophet is said to have declared: "Whoever has faith in God and in His apostle, observes regular prayers and fasts the month of Ramadan, it shall be incumbent upon God to make him enter Paradise, whether he fights in the way of God or remains in the land of his birth." Yet when the people asked if they should convey this glad tiding to others, the Prophet did not answer directly. Instead, he described the high station of the martyrs in Paradise.[22] Perhaps for this reason it was the jurist rather than the orator or theologian who determined the principle according to which a man or woman may be considered to be a martyr.

We cannot enter in detail into this technical topic of the qualifications of a martyr; a few general remarks must suffice. Three categories of martyrs may be distinguished: martyr of this world, martyr of this and the world to come, and martyr of the world to come only. The first is he who dies for a worldly cause other than that of faith. The second is he who is slain for no other reason but that "the word of God be uppermost." Such a martyr is to be buried in his clothes, without washing or shrouding — ordinarily, necessary rites for the dead. The martyr of this world is likewise buried in his clothes, since in the end his motives are known only to God, who will reward each person according to his acts and intentions. Umar Ibn al-Khattab and Ali Ibn Abi Talib, the second and fourth of the four rightly guided caliphs who were stabbed and died later of their wounds, were given regular burial. While both were considered martyrs in the way of God, such burial indicates that they were not, technically speaking, martyrs. The third caliph, Uthman, who was slain in his house, was also not washed or shrouded.[23]

Finally, the Quran counsels Muslims to make peace among themselves. Yet if one group transgresses against another, that group must be fought until it returns to the right path.[24] Thus, we are told, after the battle of Nahrawan against the Kharijites (A.D. 659), Ali had the dead on his side buried as martyrs. This principle has continued to be observed (and often abused) to the present day.

As in Christianity, the blood of the martyr in Islam washes away his or her sins. It is important to observe that even though women are exempted from actual fighting for religious and juristic reasons, the first martyr in Islam was a woman—Sumayya, the mother of Ammar Ibn Yasir, who was tortured to death with her husband and son by the Meccan Arabs before the conquest of the city. The injunction to let the blood of the martyrs be their purification is said to have been given by the Prophet regarding those slain in the battle of Uhud.[25] He said: "Shroud them in their blood and do not wash them. For no man who is injured in the way of God but that he shall come on the day of resurrection with his blood gushing out of his veins. The color shall be that of blood and the odor that of musk."[26]

The martyrs—"those who are slain in the way of God"—the Quran tells us "are not to be reckoned as dead; rather, they are alive with their Lord sustained."[27] Islamic eschatology has always been expressed in the language and the social framework of this life. Hence, tradition very early displayed great imagination in depicting the great pleasures of the martyrs in Paradise.[28] Yet the true martyr for God retains his desire for martyrdom even in Paradise. Malik Ibn Anas related that the Prophet said: "No one who enters Paradise would wish to return to this world, even if he were to possess all that is in it, except the martyr. He would desire to return to the world to be killed ten times because of the great honor [with God] which he sees in this act."[29] "The door of Paradise," we are told in another tradition, "is under the glittering swords."[30]

Tradition records numerous examples of martyrs who sensed the odor of Paradise on the battlefield and thus gladly met their death. One such example is that of a man called Abdallah Ibn Jahsh who prayed on the morning of the battle of Uhud, saying: "O God, let me today meet a strong and brave knight who will kill me and cut off my nose and two ears. Thus when I shall meet you tomorrow, you will say, 'My servant, for what were your nose and ears cut off?' I will then answer, 'It was in You [for your sake], my Lord, and in your apostle.'"[31]

Shiah Muslims have made the ethos of martyrdom and suffering a basic principle of their faith and piety. Every year during the first ten days of Muharram (the first month of the Muslim calendar), they relive the experience of Husayn Ibn Ali, the third imam, who through his death at Karbala provided for all Muslims the supreme example of self-sacrifice in the way of God. In the tragedy of Karbala in A.D. 680, the ideal of martyrdom took on new theological and pietistic significance. Thus Husayn, "the Prince of Martyrs" and "Master of the Youths of the People of Paradise," was said to have been destined for this sacrifice from the beginning of creation. History was read backward from him to Adam, and beyond and forward to the end of the world. Before him, history was a long prelude to the drama of suffering and death of which he, his friends, and immediate relatives were the central characters. After him, history is a period of intense hope in the anticipation of the return of the Mahdi (his ninth descendant and twelfth imam of the Shiah community) to avenge the death of Husayn and vindicate the faithful for their actual and vicarious sharing in the sufferings of the holy family of the Prophet Muhammad. Yet Husayn himself was said to have been told by the Prophet in a dream that "he has an exalted station with God which he cannot attain except through martyrdom."[32]

The death of Husayn, moreover, became for Shiah Muslims a source of redemption and healing. According to a well-known tradition, just before his death the Prophet said: "I am leaving with you [the Muslim community] the two weights onto which if you hold fast, you shall never go astray: the Book of God and my family, the people of my household. They shall never be separated until they come to me at the spring."[33] This paradisiacal spring shall be given to the Prophet on the day of judgment to quench the thirst of the pious "on the day of the great thirst."[34] Both the Quran and the family of Muhammad will judge and intercede before God and his Prophet for those of the Muslims who honored the two weights or neglected and mistreated them. Husayn will also stand before God on the day of resurrection as a headless body to contend with his murderers and intercede for his followers.[35] For Shiah piety it is Fatmah, the daughter of Muhammad and mother of Husayn, who has in this world embodied the suffering of her descendants and who continues to shed tears of anguish even in Paradise.[36]

This ethos of suffering stands in sharp contrast to the quick and spectacular success of the early generations of Muslims. Yet it is itself the product of that military and economic success, coming as it does out of the conviction that political justice must, in the end, reflect divine justice. God Himself, in Shiah theology, is bound only by His own justice. Hence, Shiites repeat daily in their worship the prayer: "O God, we desire of You an honorable state in which You honor Islam and its people, and humiliate hypocrisy and its people. [We pray] that in it you render us among those who call [others] to obedience to you, and that you make us leaders to your way." This ideal order will come only when human justice will approximate divine justice most closely, which can only be achieved under the leadership of an imam protected by God from error. In this hope—or rather, humanly unrealized goal —political idealism and theology meet.

It is noteworthy that Shiites, more than the Sunni majority of Muslims, have risked life and Muslim unity in this quest. They have, moreover, maintained a long and recognizable list of martyrs. The list begins with Abel (Qabil) and includes the Prophet Muhammad and all the imams but one. The twelfth imam, the Hidden Imam, will return to close this long chapter of wrongdoing and martyrdom, and establish justice in the earth. Thus the Prophet is said to have declared: "Even if there remains [only] one day of the life of the world, God will prolong that day until a man of my progeny shall appear, whose name is my name and whose agnomen is my agnomen. He shall fill the earth with equity and justice as it has been filled with inequity and injustice."[37] This tradition, with minor variations, is accepted by both Shiah and Sunni traditionists. Thus the ideal it expresses has gained official acceptance among Muslims of both groups.

This ideal of great justice was realized for a brief time only by the Prophet, Muhammad, in Medina. The Quran refers to the realization of the ideal of a good society in a statement coming shortly before the Prophet's death and after all the obligations of Islam had been instituted: "Today have I perfected your religion for you; I have completed my favor towards you and have accepted Islam as a religion for you."[38] Martyrs throughout Islamic history have been an affirmation of this hope, and a recognition that this hope remains an ideal unfulfilled because of human folly. Hence, the challenge remains as powerful today in Iran, Afghanistan, the Arabian peninsula, and even here in the New World as it was when it was first uttered.

"Surely God has exchanged with the people of faith their lives and wealth so that they shall have Paradise: they fight in the way of God, they kill and are killed. . . ."[39] This verse continues, "It is a promise incumbent upon Him in truth, in the Torah and the Gospel." Thus Islam has from the beginning recognized the place and value of martyrdom in the major scriptures revealed before it. In an earlier surah of the Quran, revealed before the principle of *jihad* was established for the Muslim community, the Quran alludes to the famous Christian martyrs of Najran[40] who became the subject of much exegetical and *hadith* scholarship. It is therefore important to ask, in conclusion, about the similarities and differences in the view of and attitude toward martyrs in the two religious traditions.

Perhaps the most obvious and important historical difference is that while in Christianity martyrdom was a glorious struggle before Christendom became a world power under Constantine, in Islam the *jihad* or struggle of the martyrs was instituted *after* Islam became a religious, social, and political order. Thus, when the symbol of supreme martyrdom, the cross, became the banner under which political wars were waged, the significance of the principle altogether became subject to question and doubt. The most intense protest against this "distortion" may be seen in the radical Reformation and the rich and moving martyrologies that Mennonites and Anabaptists have left as their legacy for posterity. The ideal martyr in Christianity was therefore he "who suffered stripes, imprisonment, crucifixion and wild beasts . . ." Is it because of this loss of the original meaning of this ideal that even among committed fundamentalist Christians martyrdom is no longer the impetus it was for the early Church?

In Islam, the ideal martyr is he who strives in the way of God "with his hand, with his tongue, and with his heart." Yet striving only with the heart is considered to be "the weakest of faith."[41] This emphasis on outward struggle does not imply wild and uncontrolled warfare, however; rather, it advocates a regulated struggle for the good and against evil. (At any rate, such is enjoined in the Quran and *hadith* tradition.) This struggle has definite priorities of concern: "If affliction befalls you," advised Abdallah Ibn Jundub, the son of a well-known Companion, "ransom your souls by your wealth. But if affliction increases, put your souls before your faith. For a truly deprived man is he whose religion is taken away from him. This is because there is no poverty after Paradise, nor is there any wealth after the Fire."[42]

In spite of this important difference, however, both Islam and Christianity agree on the basic concept of martyrdom as witness to the truth. The true martyr, the two religions also agree, is he who is free from any other motive but that witness. While the ideal martyr in Islam is the one who falls on the battlefield, actual fighting is not an absolute requirement for martyrdom. Islam, moreover, has its martyrs who silently and bravely endure torture and death. Finally, both traditions are in agreement regarding the exalted station of the martyr with God and the belief that the martyr will carry the marks of his sacrifice with him to be displayed even in heaven.[43]

In more recent Christian developments, the two ideals may yet have more in common than ever before. Liberation theology—the product of poverty, piety, and political awareness—may yet prove to be the most important phenomenon in modern Christian history. As a Muslim, I believe that piety without political involvement is at best all theory and no practice. It shall be those who feed the hungry, clothe the naked, care for the sick, and defend the wronged in prison who will inherit the kingdom of God.

Notes

1. I John 1:1. (All Biblical quotations are taken from the Revised Standard Version.)
2. Acts 7:55–56.
3. See also Acts 1:8, Luke 21:13, John 15:27, and Matt. 10:28, where the term *martyr* is also used in the sense of witness.
4. Rev. 17:6. See also Rev. 6:9–11, 20:4.
5. Cyril C. Richardson et al., eds., *Early Christian Fathers*, The Library of Christian Classics (Philadelphia: The Westminster Press, 1953), vol. 1, p. 46.
6. See Rom. 6:3, and the entire epistle that revolves around this concept.
7. See Eph. 20:2.
8. See Richardson, *Early Christian Fathers*, pp. 149ff.
9. *New Catholic Encyclopaedia*, vol. 11, 1967, p. 312.
10. Ibid.
11. Ibid.
12. Richardson, *Early Christian Fathers*, p. 156.
13. On the development of the cult of the martyrs and its relationships to Graeco-Roman antecedents, see James Hastings, ed., *Encyclopaedia of Religion and Ethics* (New York: Charles Scribner's Sons, n.d.), vol. 9, pp. 52ff.
14. Ibid., p. 53.
15. Ibid., p. 51.
16. Hasan Khalid, *al-Shahid fi al-Islam*, (Beirut: Dar al-Ilm lil-malayin, 1971), p. 75.
17. See Quran 4:69, 57:19.
18. Ahmad ibn Ali bin Hajar al-Asqalani, *Fath al-bari fi sharh sahih al-bukhari* (Beirut: Dar al-marifah, n.d.) vol. 6, p. 28.
19. Ibid., p. 28.
20. Ibid.
21. Khalid, *al-Shahid fi al-Islam*, p. 57. See also pp. 55–57.
22. Ibn Hajar, *Fath al-bari fi sharh sahih al-bukhari*, p. 11.
23. See Khalid, *al-Shahid fi al-Islam*, pp. 69–72.
24. See Quran 49:9.
25. See Khalid, *al-Shahid fi al-Islam*, p. 70.
26. Ibid.
27. Quran 3:169.
28. See Imad al-Din Abi al-Fida Ismail Bin Kathir, *Tafsir al-Quran al-Azim*, 2d ed. (Beirut: Dar al-Fikr, 1389/1970), vol. 2, pp. 153–60.
29. Ibn Hajar, *Fath al-bari fi sharh sahih al-bukhari*, p. 31.
30. Ibid.
31. Khalid, *al-Shahid fi al-Islam*, p. 138.
32. Akhtab al-Muwaffaq al-Khawarizmi, *Maqtal al-Husayn* (Najaf: Muhammad al-Samawi, 1367/1947), vol. 1, p. 187.
33. Abu Jafar al-Saduq Ibn Babawayh al-Qummi, *Ikmal al-Din* (Najaf: al-Matbaah al-Haydariyyah, 1389/1970), p. 62.
34. Mahmoud M. Ayoub, *Redemptive Suffering In Islam* (The Hague: Mouton Publishers, 1978), pp. 205ff.
35. Ibid., p. 214.
36. Ibid., pp. 144–45.
37. Ibid., p. 217.

38. Quran 5:3.

39. Quran 9:111.

40. Quran 85:4–8.

41. Abu Isa Muhammad bin Isa bin Sawrah al-Tirmidhi, *Sunan al-Tirmidhi,* Abdul Rahman Muhammad Uthman, 3d ed., (Beirut: Dar al-Fikr, 1398/1978) vol. 3, p. 318.

42. Khalid, *al-Shahid fi al-Islam,* p. 138.

43. I have already cited Muslim tradition in support of this idea. For the Christian tradition, see Ayoub, *Redemptive Suffering in Islam,* pp. 199, 282 (n.7).

4

Charismatic Leadership
in Messianic and Revolutionary Movements

The Mahdi (Muhammad Ahmad) and
the Messiah (Shabbatai Sevi)

R. HRAIR DEKMEJIAN

This chapter aims to develop a theoretically eclectic framework to analyze the psychological, social, and political processes by means of which charismatic founders of revolutionary and religious movements emerge in environments of acute social crisis. The validity of this framework will be tested through two case studies of leaders of messianic movements.

At the most general level of comparative inquiry, the epicentric role of personal leadership has been a persistent characteristic of religious/ideological movements throughout history. The universality of the single-leader imperative also applies to various revivalist or millenarian religious movements that seek to reinvigorate a particular religious tradition either by remaining within it or by breaking away as cults or sects. In view of the overwhelming centrality of leadership, religious and ideological movements may be fruitfully studied as extensions of the leader's personality as it reacts with the social milieu of his time.

The leader-movement interaction may be explored at three interrelated levels of analysis:

1. The movement as a projection of the leader's personality, whereby his inner conflicts seek resolution outside his self at the societal level.

2. The movement as the repository of the leader's values, beliefs, and message of salvation.

3. The movement as an organizational mechanism to propagate the leader's message and to administer the newly founded community.

These three levels or dimensions of analysis cover the whole continuum of the birth and development of new-founded or revivalist movements, beginning with the formative period of the leader, his response to the environment, his self-manifestation through propagation of a revivalist message, and finally the process of conversion to the new faith and the institutionalization of the movement. Clearly, the complexity of this process requires the application of psychological, social-psychological, and leadership theories, along with the theological and historical analysis of specific revivalist movements. In specific terms, Erikson's psychological theories and Weber's theories of leadership offer promising results when combined with theories of leadership, crisis, alienation, and group behavior. The analytical problem is to integrate these theoretical approaches in a complementary manner in order to achieve a comprehensive theoretical framework that lends itself to generalized application to the comparative study of religious, ideological, and revivalist movements.

Charisma and Psychohistory: A Theoretical Synthesis

The contributions of Erikson and Weber constitute the two most important components of the proposed theoretical synthesis. Significantly, both men (along with Freud) derived some of their most valuable insights from their studies of religious movements. Weber's work on the prophetic tradition and Erikson's studies of Luther and Gandhi are cases in point in terms of providing theoretical guidance to scholars seeking to analyze comparatively leaders' roles in revolutionary settings and in fundamentalist movements.[1]

Despite the analytical power of their respective theories, however, neither Weber nor Erikson singly can provide the theoretical depth and comprehensiveness necessary to study religious and ideological movements. Nevertheless, each provides complementary components for a composite theory of inspirational leadership—a prospect first suggested by Dankwart A. Rustow.[2] The task here is to develop a synthesis combining Erikson's psychology with Weber's sociology, along with other relevant theories. This synthesis can be achieved by treating the leader-movement relationship as a cyclical or dialectical process of stages that begins with the leader's appearance and culminates in the institutionalization of his movement. The conceptual outlines of this approach are suggested in Weber's typology of authority—charismatic, legal-rational, and traditional—where the leader's charisma is progressively "routinized" and diffused into legal-rational institutions that acquire traditional legitimacy with the passage of time. An earlier statement of this dynamic conceptualization of the leader's role is to be found in Montesquieu: "At the birth of societies, it is the leaders of the commonwealth who create the institutions, afterward it is the institutions that shape the leaders."[3]

The Montesquieu-Weber conceptualization implies a progressive change in the leader's role and influence vis-à-vis the movement and its general milieu. At the outset, the leader is the *founder* and *legitimizer* of the movement, which in time acquires organizational structure and bureaucratic leadership consisting of the leader's disciples. In a more general sense, Montesquieu and Weber occupy a midway position between Carlyle and Marx. While Carlyle makes the hero-leader the primary architect of history, Marx and other economic and historical determinists relegate leadership to a position of subservience to social forces. The formulation presented here proposes to subsume Carlyle and Marx; the leader can be both a *product* of social forces and a *shaper* of social forces, *depending on the particular developmental phase of his social environment.* In the institutionalized setting of a legal-rational or traditional society, the impact of leadership is likely to be limited. At the other end of the spectrum, however, in milieus of social crises, Carlyle's hero will emerge as the prime architect of the historical process.[4] It is precisely at this juncture that Weber's theory of charismatic authority becomes salient in its explanatory power to elucidate the leader's all-important role "at the birth of societies. . . ."

Crisis Milieu

In contrast to legal-rational and traditional-type leaders, the charismatic is both *intensely affected* by his crisis milieu and powerfully *affects it* (by presiding over its destruction and transformation). He is at once the product of a crisis-torn society and the builder of a new order. Thus, the charismatic's sequential compulsions to destroy and create focus attention on the nature of the crisis environment and its influence on the leader's personality and motivational base.

The existence of social crisis is a prime prerequisite for the emergence of charismatic leadership and the concomitant spread of revolutionary movements of both a religious and ideological nature. Newly established religions and revivalist or ideological movements always possess a fundamentalist character that readily transforms them into "totalitarian" revolutionary creeds seeking a radical transformation of society. Consequently, these movements and their leaders are unlikely to succeed in a stable environment; hence, the functional necessity of crisis. Indeed, an empirically powerful case can be made regarding the incidence of crisis as prelude to transformational movements whereby the propagation of the new faith or its revival is a response to the crisis itself. Examples abound in history:

- Moses and the tribes in the desert
- Muhammad's Meccan environment

- Al-Hakim's Fatimid Cairo
- Luther and German Catholic society
- Shabbatai Tzvi in the Jewish Dispersion of the 1600s
- Abd al-Wahhab's tribal Arabia under Ottoman rule
- Muhammad Ahmad's Sudan under Anglo-Ottoman-Egyptian rule
- Gandhi in India under British rule
- Hasan al-Banna in interwar Egypt
- Nasser in postwar Arab society
- Elijah Muhammad in twentieth century black America
- Khomaini in monarchical Iran

In view of the importance of the crisis milieu, a theoretical framework would have to specify its attributes—a subject that does not receive extended attention in Weber's theoretical writings. Indeed, Weber does not present a detailed analysis of the historical conditions and the social processes that precede charisma.[5] Among the preconditions to charismatic development, Weber points to moments of distress and collective excitement that are often produced by extraordinary events.[6] Furthermore, in his work *Ancient Judaism*, Weber suggests that the rise of the Hebrew prophets was a response to the decline in kingly power, external insecurity, and economic crisis—all pointing to a decline in the dominant cultural values of the social system.[7] Despite this lacuna, the Weberian framework readily lends itself to the introduction of supplementary theories to fill the gap. This may be accomplished by utilizing six interrelated conceptual clusters derived from the contemporary literature on crisis which, taken together, characterize the anatomy of the crisis milieu:

1. Breakdown in mechanisms of conflict resolution
2. Crisis in legitimacy of elites, ideology, and institutions
3. Alienation/anomie
4. Identity crisis (individual and collective)
5. Insecurity and pathological mass behavior
6. Vulnerability to mass appeals[8]

The foregoing formulation along with Weber's insights clearly suggest that the milieu preceding the onset of charisma would be one of the multidimensional crises encompassing the social, economic, cultural, political, and— more basically—the spiritual realms.[9] A prime manifestation of crisis is the inability of the social system to manage and resolve conflicts within society as well as with other societies. Such persistent failure triggers a crisis in the legitimacy of the political system, particularly when accompanied by the arbitrary use of force by elites to maintain control.[10] Such situations tend to generate popular alienation from the regime.

The concept of alienation is an essential component of the theoretical framework because of its explanatory potential in the analysis of the psychological-spiritual dimension of the crisis environment. Alienation signifies an end-of-ideology[11] setting characterized by doubt in the truth of the "old faith" and the erosion or atrophy of its norms and values. Progressive alienation is bound to deepen and widen the crisis in the legitimacy of elites and institutions, thereby creating an active opposition to the regime along with a nebulous mass of alienated individuals characterized by powerlessness, normlessness, isolation, and self-estrangement.[12] This state of being can be further characterized by combining Durkheim's anomie[13] and Erikson's identity-vacuum.[14] Anomie refers to a state of individual social-psychological withdrawal from society that is even deeper than alienation. In extreme cases, anomie and alienation lead to an identity-vacuum in which people lose their sense of who or what they are. Erikson's notion of identity-vacuum is an extension of his concept of identity crisis applied to members of society, who experience it individually and collectively in times of distress. This collective identity crisis may be accompanied by a growing sense of physical and/or psychological insecurity. A related attribute of mass distress is Erikson's notion of existential dread, where the rituals of existence have broken down.[15] At this advanced stage of crisis, irrational, schizophrenia-like disorientations are likely to occur, creating a deep feeling of psychological dependence and heightened expectation.[16] Devereaux and Langer insightfully theorize that crises "infantilize" the people who demand a leader who conforms to their childish expectations.[17] Indeed, the intensity of the crisis renders the people "charisma-hungry," in Erikson's phrase, and vulnerable to mass appeals.[18]

An Exemplary Personage

The foregoing anatomy of the crisis environment sets the stage for the manifestation of the charismatic leader. In the absence of a leader with charismatic potential, the process of charismatic development cannot be initiated regardless of the intensity of crisis. Conversely, the charismatic cycle cannot be triggered without circumstances of turmoil, regardless of the leader's charismatic potential. However, the simultaneous occurrence of these initial prerequisites — the exemplary personage and a crisis milieu — is a necessary but *not sufficient* condition for development of charisma and a charismatic movement. The intervening variables include the leader's psychological attributes, his style of leadership, the content of his message, and the matrix of leadership opportunities — all of which relate to the process by which the leader projects himself upon the society in crisis. Once again, Weber provides the framework and certain conceptual outlines of analysis, although the explication of the complex dynamics of the leader's interaction with society will require supplementary theories and paradigms derived from developmental psychology, social psychology, and political science.

Attributes of Charisma

The specific attributes of charismatic authority are interspersed throughout Weber's voluminous writings. The conceptual essence of Weber's theory of charisma, however, is contained in several key passages:

> . . . a certain quality of an individual personality by virtue of which he is set apart from ordinary men and treated as endowed with supernatural, superhuman, or at least specifically exceptional qualities. These . . . are not accessible to the ordinary person, but are regarded of divine origin or as exemplary, and on the basis of them the individual concerned is treated as leader.[19]

> . . . "Charisma" shall be called a quality of a person that passes for something outside the everyday, . . . because of which the person is appraised as equipped with powers or pecularities that are not accessible to just any other person and which are super-natural or super-human or at least specifically outside of the everyday. . . .[20]

Elsewhere, Weber sees charismatic legitimacy as "resting on devotion to the exceptional sanctity, heroism, or exemplary character of an individual person, and of the normative patterns or order revealed or ordained by him."[21]

In the foregoing passages, Weber's emphasis is on the unique personal attributes of the leader. Weber's terminology reflects the origins of his intellectual inspiration, which came from his systematic study of the prophetic tradition, Christianity, Islam, and Oriental religions. Weber explicitly refers to Rudolph Sohm's work on the leadership and organization of the early Christian Church, which led him to the adoption of the term *charisma* as a dynamic explanatory concept.[22] In order to appreciate the unique relevance of charisma to the study of religious and millenarian movements, it is important to trace the etymological and biblical origins of the word.

In response to scholars who are distrustful of "Western" social science theory, it should be noted that the term *charisma* is derived from the Greek original of the New Testament. The precise derivation is from the old Greek verb *charezoma* or the noun *charis*, meaning grace, favor, beauty; thus, charisma means "gift of grace."[23] In his seminal analysis of the theological origins of charisma, Daniel Bell observes that the term is not found in classical Greek except in Philo and the early Christian literature.[24] In the New Testament, *charisma* is used seventeen times, all but once (1 Peter) in the

Pauline corpus—specifically, in his Epistles to the Romans, 1 and 2 Corinthians, and 1 and 2 Timothy.[25] In its Pauline usage, *charisma* connotes extraordinary giftedness, particularly the "gift of prophecy"—the ability to foretell the future. But what is the source of these "gifts," and what are the attributes of these gifted people?

To Paul, the common source of charisma is the Holy Spirit, which distributes the *charismata* that enable one to perform certain functions (*praxis*) among the faithful.[26] Paul proceeds to set a supreme criterion to validate the possession of charismata:

> . . . Though I speak with the tongues of men and of angels, and have not charity, I am become as sounding brass. . . . And though I have the gift of prophecy, and understand all mysteries, and all knowledge; and though I have faith, so that I could remove mountains, and have not charity, I am nothing. . . . For we know in part, and we prophecy in part. But when that which is perfect is come, then that which is in part shall be done away. When I was a child I spoke like a child, I understood as a child, I thought as a child: but when I became a man, I put away childish things. For now we see through a glass, darkly; but then face to face: now I know in part; but then shall I know even as also I am known. And now abideth faith, hope, charity, these three; but the greatest of these is charity.[27]

Thus Paul recognizes a hierarchy of gifts, among them wisdom (*sophias*), knowledge (*gnoseos*), and inspiration (*pneumatika*)[28]—all of which are subsumed in charisma, which, however, will become transitory unless validated by charity—love—which opens the way to prophecy.[29]

Paul provides two additional insights that are applicable to the study of charismatic leaders and movements. First, he admonishes against the indiscriminate use of revelational ecstasy by persons "speaking with tongues"—an attempt by Paul, the chief "routinizer" of the Christian faith, to prevent the rise of charismatic pretenders after Christ. Second, Paul stresses the centrality of the communication process between the prophet and his followers—the necessity to "utter . . . words easy to be understood . . ." instead of the trumpet with its "uncertain sound."

According to Daniel Bell, the charismatic phenomenon is found in diverse religions and cultures.[30] The Islamic tradition is particularly rich in conceptual equivalents of charisma. Gustave von Grunebaum equated charisma to *barakah,* in reference to the Prophet Muhammad.[31] (This term is given a deeper meaning in Sufism.)[32]

While Weber and his followers extended the conceptual range of charismatic theory to cover social, political, and artistic leaders, the religious type of charisma was fundamental in his thinking since it provided the source of legitimacy for the initial exercise of authority by the "gifted one."[33] The question remains one of recognizing someone's possession of these "gifts"— validation of charisma. While all charismatics claim a sense of mission independent of social recognition of their giftedness, in practice their claim to charisma will not have a social impact unless it is socially recognized and accepted. Thus, the leader's possession or lack of exemplary qualities is always determined by *his* followers according to his society's culturally based criteria. Unbelievers who fall outside the pale of the charismatic experience are unable to recognize and evaluate this subjective and mystical phenomenon.

Equally serious is the intellectual dilemma that inescapably confronts scholars of charismatic movements who approach their evaluative task with Western or Marxist scientific rationalism and the perspective of bureaucratic cultures. All too often, Western scholars and observers have reacted *personally* to charismatic phenomena and promptly judged them to be "fanatical." The scholar should never forget that he is an outsider to the situation, and should abstract his ego and values from the evaluation process; the determination of the genuineness of the leader's charisma should be left to his followers. Whatever the leader's personal qualities or morality, the fact remains that these were acceptable to the communicants and proved instrumental in convincing them of the truth of his message.[34] The scholar's task is not to worry about determining the genuineness or spuriousness of the leader's charisma, but rather to inquire into the cultural, situational, and personal determinants of charisma and its dispersion into the society. To pose the fundamental question: What types of social milieus give rise to charismatics who proceed to reshape those social environments? Having explicated the attributes of the crisis milieu, it will be necessary to turn to its formative impact on the prospective leader—to analyze the configuration of his personality and its impact on the society in crisis.

The Leader's Personality

Weberian theory is not concerned with psychological analysis; it emphasizes the revolutionary, innovative, and transforming nature of charismatic leadership but does not explain why certain types of leaders claim a sense of mission and proceed to infuse society with their beliefs, values, and vision. It is at this crucial juncture that Weberian theory requires an infusion of psychological theory centering on the personality of the leader and its interaction with society. A viable theoretical construct will have to possess sufficient depth and breadth to explicate the impact of society on the leader's personality development; the attributes of the leader's personality; the modality in which the leader projects himself upon society; and the interaction between the leader's personality and the crisis milieu. To fill this theoretical lacuna, Erikson's work on personality development is singularly appropriate. However, as a prelude to Erikson, the early contributions of Harold Lasswell merit attention. In his formula $p)d)r = P$, Lasswell theorized that political man's private motives are displaced onto public objects and rationalized as being in the public interest.[35] This relationship between private motivations and public acts constitutes the focal point of the study of leadership—religious, social, and political. Significantly, Erikson's attempt to bridge the gap between the dynamics of individual behavior and the forces of history centered on two religious charismatics—Luther and Gandhi.[36]

Despite the inherent complexity of Erikson's theoretical approach, his case studies of Luther and Gandhi demonstrate its applicability to the study of other leader-centered religious and ideological movements. Erikson posits eight development stages marked by successive crises:

1. Early Infancy—The outcome of this crisis (trust versus mistrust) will be determined by the quality of maternal care.

2. Infancy—This crisis develops the infantile sources of what later becomes the person's will. The resolution of this crisis will determine whether an individual will develop a sense of autonomy or a sense of shame and doubt. The way in which this doubt is met by grownups determines the individual's ability to combine an unimpaired will with self-discipline, and to temper the inclination to rebellion with responsibility.

3. Play Age—This stage (initiative versus guilt) is based on Freud's oedipus complex. It involves the unconscious association of sensual freedom with the mother's body and its prohibition by the father.

4. School Age—The resolution of this crisis decides the balance between a sense of industry and a sense of inferiority, and prepares the person for his ethos by giving him tools and rationalizations to collaborate with others.

5. Adolescence—For Erikson, this is the critical stage, in which an identity crisis occurs as each youth must forge for himself a life-direction through a synthesis of the remnants of childhood and the hopes of his anticipated adulthood. In some young people the identity crisis will be minimal, while in others it will produce neurotic and psychotic behavior until a "second birth"; others will resolve their identity crises through participation in religious and ideological movements, while still others may experience a prolonged adolescence. The failure to find an identity is a state of identity diffusion and will lead to danger.

6. Young Adult—This crisis will decide the dichotomy between intimacy and isolation.

7. Adulthood—This stage is marked by a crisis of generativity when the

adult looks at his life-work and finds it wanting. If satisfied, he has resolved the problem. The alternative is self-absorption.

8. Mature Age—As the person gets older, he is concerned with how to escape corruption in living and how to give meaning to life in death. This is the integrity crisis, which if unresolved leads to despair.[37]

The foregoing stages of development are what Erikson calls *the metabolism of generations*. The crucial stage for the emergence of the leader is that of identity crisis and its social consequences.

Projection

The theoretical utility of Erikson's work for the Weberian framework transcends the mere explication of the leader's personality development; indeed, Erikson offers a unique explanation of the process by which the emerging leader manifests himself and proceeds to establish a charismatic bond with his followers. The process begins with the identity crisis when the future leader enters a "moratorium"—a period of withdrawal, loneliness, moodiness, and uncertainty during which the young person gropes for a dominant skill or faculty in his search for an identity.[38] The moratorium is a stage of preparation for his forthcoming mission; it might be called the leader's "springboard" for action, the "trigger" being provided by the resolution of his identity crisis. Once the leader succeeds in breaking out of the moratorium by having found an identity, he will proceed to use his special gifts to achieve the "great moment" in history. He is now convinced of his possession of extraordinary powers; the next task is to convince others that he is indeed "the gifted one."

But why does the leader seek to convince others of his gifts? Why does he seek a revolutionary mission dedicated to changing society? In a religious context, the answer will be theological in terms of a divinely inspired mission to seek social change. However, the psychological explanation for his compulsion to preach and to transform springs from the leader's "need to settle a personal account on a large scale and in a grand context,"[39] in compensation for deprivations suffered in the spheres of family and society.[40] It follows that the leader's emergence from the moratorium is *only the beginning* of the resolution of his identity crisis; a complete resolution can only be achieved on a social scale. In Erikson's classic formulation: "Now and again however, an individual is called upon to lift his individual patienthood to the level of a universal one and to try to solve for all what he could not solve for himself alone."[41]

This projection of the leader's continuing patienthood onto society is the very nexus by which the leader's personality and the social forces of the crisis environment come together. This is where the individual identity crisis of the leader and the collective identity crisis of society meet in search of a shared resolution. However, complete resolution of the identity crisis depends on the effective interaction between the leader's personality and the crisis environment—a process governed by the operation of three intervening variables.

Message, Performance, and Opportunity

The process of projection, in an instrumental sense, is effected through the "message which the leader propounds to reveal himself and his vision."[42] The content of the message is determined by the leader's world view synthesized during his moratorium from the cumulative experiences of his formative years—the sum total of his past pleasures and pains, rewards and deprivations, as *he* perceives them. On balance, these experiences, endured in the crisis milieu, are of a negative nature. The emerging leader, as a product of his crisis-torn social and familial environment, is typically an acutely alienated individual whose gifts have gone unrecognized and aspirations unfulfilled. This identity crisis is reinforced by a feeling of "marginality" in society, in terms of his "station in life" and his perception of his opportunities for success—all of which propel him toward revolutionary action as prescribed in the message.[43] This message typically contains a bold prescription to remedy the prevailing crisis situation, as well as a utopian promise for a bright future.[44] The message also possesses a rhetorical dimension that the charismatic leader employs with great virtuosity to convince the people of the truth of his path.[45]

Another intervening variable that affects the leader's ability to establish charismatic appeal is his behavior or performance as leader. To be effective, the message needs constant reinforcement from the leader's heroic performance, as this represents the unfolding of his message—or, conversely, the message shall contain his program of exemplary or heroic activity.[46] In practical terms, for the message to be heard and the performance to be seen the leader has to have the opportunity to project himself personally onto society; indeed, the leader-follower interaction will be aborted without this intervening element. One may realistically expect the ruling elite to attempt to silence the aspiring charismatic at the onset of his mission. Under such circumstances, the emerging leader may attempt a temporary accommodation to the ruling order or remove himself to a secure base; he may even attempt to move against his enemies to capture political control.[47]

Value Transformation: The Charismatic Breakthrough

The achievement of a charismatic breakthrough, therefore, is not a common phenomenon. The charisma cycle is triggered by the coincidence of a

crisis environment and a particular type of gifted personage who, at the op-
portune moment, is motivated to project his patienthood onto the mass level
through a salvational message that is correctly attuned to critical social needs.[48]
At the most elemental level, the message will be received and internalized
only in a milieu where there is a "fit," or convergence, between the leader's
identity crisis and the collective identity crisis of the people.[49] One may extend Eriksonian terminology to state that the message is the connecting link
between the patienthood of the leader and the patienthood of the masses.

The effective interaction of the foregoing factors creates an initial charismatic bond. On the basis of the legitimacy flowing from this nascent charisma, the leader proceeds to exercise an increasingly diffuse and intense
influence over the normative orientations of people.[50] Initially, he will typically draw to himself a small number of alienated individuals who are dedicated to enlarging his congregation (*gemeinde*) to include the alienated masses.

In sharp contrast to traditional or legal types of authority under which the
people's criteria remain unchanged, the charismatic is able to affect a significant change in the values of his followers.[51] Thus, the leader will proceed to
fill the existing value vacuum with his own values or ideology as promulgated
in the message. In Erikson's terms, in his quest for identity the leader shapes
the identities of his followers in accordance with his own. Thus, they become
subject to *his* charisma, and he becomes *their* charismatic leader. In view of
this reciprocal relationship, the notion that the charismatic "is always the creation of his followers"[52] becomes a half-truth. It is necessary to add that, to
the extent the leader succeeds in imparting his own values to his followers,
they are *his* creation.[53] One of the most distinctive characteristics of charismatic authority—and one that sets it apart from other types—is the highly
spiritual relationship that develops between the leader and his followers. Based
on a bridge of leader-inspired values, the charismatic relationship places the
leader "in communion" with his followers, in a state of intense spiritual union.
Both the leader and the followers receive psychological satisfaction from this
union as their egos become *fused* in the context of an expanding mass movement characterized by what Jung called "mass psychoses," in the throes of
"psychic epidemics."[54]

Routinization of Charisma

Weber saw legal and traditional systems of authority as somewhat permanent or stable structures that provide for everyday social needs. In contrast,
charismatic domination is conceived as being less enduring and unstable, since
it arises in response to crises or emergencies to satisfy extraordinary social needs.
Therefore, the intense emotional experience of the followers' spiritual sub-

mission to the leader is of relatively short duration, usually occurring outside the framework of established rules and institutions. Indeed, Weber believed the "waning of charisma" to be a dominant historical tendency.[55]

Transformation of Charisma

The decline of charisma may follow different patterns, depending upon the specific circumstances of a given situation. The leader may feel that his mission is at an end,[56] since his God has forsaken him and his "gifts" have been taken away.[57] In the case of a specifically political charismatic leader, he may not be able to satisfy the expectations of his followers beyond such immediate psychological payoffs as dignity, identity, and a sense of belonging; yet in the long run he will have to produce social and economic payoffs as well, which can only be done through establishment of a new order of bureaucratic structures and processes.[58] Thus, charismatic leadership inescapably gives way to "routinization"—a process that could occur either after the leader's demise or as a consequence of his active participation. In order to perpetuate the social impact of his advent, the leader may consciously initiate the routinization process by *infusing* his charisma into new organizational forms and processes that will bear the halo of his blessing.[59] One might suggest that routinization involves the "depersonalization" of charisma and its institutionalization, whereby the leader's charismatic legitimacy is expanded to embody the new order.

Logic suggests that to insure continuity and stability, routinization should take place at the height of the charismatic relationship; not all charismatics, however, are necessarily effective routinizers. Their spiritual and rhetorical temperament and self-view may not incline them to undertake bureaucratic and organizational endeavors, which are often delegated to disciples. Indeed, the self-imposed transition from an inspirational-rhetorical style to a bureaucratic one requires a painful psychological readjustment on the leader's part that ultimately transforms his role within an increasingly rationalistic environment.[60] At the culmination of the cycle, the leader will have presided over a transition from charismatic domination to one increasingly based on rational-legal legitimacy which, over time, may also acquire traditional legitimacy. It is important to note that Weber did not himself posit an explicitly developmental sequence between his three types of authority, although he did discern a "dialectical" relation between charisma and bureaucracy.[61] Moreover, Weber explicitly states that his threefold classification of authority consisted of "ideal" types that in practice occur in combination. Only at the very onset of the charismatic outbreak can one conceive of the manifestation of "pure" charisma.

Agents of Routinization: Disciples, Priests, and Bureaucrats

The atrophy of charisma and the concomitant tendency toward routinization characterize the process by which the leader's following is transformed into an organized movement or party. The primary agents or vehicles of this transformation are the leader's disciples who, as early believers in the truth of the message, constitute a "charismatic aristocracy."[62] Initially, the disciples are bound together in their personal allegiance to the leader and commitment to his mission, without regard to everyday familial and economic concerns.[63] Instead, the leader and his disciples live in a primitive communism of spiritual union and economic sharing (of donated money) as the disciples partake in the leader's charisma. As routinization takes hold, the leadership functions are divided among the disciples, who now act as the *carriers* of the leader's gifts-of-grace as well as the *implementers* of his grand design. Progressively, the disciples assume specialized functional roles and rank along with a growing manifestation of self-interest in the acquisition of power, wealth, and privilege. Consequently, the disciples' self-interest in terms of appropriating the leader's power dictates their advocacy of routinization and depersonalization of charisma, which transforms them into bureaucratic functionaries.[64] This points to the inevitably stressful relationship between leader and disciples, between prophets and priests, in terms of their functional roles within the movement — the prophets as the creators of the movement and the priests as its routinizers. The priests, even more than disciples, represent rational-legal and traditional authority.

However, neither disciple nor priest is able to function outside the charismatic's influence. The disciples draw their legitimacy directly from the leader's charisma while priests (and, to a degree, bureaucrats and elected officials) derive their authority through an "apostolic succession" effected through the act of ordination. The act of ordination centers on a laying on of hands and anointment with oil — both of which represent the transference of the leader's or prophet's charisma to successors who now bear the halo of his legitimacy. This act of transference by infusion with *charis* is in itself an act of routinization of charisma whereby the priests, as the carriers of grace, will perpetuate the faith in an increasingly bureaucratic context. Here, charisma declines and blends into bureaucratic forms which, however, eventually lose their rational-legal/traditional legitimacy without the continued infusion of the original grace.[65] With the passage of time, these charismatic infusions may solidify around certain offices of leadership, such as the Roman papacy, the American presidency, the British Crown, the Ecumenical Patriarchate, the Armenian Catholicosate, or the Japanese emperorship. These offices become the repositories of charisma whereby the "charisma of office" may be transformed into traditional legitimacy. (Exceptions to this phenomenon are found in such nonhierarchical religions as Sunni Islam and Judaism, where the repositories of charisma are multiple and where the acquisition of charisma is effected primarily through informal processes of religious learning, reputation, and popular consensus.)

The phenomenon of office charisma is also manifest in Shiite Islam, where both consensual and appointive determinants of religious office operate. Thus, the titles of *Hujjat al-Islam, Ayatollah, Mujtahid* and *Imam Jomeh* carry a certain office charisma, which often transcends the religious sphere to influence political affairs. Similarly, the Islamic caliphate possessed office charisma that individual caliphs reinforced by claiming legitimacy through "genealogical charisma"—the transference of prophetic grace by virtue of being from Muhammad's "seed."

The renovative role of charisma as a periodic revitalizer of bureaucratized religious and political systems constitutes a significant application of Weberian theory. This is particularly relevant to situations of longterm bureaucratic decline that have not reached the crisis state where the creativity of a "charismatic reformer" may revitalize the system. In the Islamic context, the need for periodic revitalization is recognized in the popular expectation of the renewer (*mujaddid*) who will come forth every century or millennium. Clearly, the charisma of the renewer is not as revolutionary or intense as the charisma of the Mahdi or Messiah.[66] Indeed, mahdiship connotes an *end and a beginning* —a clear break with the past and the outbreak of revolutionary force emanating from the leader to transform the foundations of society.

Self-evaluation

A fitting finale to the proposed cyclical framework of charismatic development is embodied in two related Eriksonian concepts centered on the last phases of his stages of personality growth—generativity crisis and integrity crisis.[67] The universal relevance of these concepts transcends charismatic movements to include all leadership situations, in the sense that the consequences of leadership become the foci of assessment and evaluation by the principal actor. This task of self-evaluation becomes particularly relevant if one shares this writer's view that failure is an inescapable concomitant of leadership. Indeed, the human condition circumscribes the impact of effective leadership, whereby success becomes partial in scope and temporary in duration.

The crisis of generativity occurs when the leader looks at his life-work in terms of his own criteria of success and failure. If dissatisfied, the person is likely to experience stagnation and manic depression. The leader may feel disappointed in his ability to effect total change or to realize the discrepancy between his intentions and the consequences of his deeds; indeed the leader's handiwork may well be the opposite of what he intended. As examples, Erikson cites Luther, Darwin, Einstein, and Freud, and the list can be extended to include Lenin, Franklin D. Roosevelt, Woodrow Wilson, Ben Gurion, Nasser, and Mao (who continued in vain to try to *recharismatize* Chinese society until his death). The negative consequences of self-evaluation will lead to the *integrity crisis* — to the "portals of nothingness, or a feeling of having been."[68] The integrity crisis is likely to be a lifelong and chronic crisis in religious individuals who are persistently concerned with "how to escape corruption in living and how in death to give meaning to life."[69] Such men experience a breakthrough and perceive these problems early in life, and may succeed in adapting themselves to the triumphs and disappointments of their leadership experience, depending on resolution of childhood crisis. However, there is no escape from the generativity/integrity crisis. To Erikson, the leader is seduced by the people's existential anxieties when they feel an intense need for new meaning and rejuvenation. (One might add that the leader in turn seduces his followers, at least for a period.) In either case, the evolving relationship between the charismatic founder and his disciples and followers often contains the seeds of discord, especially toward the end of the cycle, during and after the routinization phase.

In both revolutionary and religious movements, *the inescapable pattern is for revisionism to set in* at the end or soon after the leader's departure, and — ironically — the main architects of revisionism are the disciples themselves. Indeed, the very act of routinization entails revisionism of the original creed. Moreover, the leader-disciple relationship is inherently dissonant, since it pits the leader's charisma against the increasingly bureaucratic behavior of the disciples. In the end, it is difficult to escape the generativity crisis, since the leader's disciples and followers will rarely, if ever, live up to his expectations. Erikson captures this in the following words: "The best of them will fall asleep at Gethsemane; and the worst will accept the new faith only as a sanction for anarchic destructiveness or political guile."[70]

Having set forth the various components and stages of the framework, two brief applications will be attempted, centering on the movements of religious resurgence led by the Sudanese Mahdi and the Shabbatai Tzvi (Sevi) of Smyrna. The analysis will focus on the extent to which the theoretical model is useful in studying the historical evolution of the two situations. A major limiting factor, however, is the general paucity of historical data, particularly on the two leaders' formative years.

The Mahdi

The mahdist revolution that began a century ago continues to attract widespread scholarly interest. As the only successful third world revolution of the nineteenth century, the Mahdiyya was a shattering experience for the Sudan's British, Turkish, and Egyptian rulers. The present inquiry will center on the crisis situation, the leader's attributes, his claim to mahdiship, the popular reaction, and the routinization process.

The Sudan in Crisis

The existence of a situation of conflict and crisis in the Sudan of the mid-nineteenth century is documented in memoirs, histories, and official records. Because of its multidimensional nature, the crisis that engulfed Sudanese society, beginning in the early 1800s, was both pervasive and total — at once political, economic, demographic, and psychological. While it is difficult to state with certainty which came first, it is clear that the various components of conflict were closely interrelated and that their convergence after the 1850s set the stage for the rise of the Mahdi.

At the political level, the predominantly tribal Sudan had been subjected to repeated waves of conquest begun in 1820 by the Albanian ruler of Egypt, Muhammad Ali. By 1879, virtually all of the country had been occupied by the Cairo-based Khedival regime, which utilized British and Ottoman military and bureaucratic officials to sustain its hold on the Sudan. The general abhorrence of the Ottoman flag and the Turks it represented was deepened by the cruel and exploitative behavior of the soldiers and administrators sent from Cairo. Burdened by the government's policies of extortionate taxation and recruitment of slaves into the army, the Sudanese were also victimized by enterprising northerners who had come from Egypt to amass large fortunes. Service in the Sudan was considered by officialdom as a form of exile made bearable only by the opportunity for financial gain.[71] The situation was further compounded by the very rapid turnover of administrators; between 1825 and 1885 no less than twenty-five governors-general ruled in Khartoum, most of whom had very brief tenures.[72]

Severe economic distress had exacerbated tribal conflict and caused population movements even prior to Muhammad Ali's conquest. In the north, the narrow strip of cultivable land by the Nile was insufficient to provide enough food for a growing population. This factor, combined with the pressures generated from tribal in-fighting, had been responsible for the migration of the Danaqla tribe in the eighteenth century and the Jaaliyin in the early nine-

teenth century. One major consequence of the breakdown of the tribal structure was accelerated urbanization, a process that almost always generates great
stress. Concomitantly, there was the gradual atrophy of the traditional authority exercised by tribal chiefs. The very fact that certain of these native elites
were permitted to retain their power positions under foreign rule automatically brought their tribal legitimacy into question.

The most basic and fundamental dimension of the Sudanese crisis situation was socio-psychological. While closely related to the political, economic,
and demographic aspects, crisis in the socio-psychological realm is more significant, since it represents the focal area at which the potential charismatic
directs his message. Specifically, this brings into focus the prevailing belief
system in the Sudan along with the attendant problems of alienation, identity crisis, and psychological insecurity.

The eighteenth and early nineteenth centuries saw the emergence of
puritanical movements in Islam, mostly at the periphery of the Ottoman imperial realm, such as the Wahhabis in Arabia, the Sanusis in Libya, and the
Khatmiya in the Sudan.[73] At the general level, these religious orders constituted a reaction against the orthodoxy of caliphal authority as exercised
by the Ottoman sultan, and the growing pressure of European influence
within the empire. Within the Sudanese context, the proliferation of Sufi
(Islamic mystic) orders had, since the Funj period, reflected the free-flowing
mysticism of "frontier" Islam, unencumbered by the homogenizing weight
of Islamic orthodoxy. The orders were founded by individual religious teachers who proselytized among Muslim and pagan alike; often they came to be
regarded as saints possessing miraculous powers. Frequently, a successful
teacher would establish his own suborder by proclaiming his independence
from the parent group. The upshot was a continuing fragmentation of society based upon differing interpretations of the Islamic belief system as provided by each Sufi shaykh. Not only did authority become fragmented, but
the great diversity of "truths" produced conflicts and spiritual uncertainties
among the faithful.

The mood of psychological dependence and heightened expectation arising from the crisis situation found additional reinforcement in the Sudanese
concept of the Mahdi. The notion that "the guided one" would come to save
the Islamic community had been a part of the popular Sunni belief system.
This was especially true in tribal North Africa, where, among others, Muhammad Ibn Tumart (1130) of the Maghrib and Uthman dan Fodio (1754–1817)
of the Fulani had established precedents in successfully invoking the mahdist
idea.[74] Popular belief held that the Al-Mahdi Al-Muntazar, the Expected
Mahdi, would appear at the end of each century. In the Muslim year 1298
(A.D. 1881), Muhammad Ahmad of Dongola proclaimed himself as Mahdi

and proceeded to propagate a message of militant puritanism in a crisis-torn society.

Formative Years

Muhammad Ahmad's childhood was marked by personal misfortune and family mobility and instability. He was one of the four sons of a poor Dongolese boatbuilder, Abdallah, who moved his family southwards to Karari near Khartoum, where there was suitable timber. Muhammad Ahmad was soon orphaned and forced to live with an uncle in Aba. While his brothers followed their father's trade, the future Mahdi displayed an unusual motivation for religious studies. As a child, he possessed a prodigious mind that enabled him to recite the entire Quran at the age of nine.[75] At sixteen he was already a *darwish* (mystic) and an ardent student of Sufism.[76]

Although the Mahdi's family claimed descent from the Prophet, this did not alter the young mystic's status of marginality or accord him opportunity for advancement. Moreover, despite his prodigious quranic knowledge, he was not among the numerous Sudanese youth who went to Cairo's Al-Azhar to study. It is unclear why this officially approved path to success was not followed by Muhammad Ahmad. In any event, the lack of such an education may have reinforced his feeling and status of marginality, whereas Azharite training might have destroyed his early revolutionary tendencies through co-optation. Whether by personal choice or through force of circumstance, then, he remained in the Sudan to pursue a life of strict asceticism under Shaykh Muhammad Sharif Nur al-Daim of the Samaniya order.

There is no evidence that Muhammad Ahmad felt bitter about his lonely lot in the Sudan, for he had found himself and his true path, his "medium of salvation," in Islamic mysticism. In fact, in the context of poverty and misfortune, he embraced extreme asceticism with such intensity and rigor that by his late childhood years he had already acquired an unshakable but "premature integrity."[77] Such early and total commitment to a value system characterizes all ideological and religious leaders who seek comprehensive social change.[78] In the case of Muhammad Ahmad, the child mystic chose to withdraw from life into a cave for study, prayer, and meditation — in societal terms, to a state of "nothingness." However, as he grew into adolescence and adulthood, the realities of life began to impinge upon his prematurely acquired integrity of puritanical values and beliefs. This clash between his personal puritanism and societal "decadence" had two foci: his religious teachers and the governmental authorities.

Muhammad Ahmad's abhorrence of Ottoman rule was a widely shared feeling among the Sudanese. However, his personal and total rejection of the Turks flowed from their desecration of the Islamic faith, both in theory and practice; in his eyes they were as much infidels as their European mercenaries. More acute for the young ascetic were the deviations that became increasingly manifest between his beliefs and those of his teachers. These tended to threaten his integrity—his very being. As a student of Shaykh Muhammad Khujali he refused to eat with his master, since the food was provided through government subsidies.[79] This conflict of values became exacerbated when Muhammad Ahmad went to study under Muhammad Sharif in 1861. After serving his master for seven years with utmost humility—the mutual affection between the two men had produced a father-son relationship—he was licensed as a shaykh at the age of twenty-four.

In 1870 he settled with brothers on Aba Island, which became his headquarters, and during the next decade proceeded to acquire a large following on the strength of his preaching and his reputation for humility and piety. However, his increasing popularity brought him into conflict with his master, Muhammad Sharif, which in 1878 led to a fight between their respective followers. After a brief reconciliation, Muhammad Ahmad's revulsion came to a head when Muhammad Sharif permitted dancing and music during the circumcision of his sons. Such conduct was an abomination to Muhammad Ahmad's puritanical soul as well as a breach of the Islamic law. In response to Muhammad Ahmad's public denunciation of Muhammad Sharif, the former was expelled from the shaykh's order. Repeated attempts to seek forgiveness and readmission were refused by the master, and Muhammad Ahmad eventually joined a rival Samaniya order under Shaykh al-Qurashi. The shaykhly teachers in general and Muhammad Sharif in particular had become the young preacher's surrogate fathers, against whom he now rebelled in the name of religious puritanism. Soon, he would raise the level of his rebellion against authority to reject, in the name of God, the Egyptians, the Ottoman Turks, the British, and the world beyond.

In 1880, Muhammad Ahmad assumed the leadership of the order as shaykh after Qurashi's death. A year later, he was to claim a rank above and beyond that of shaykh—that of Mahdi—to effectively settle a personal score on a large scale. Indeed, his conflict with Muhammad Sharif was a chastening experience that brought to Muhammad Ahmad the realization that moral corruption now permeated even the ascetic orders. At that juncture he appears to have faced three possible alternatives: (1) to retreat into asceticism—to "nothingness"; (2) to continue to preach, as shaykh, with a salutary but limited social impact; or (3) to make society conform to his own unchangeable puritanical values through a revolutionary takeover of power. By 1881, he had chosen the latter course, which entailed a switch in his medium of salvation from ascetic shaykh to Mahdi—from "nothingness" to "allness."[80] This claim to mahdiship unified the religious and political realms in one person, in keeping with the Prophet's precedent. It also implied a revolutionary takeover of power from the "infidel" Turks, as well as a radical renovation of the faith. In this sense, the Mahdi was a political revolutionary as well as a religious renewer.

Claim to Mahdiship and Personal Attributes

Muhammad Ahmad's claims to mahdiship were based on a number of specific and general criteria, found in the Sudan's Islamic/tribal cultural system in the form of *hadith* (traditions of the Prophet):

1. Appointment by the Prophet Muhammad in a vision as the Mahdi and as the Prophet's *khalifa* (successor), reinforced through divine voices and messages.

2. Descent from the Prophet's family through Ali and Fatimah.

3. Resemblance to the Prophet in nature (although not in physical attributes).

4. Birth from a father called Abdallah — the name of the Prophet's father.

5. Possession of specific physical attributes: Bald forehead; aquiline nose; Arab complexion; cleft between front teeth; birthmark on right cheek; and countenance like a brilliant star.

6. Emulation of the Prophet's activities in Arabia: Preaching God's word; call to puritanism; unifying the tribes in holy war against the infidels; fleeing when threatened; working miracles while leading the people to victory in battle.

7. Appearance as the Expected One at "the End of Time and the Hour" around the end of the Islamic century—1298 (A.D. 1881).[81]

Muhammad Ahmad's claim to mahdiship was reinforced by his spectacular victories against the Anglo-Ottoman-Egyptian armies, as well as by his display of the puritanical attributes of a holy man (*qutb*). Thus, in the perceptions of his followers, the Mahdi possessed certain unique attributes and abilities: Deputy of God, Deputy of the Messenger of God, The Caller of God, The Sword of God, The Expected Mahdi, The Expected Imam, The Expected Fatimid, Master of Time, Master of Saints, Renewer of the Faith of Prophecy, Being Created of the Prophet's Light, Possessor of Barakah, Worker of Unique Miracles, Mediator between the Prophet and the People, Interpreter of the Prophetic Vision, Infallible, and Perfect Man.[82] It should be noted that the Mahdi and his followers were working primarily under the Sunni perception of mahdiship, which in contrast to the Shiite notion of the Mahdi is not rigorously defined.[83]

Conclusion

There exists substantial fit between the stages of the theoretical framework and the Mahdist case. This is particularly true regarding the milieu of the Sudanese crisis and its "existential dread" in terms of mass alienation and expectancy. However, due to lack of information, the Mahdi's phases of personality development cannot be fully analyzed. Moreover, Erikson's eight phases of personality development may not fully correspond to those in the Sudanese culture.

The Mahdi was not destined to preside over the new order; he died soon after his victory over General Charles Gordon in January 1885. Yet the Mahdi had forged a dynamic Islamic state out of a puritanical movement; the process of routinization had already begun at the time of the Mahdi's death, and the Mahdiyya continued as a functioning theocracy until its defeat by Great Britain in 1899.

Shabbatai Sevi

The case of Shabbatai Sevi offers a prime example of a revivalist movement in which charismatic leadership became a central factor. Here was a millenarian movement of Jewish revivalism in which two charismatics played mutually complementary roles: Sevi as the Messiah and Nathan Ashkenazi of Gaza as his precursor/prophet.

The Crisis Milieu: Identity Crisis and Cognitive Dissonance

The history of the Jews had been characterized by protracted crises and persecutions. However, the immediate period before the appearance of Sevi was marked by several specific events that contributed to the deepening and intensification of the social-psychological crisis of the Dispersion. The most traumatic upheaval was the expulsion from Spain (1492), which created a new Diaspora and marked the onset of "Messianic birth pangs."[84] During the sixteenth century, the Jewish Dispersion found itself caught in the confrontation between the Ottoman state and the emerging nation-states of Europe. The Jewish situation in the European sphere was even worse than that of the Islamic realm. The Thirty Years War brought great suffering to Jews living in Germany, while in Poland the Cracow massacre of 1637 was only a prelude to the Chmielnicki massacres of 1648 and to other acts of repression and *po-*

grom that continued until 1655 in the context of the Swedish-Russian War.[85]

The main reaction to this extended period of crisis was Lurianic kabbalism, based on the mystical teaching of Isaac Luria of Safed (1534–72). The kabbalists produced effective symbols, myths, and images of historical realities, which readily appealed to the unsophisticated masses in the throes of crisis. The kabbalists provided a social ideology—a popular religion—the essential breeding ground for the Shabbataian movement. The religious revivalism of the kabbalists as a response to crisis was instrumental in defining a new Jewish identity as a prelude to spiritual and political salvation. During the early 1600s, there was a pervasive sense of expectation throughout the Dispersion, with the year 1648 as the focus of hopes for messianic redemption. In vain, they waited as several messianic dates passed without any sign of the expected Messiah.

Then the kabbalists seized upon the passage in Zohar: "In the year 408 of the sixth millennium they that lie in the dust will arise. . . ."[86] Instead of salvation, however, came more massacres, necessitating another painful readjustment of messianic chronology with all of its attendant crises in identity. Shabbatai Horowitz lamented: "In the Year 408 of the sixth millennium I had hoped in my heart to go out free, but [instead] they have taken crafty counsel to destroy the people."[87]

At this juncture, a classic case of "cognitive dissonance"[88] is discernible. The failure of prophecy often produces cognitive dissonance among the believers, whereby in order to achieve greater "consonance" or consistency between beliefs and reality their beliefs are changed or reinforced by new cognitions. One consequence of such reduction of dissonance is an increase of religious fervor—a call to prayer, penitence, and charity until the Messiah's revelation.

The Messianic Personage: Shabbatai Sevi

Born in a family of commercial agents in Smyrna, Shabbatai did not follow his two brothers into his family's increasingly prosperous business. Instead, he received talmudic training under the well-known Joseph Eskapha, He was ordained as *hakham* at the age of eighteen, but never served as rabbi of a congregation. Supported by affluent brothers, Shabbatai preferred the ascetic life of the mystic. He possessed a quick mind, a solid knowledge of the law, and a reputation as an inspired man. However, he lacked the ability and discipline of a writer. His distinguishing attributes included a beautiful singing voice and a majestic countenance.[89]

At the age of twenty, Shabbatai developed the clear signs of mental illness marked by paranoia, manic depressive psychosis and hysteria. He began to experience cyclical stages of ups and downs — periods of mental illumination accompanied by great outbursts of energy, ecstasy, and exaltation followed by periods of dejection, agony, and childish behavior.[90] During his periods of illumination, he acted in a strange manner and openly transgressed the Law. It appears that during one of his "illuminations," Shabbatai revealed himself in 1648 as the Messiah. In a vision he claimed to have been anointed by the Patriarchs as the Amirah, and proceeded to utter the "Ineffable Name of God" (which brought rebuke from his teacher, Joseph Eskapha).[91] Since there is no clear evidence of these early claims, it is possible that Shabbatai revealed himself in 1648 only to close associates, or that he laid claim to this crucial date retrospectively when he became the leader of a mass movement. Whatever the case, around 1651 he was forced by the rabbis to leave Smyrna to spend the next fifteen years as a persecuted wanderer. During his extended moratorium Sevi continued to suffer anguish and persecution, but he also attracted some followers through his personal charm and magnetism, noble bearing, and songs of divine love. His two marriages in Smyrna were not consummated and during his next stop, Salonika, he married the Torah in public, an act prompting his expulsion by the rabbis. In 1658, Shabbatai reached Constantinople, where he abrogated the "old Law," promulgated "the new law of Isaiah," and decreed a change in the dates of major feasts — all of which caused the rabbis to have him flogged. In the course of the next two years he returned to Smyrna and went on to Jerusalem for a year's visit. Despite opposition from local rabbis, Sevi was successful in attracting some followers as an ascetic, often living as a hermit in caves. Late in 1663 he proceeded to Egypt to collect donations from the affluent Jewish community of Cairo for the destitute Jewry of Palestine, who were suffering under heavy Ottoman taxation. He was welcomed in Egypt, where he stayed for two years and took a third wife, Sarah, despite her questionable reputation. Yet the successful sojourn in Egypt did not end Sevi's moratorium. The strange illness persisted as he left Egypt for Gaza to seek a cure in the blessing of a rising prophet, Nathan Ashkenazi.[92]

It was the prophecy of Nathan of Gaza which confirmed Sevi's mission as Messiah. Nathan was a mystic of excellent reputation who had discovered during an ecstatic vision in 1665 that Sevi was the expected saviour. Nathan was a brilliant Lurianic kabbalist who acted as the precursor of the Messiah. During Sevi's visit to Gaza, Nathan declared him the Messiah and Sevi responded with laughter. Only Nathan's repeated urgings convinced Sevi that he was indeed the chosen one.[93] Nathan's prophetic role was crucial: increasing numbers of converts flocked to Sevi for the first time. In convincing Sevi of the divine validity of his calling, Nathan brought him out of his moratorium. Subsequently, Nathan served as the ideologist and propagator of the

Shabbatian faith. Nathan's strengths complemented Sevi's weaknesses of character as the two men pressed on with their common spiritual mission.

After being proclaimed Messiah in Gaza (May 1665), Sevi chose twelve rabbinic scholars to represent the tribes and proceeded to march into Jerusalem sitting upon a horse with great pomp.[94] Now Sevi began to preach a message of redemption and spiritual renewal, while altering the feast days, forbidding all fasting, encouraging the eating of animal fat, and changing liturgical procedures. Finally, his explicit claim to messiahship prompted Sevi to substitute his name as king of Israel in place of the sultan in public prayers — an act of rejection of Ottoman authority. These acts infuriated the rabbis who asked the Ottoman judge to arrest Sevi. In a personal appearance before a Muslim judge, Sevi "miraculously" convinced him of his innocence, whereupon the rabbis excommunicated the Messiah and expelled him from Jerusalem.[95] However, rabbinic opposition could not stop the growth of a movement that was supported by an accredited prophet like Nathan. After leaving Jerusalem, Sevi was received in Aleppo with great honor and enthusiasm, where his manifestation of manic "illumuniation" was not marred by strange behavior. In September 1665, Sevi returned to his native Smyrna where he assumed a passive role until December, perhaps due to his depressed mental state. Suddenly, during Hanukkah, Shabbatai appeared in the synagogue in royal dress and a state of exaltation and illumination, and intoned prayers and hymns with his marvelous voice. Once again Sevi transgressed the law by pronouncing the "Ineffable Name of God," inventing new rituals, and calling upon women to read the Torah.[96] He then proceeded to march on his opponents' synagogue, which he proceeded to occupy after axing the door open.[97] A wave of messianic excitement swept over Smyrna as the faithful saw miracles and heard the prophets. (Elijah was seen walking the streets.)[98] It is said that Sevi's message attracted a wide following that included not only the common people but also scholars and the affluent.

In late December 1665, Sevi departed for Constantinople where the tidings of the Messiah's arrival had created an atmosphere of great fervor and tension. Amid Jewish rejoicing was the fear of Turkish massacre. Sevi's charismatic appeal had reached its zenith, and its economic and political consequences were becoming a governmental concern. Indeed, the messianic involvement of the Jewish population was causing a precipitous decline in the empire's commerce as the gathering support for Sevi's kingship seemed to threaten imperial authority. In actual fact, Shabbataism did not constitute an immediate revolutionary threat to the Sultan, although it was socially and economically disruptive as Jews began making plans to follow the Messiah to Palestine. Yet the rhetoric of both Nathan and Sevi was potentially threatening as they spoke of Sevi's imminent assumption of the crown from the sultan; however, this would occur by singing songs, without fighting.

Upon his arrival in Constantinople, Sevi was arrested by the grand vizier, Ahmet Koprulu, with the connivance of some local Jewish leaders.[99] The vizier was lenient with Sevi, who was eventually sent to a comfortable jail in the fortress of Gallipoli, where thousands of believers came to pay homage to "the Lord's Anointed."[100] In this "tower of strength" Sevi received emissaries, issued new laws, and continued to exhort his followers. Both the European and Eastern Jewish communities were aflame with messianic fervor.

In September 1666, at the height of his messianic career, Sevi was accused of lewdness and other charges by one Rabbi Nehemiah of Poland. The charges were presented to Sultan Mehmet IV by Nehemiah who, an apostate, might have been used as a government agent to destroy Sevi's credibility. Given the choice of apostasy or death, Sevi chose to accept Islam with passivity, after which he led a life of duplicity. In 1672, Sevi's suspicious behavior prompted the Turks to rearrest him and banish him to a fortress in Albania. The apostasy was a serious blow to the believers, many of whom regressed into a new phase of identity crisis. Some followed Sevi into apostasy, while others continued to believe in his mission and remained Jews under Nathan's guidance. The prophet Nathan's vain efforts to routinize the remnants of Sevi's charisma centered on his scriptural reinterpretations in an attempt to justify Sevi's apostasy. However, Nathan's repeated adjustments of his prophecy to conform with Sevi's actions could not reduce the manic cognitive dissonance which the apostasy had generated among the faithful. During 1678–79, Nathan introduced the notion of "occultation" in reference to Sevi's death. Nathan himself died in 1680.

Conclusion

When examined from the Weberian/Eriksonian perspective, the Shabbataian case offers several significant insights. The crisis milieu is clearly visible, as is the Jewish compulsion to seek a saviour. As to Sevi's extreme patienthood, Erikson's theory offers only a partial answer, due to the possible existence of psychophysical infirmities afflicting the "false Messiah." Yet Sevi's message conforms with our framework in terms of its radical content, utopian promises, and powerful influence upon the expectant masses. The historical evidence presented by Scholem points to the overwhelming value transformation in a majority of Jewry as a consequence of the charismatic bond between Sevi and his followers. However, it should be noted that Sevi was a largely passive leader in contrast to the Mahdi and other charismatics. The roles of propagator of the message and routinizer of the movement devolved upon Nathan of Gaza, a charismatic in his own right. Sevi's extraordinary qualities of body and soul were also essential to the success of the movement, as was his persistence in projecting his desperate inner patienthood to the mass level in search of a cure. At the point of convergence of Sevi's patienthood and that of the Jewish Diaspora was the prophetic personality of Nathan—the precursor, the validator, and the routinizer of Shabbataian charisma.

The foregoing comparative analysis of the Mahdist and Shabbataian movements has illustrated some of the dynamic factors associated with the rise of charismatic personages in messianic and millenarian movements. To the extent that charisma plays a role as a dominant force in social transformation, the framework presented here may be utilized to study the genesis and evolution of various cultic, revivalist, and revolutionary movements. In each case, however, the analysis should be anchored on the cultural system surrounding particular leaders and their societies. Therefore, sensitivity to cultural equivalence should become a central consideration in any comparative study of charismatic phenomena in different sociocultural settings.

Notes

1. Max Weber, *Ancient Judaism,* trans. and ed. Hans H. Gerth and Don Martindale (New York: Free Press, 1952); Sigmund Freud, *Moses and Monotheism* (New York: Vintage Books, 1939); Erik Erikson, *Young Man Luther* (New York: Norton, 1958); and idem, *Gandhi's Truth* (New York: Norton, 1969).

2. Dankwart A. Rustow, "The Study of Leadership," in D. A. Rustow, ed., *Philosophers and Kings* (New York: George Braziler, 1970), pp. 14–15.

3. Charles L. Montesquieu, "Considerations sur les Causes de la Grandeur des Romains et de leur Decadence," *Oeuvres Complètes de Montesquieu* (Paris, Gallimard, 1951), p. 70.

4. For a modified view, see R. Hrair Dekmejian, "Marx, Weber, and the Egyptian Revolution," *Middle East Journal* 30, no. 2 (Spring 1976): 161–62. Ironically, it was Lenin who supplied Marxist revolutionary doctrine with a theory of leadership in the form of the Vanguard Party and put it into practice in the Russian Revolution.

5. Max Weber, *The Theory of Social and Economic Organizations,* trans. A. M. Henderson and Talcott Parsons (New York: Oxford University Press, 1947), pp. 70–71, and Peter Blau, "Critical Remarks on Weber's Theory of Authority," *American Political Science Review* 57, no. 2 (June 1963): 309.

6. Max Weber, *Economy and Society,* trans. and ed. Guenther Roth and Claus Wittich (New York: Bedminster Press, 1968), pp. 1111, 1121. On the relationship between situations of

distress and the rise of charismatic leadership, see Robert C. Tucker, "The Theory of Charismatic Authority," in Rustow, *Philosophers and Kings,* pp. 80–84.

7. Weber, *Ancient Judaism,* p. 283. On this question, see the insightful analysis by R. Hummel, "Charisma in Politics" (Doctoral diss., New York University, 1972).

8. R. Hrair Dekmejian, *Egypt Under Nasir* (Albany: SUNY Press, 1971), pp. 14–15.

9. This point receives lengthy treatment in Hummel, who bases his analysis on Weber, *Economy and Society,* 1111, 1121. See Hummel, "Charisma in Politics," p. 378.

10. Dekmejian, *Egypt Under Nasir,* pp. 9–13.

11. Daniel Bell, *The End of Ideology* (New York: Free Press, 1962).

12. For a critical analysis of alienation, see Daniel Bell, "Sociodicy: A Guide to Modern Usage," *The American Scholar* 35, no. 4 (Autumn 1965): 700–1.

13. Emile Durkheim, *Suicide,* trans. J. Spaulding and G. Simpson (Glencoe, Ill.: Free Press, 1951). For the relevance of anomie to charisma, see S. N. Eisenstadt, *Max Weber: On Charisma and Institution Building* (Chicago: University of Chicago Press, 1968), p. xxiii.

14. Tucker, "Charismatic Authority," p. 83.

15. Ibid.

16. George Devereux, "Charismatic Leadership and Crises," *Psychoanalysis and the Social Sciences* 4 (1955): 146–551. Often, this expectancy is reinforced by a precursor such as John the Baptist.

17. Ibid., pp. 149–51, and William Langer, "The Next Assignment," in Bruce Mazlish, ed., *Psychoanalysis and History* (New York: Grosset and Dunlap, 1963), p. 103.

18. On Erikson see Tucker, "Charismatic Authority," 83. On psychological vulnerability in mass society, see William Kornhauser, *The Politics of Mass Society* (Glencoe, Ill.: Free Press, 1959), pp. 114–15, and Hans H. Toch, "Crisis Situations and Ideological Reevaluation," *Public Opinion Quarterly* 19 (Spring 1955), pp. 53–67.

19. Weber, *Social and Economic Organizations,* pp. 358–59.

20. Weber, *Economy and Society,* p. 24.

21. Ibid., p. 215. Edward Shils states that a leader's charismatic quality lies in what is perceived to be "his connection with some very central feature of man's existence and the cosmos in which he lives." See Shils, "Charisma, Order and Status," *American Sociological Review* 30 (April 1965): 199–213.

22. Rudolph Sohm, *Kirchenrecht* (Munich: 1923).

23. See Dekmejian, "Marx," p. 162. Also relevant is the term *chrisma,* meaning to rub or anoint with unguents. Thus, *chrisma* means baptismal oil while *Christos* means Christ, the Anointed One.

24. Bell, "Sociodicy," p. 702.

25. Charisma is used six times in Romans; seven times in 1 Corinthians (five times in chapter 12); and once each in 2 Corinthians, 1 and 2 Timothy, and 1 Peter. See Bell, "Sociodicy," pp. 702–3. Also see Francis A. Sullivan, *Charisma and Charismatic Renewal* (Ann Arbor, Mich.: 1982), pp. 17–18.

26. Sullivan, *Charisma,* p. 42.

27. 1 Cor. 13:1–13.

28. Sullivan, *Charisma,* pp. 28–29.

29. 1 Cor. 14:1–12.

30. Bell, "Sociodicy," p. 702.

31. Gustave E. von Grunebaum, *Medieval Islam,* 2nd ed. (Chicago: University of Chicago Press, 1953), p. 92. See also Annemarie Schimmel, *And Muhammad is His Messenger* (Chapel Hill: North Carolina University Press, 1985), pp. 55, 67.

32. Idriss Shah, *The Sufis* (Garden City, N.Y.: Doubleday, 1953), p. 92.

33. Bell, "Sociodicy," p. 703.

34. Dekmejian, "Marx," pp. 164–65, and R. H. Dekmejian and Margaret J. Wyszomirski, "Charismatic Leadership in Islam: The Mahdi of the Sudan," *Comparative Studies in Society and History* 14, no. 2 (March 1972): 198–99.

35. Harold D. Lasswell, *Psychopathology and Politics* (Chicago: University of Chicago Press, 1930), pp. 74–76.

36. For a cogent analysis of these problems, see Lucian W. Pye, "Personal Identity and Political Ideology," in Mazlish, *Psychoanalysis and History.*

37. Erikson, *Young Man Luther,* pp. 253–62.

38. Ibid., p. 43.

39. Pye, "Personal Identity," p. 165.

40. Erik Erikson, "The First Psychoanalyst," *Yale Review* (Autumn 1956): 50.

41. Erikson, *Young Man Luther,* p. 67.

42. Dekmejian and Wyszomirski, "Charismatic Leadership," pp. 195–96.

43. Ibid., pp. 196–97. On the role of marginal and *déclassé* individuals in the founding of new states, see Rustow, "Study of Leadership," p. 21.

44. Dekmejian and Wyszomirski, "Charismatic Leadership," p. 195.

45. On the impact of the message, see Tucker, "Charismatic Authority," pp. 86–90.

46. Dekmejian, *Egypt Under Nasir,* 5–6. The revolutionary nature of the message does not preclude the selective incorporation of certain prevailing values and symbols. Thus, there is a degree of continuity between the old and the new. The leader selectively invokes history, myth, and heroes to reinforce the sanctity and validity of his mission.

47. Ibid., p. 6.

48. On the content of the message, see ibid., pp. 5–6.

49. In Rustow's more general formulation: "Successful leadership . . . rests on a latent congruence between the psychic needs of the leader and the social needs of followers." See Rustow, "Study of Leadership," p. 23.

50. Amitai Etzioni, *A Comparative Analysis of Complex Organizations* (New York: Free Press, 1961), pp. 203–4.

51. Ibid.

52. Richard R. Fagen, "Charismatic Authority and the Leadership of Fidel Castro," *Western Political Quarterly* 18, no. 2 (June 1961): 275.

53. Dekmejian, *Egypt Under Nasir,* p. 7.

54. See Langer, "Next Assignment," p. 93.

55. Reinhard Bendix, *Max Weber: An Intellectual Portrait* (Garden City, N.Y.: Doubleday, 1960), pp. 299, 326.

56. Max Weber, *From Max Weber: Essays in Sociology,* ed. and trans. Hans Gerth and C. Wright Mills (New York: Oxford University Press, 1958), p. 253.

57. Bendix, *Max Weber,* p. 303.

58. Dekmejian, *Egypt Under Nasir,* pp. 7–8.

59. Ibid.

60. Ibid.

61. For a reinterpretation of Weber in terms of dialectical theory, see Dekmejian, "Marx, Weber," pp. 160–63. See also Weber, *From Max Weber,* pp. 51–55.

62. Bendix, *Max Weber,* p. 302.

63. Ibid.

64. Ibid., pp. 304, 308.

65. According to Rustow, this less intense form of charisma is seen in "the daily miracle of the Mass" that is performed by the priests in commemoration of Christ. See Rustow, "Study of Leadership," p. 18.

66. Weber does not draw a distinction between a "renewer of religion" and a "founder of religion." See Max Weber, *The Sociology of Religion*, trans. Ephraim Fischoff (Boston: Beacon Press, 1964), p. 46.

67. See Erikson, *Young Man Luther*, pp. 243, 260–61.

68. Ibid., pp. 260–61.

69. Ibid., p. 261.

70. Ibid., p. 262. For a discussion of the evolution of Islamic societies from charismatic to bureaucratic organizations, see R. Hrair Dekmejian, *Islam in Revolution* (Syracuse, N.Y.: Syracuse University Press, 1985), pp. 67–68.

71. Muhammad Bin Abd al-Majid Bin Muhammad al-Sarraj, *Shaqaiq al-Numan fi Hayat al-Mahdi wa Waqaa al-Sudan* [Highlights in the life of the Mahdi and events of the Sudan] (Cairo: 1947), pp. 16–17.

72. P. M. Holt, *The Mahdist State in the Sudan, 1881–1898* (London: Oxford University Press, 1970), pp. 13–14.

73. J. Spencer Trimingham, *Islam in the Sudan* (London: Barnes and Noble, 1949), pp. 187–241.

74. Holt, *Mahdist State*, p. 31.

75. Richard A. Bermann, *The Mahdi of Allah* (New York: Barnes and Noble, 1932), p. 53.

76. Byron Farwell, *Prisoners of the Madhi* (New York: Barnes and Noble, 1967), p. 5.

77. Erikson, *Young Man Luther*, p. 108.

78. Ibid.

79. Holt, *Mahdist State*, p. 45.

80. Erikson, *Young Man Luther*, pp. 108–9.

81. Haim Shaked, *The Life of the Sudanese Mahdi* (New Brunswick, N.J.: Transaction Books, 1978), pp. 51–61.

82. Ibid., pp. 204–7, 213–23. On the Mahdi's qualities, see also al-Sarraj, *Shaqaiq*, p. 99, and Naum Shuqayr, *Al-Jughrafiya wa Tarikh al-Sudan* [The geography and history of the Sudan] (Beirut: 1967), p. 939.

83. Holt, *Mahdist State*, p. 23.

84. Gershon Scholem, *Shabbatai Sevi: the Mystical Messiah, 1626–1676* (Princeton, N.J.: Princeton University Press, 1973).

85. Ibid., p. 88.

86. Ibid.

87. Ibid., p. 92.

88. Leon Festinger, *A Theory of Cognitive Dissonance* (Stanford, Connecticut: Row, Peterson, 1957).

89. *The Encyclopedia of Jewish Knowledge*, ed. Jacob De Haas (New York: Behrman's Jewish Book House, 1944), p. 507.

90. Scholem, *Shabbatai Sevi*, pp. 126–27.

91. *Encyclopedia of Jewish Knowledge*, p. 508.

92. Scholem, *Shabbatai Sevi*, p. 207.

93. Ibid., pp. 214–15.

94. The parallels between Sevi and Jesus should be obvious.

95. Scholem, *Shabbatai Sevi*, pp. 242–43.

96. Ibid., pp. 402–3.

97. Ibid.

98. Ibid., pp. 431–32.

99. Ibid., pp. 448–49.

100. Ibid., p. 604.

5

Indices of the Islamic Resurgence in Malaysia
The Medium and the Message

JUDITH NAGATA

The very term *ideology* conveys a sense of intensity, conviction, and sometimes even passion, suggesting a capacity to modify existing or conventional social relationships and boundaries or even to create new ones. Ideas are often credited with the power of overriding or at least controlling the groups that bear or accept their message, thereby becoming subject to their engulfing forces.

It is tempting to make such assumptions in the examination of new, lively social or religious movements, measuring them on the basis of an ideological index. There is an implicit *a priori* premise that such movements can be known and evaluated by their very zeal. Such assumptions may arise partly from the Judaeo-Christian heritage of many social scientists, whose approach to religion often reflects the theological notion that belief and conversion, especially of the "born again" variety, spring from an inner spiritual/ideological motivation and force, and that commitment goes deeper than outward social expressions and rituals.

Another common underlying premise seems to be that normative change and consensus precede and even determine patterns of social interaction — or at least that shared norms predispose shared activity. Further, the zeal and activity of intensely motivated and often socially isolated but ideologically committed individuals — the ideas of the great charismatic movers and shakers of history — can, if only temporarily, rearrange social boundaries or dissolve them into unstructured "communitas."[1] Finally, such assumptions probably reflect the tendency of the Western intellectual to stress the role of ideas as an explanation for social movements and mobilization.

A further tendency — or, possibly, a methodological constraint — of the social science (as opposed to the theological) approach is to concentrate on broad, collective patterns and directions — on leadership, and on what appears to be the overall "structure" of a movement. Sometimes, this approach is at the expense of a fuller understanding of the grass-roots followers of movements, and obscures the importance of nonideological pressures for the average participant. However, if one reverses the usual procedure and views the religious movement from the "bottom up" instead of from the top down, what at first sight may appear as a monolithic entity with a clearly definable structure may dissolve into an amorphous aggregate of small social fragments. It then becomes imperative to understand the informal, personal ties by which these fragments are knit together.

This vantage point has implications for the value/ideological question and the measure of how far recruitment and commitment are matters of theology and moral principle, or of personal relationships and social pressures. Further, a distinction must be preserved between the declared public platform and rhetoric of leadership and the apparent interpretations and interests of the rank and file, for the two may be substantially different. Variation in ideological understandings may exist between the leaders and the grass roots, and may also emerge between different cells of the followers themselves, caused by imperfect communication down the lines. During the communication process, messages may become distorted, as in the familiar party "whisper game," with the result that ideological content varies locally and also may be subject to the character and predilections of the message-bearer.

Initially, I was tempted to play devil's advocate by suggesting that the "medium is the message," and that religious revival could be analyzed without reference to any ideological/theological component whatsoever. In this vein, a revival could be explained almost mechanistically, in terms of patterns of social interaction and sanctions and pressures toward conformity within traditional society. The interpretative cue here comes from Shils,[2] who was able to explain the patriotism of soldiers in wartime on the basis of their loyalty to and pressures from the immediate, small platoon of comrades, with little reference to ideology. According to Shils's findings, the minds of ordinary men are likely to be swayed less by appeals to abstract values, virtues, and ideologies than by obligations and conformity to their closest colleagues in face-to-face relationships. To take a more specifically "religious" example, Jackson[3] has claimed that the decisive factor in determining whether or not individual Javanese villagers supported the Darul Islam movement in its heyday in Indonesia was in large measure their personal tie to the local headman; the man as much as the views themselves drew their loyalty. With this interpretation, awareness of the strength and effectiveness of small cliques and networks is essential to an understanding of both recruitment motivation and the processes of communication. (A shortcoming of this approach, however, is its avoidance of the more basic question of why the processes started in the first place.)

Studies of the development and cycles of social and religious movements[4] have demonstrated that the articulation of a coherent ideology often occurs at a later stage, after the initial stirrings of social agitation. Such timing suggests the presence of a nurturant social environment for new ideas. Thus, normative consensus may follow rather than precede social mobilization and may even depend upon it.

In my discussion of the Islamic revival in Malaysia, I shall be less radical than threatened in the devil's advocate proposition above and will try to do justice to both faces of the resurgence. First, I shall try to sketch some of the characteristics of the "message" and of the constituencies to which it appeals, and to show how far the revival has adapted to uniquely Malaysian conditions. Second, I shall return to the "medium"—the processes by which the message is actually adopted, transmitted, and interpreted somewhat independently of its strictly theological content.

The Malaysian Scene

At the risk of oversimplification, Malaysia can be said to be a country of immigrants—a plural society in which the indigenous Malays form a bare majority of just over 50% of the population. Collectively, the other populations, including the Chinese (36%), Indians (10%), and a few aboriginal peoples, are barely small enough in number to be a numerical minority, although politically they may be so. The Malays, both in the constitution and in the political structure, have the edge in terms of power and privilege,[5] which they are attempting to convert to economic advantage partly at the expense of the traditional Chinese and other entrepreneurs and traders. Numerous plans and programs provide special quotas for Malays—in government and of civil service positions, in commerce and industry, and in a variety of professional occupations, education and scholarships, and eligibility for special loans and licenses.[6] The Malays are a people intent on becoming a true "nation" in the strict sense of the term, and on asserting their identity politically and culturally. Malay is the national language and the medium of education and the civil service, and Malay cultural symbols are increasingly those of the state of Malaysia. Islam, the faith to which all Malays adhere (if in some cases only nominally), is the official religion, although Malaysia is not an Islamic state. The definition of *Malays* in the constitution in terms of the practice of Malay custom and language and Muslim identity sets up broad cultural boundaries between them and their non-Malay compatriots.

Whereas the Malays are prescriptively Muslim, each of the other communities in Malaysia has its own faith that it is free to practice without restraint, short of evangelism among Muslims and Malays. Most of the Chinese follow an eclectic mixture of Buddhism, Taoism, Confucianism, and some Christianity, while the Indians are largely Hindu (a few are Christians). There is, however, a small but significant body of Indian Muslims, in principle providing a gate in the boundary wall between them and the Malays. In the broad sweep, each of the principal communities in Malaysia is thus distinguished by its own culture, language, and religion. Given the political dominance of the Malays and the remaining economic influence of the Chinese, even the occupational traditions and life-chances for the future tend to follow ethnic lines.

Traditional Malay Social Organization

Until the impact of modern economic and political programs began to have some effect, the Malays were largely an agricultural people living in villages. There, kinship and neighborhood were the principal foundations of social life, while outside the villages the peasants were traditionally appended to a social hierarchy incorporating every Malay, from slave to sultan. Between these levels was a proliferation of intermediate titles and status divisions, including the military, both hereditary and acquired. Peasants were also attached to a parallel hierarchy of *ulama* (religious specialists) and *guru* (teachers) who formed a distinct status group in themselves, with some tendency toward closure as an endogamous[7] local elite exerting powerful moral, social, and even political pressure on the villagers.

Equal Status Age/Generation Sets

Among village Malays, the most salient divisions or principles of social cohesion and common activity revolve around the equal-status age or generation set and around the neighborhood or residential unit. Many daily, cooperative work and recreational activities, relating to mutual aid, work groups, sports, coffee shop, and mosque, are pursued within the "horizontal" age-set, stratifying the population roughly along lines of old age, middle age, unmarried adults, and youth and children. The age-set is also the basis of such marginal groups as gangs, and finally of the ties formed between fellow students in schools and colleges. These patterns tend to underscore quite distinct generation gaps; persons from different generational groups are occasionally reluctant to mix or to accept willingly each other's advice. Before young people marry, the parent-offspring relationship is often ambivalent, and the authority of the former may be threatened by rebelliousness and antagonism. Age distinctions receive formal expression in a kinship terminology used as a marker of appropriate address, behavior, and even of potential marriage partners.

Neighborhood/Residential Groups

Obviously, some social activities recruit participants across generation lines, especially within local neighborhoods and residential institutions. Included are the many ceremonial and ritual events involving village neighbors. In Malay life, coresidence creates its own obligations and on some occasions — particularly, in rites of passage and feasts — precedence is accorded to neighbors over kin. The importance of common residence recurs in urban and institutional settings in such contexts as hostels, dormitories, and police and soldiers' quarters, where the individual is encapsulated away from effective family and home influence.

Authority Relationships

Of the traditional relationships of authority in Malay society, those of royalty, military/police, and teachers concern us most for present purposes. The authority of officers over the ranks in the armed forces often extends to matters beyond the strictly professional. The tendency of the rank and file to emulate their superiors is reinforced by the effect of residential closeness and of peer-group solidarity and sanctions.

Spanning both secular and religious hierarchies, the *guru*-pupil relationship is particularly influential in both traditional and modern Malay circles. The prototype of this relationship derives from the traditional religious school, where the authority of the teacher is not questioned and study is characteristically passive, repetitive, and based on rote learning. Whether young or old, the teacher commands great respect. Sometimes, his intellectual and religious qualifications are reinforced by such extracurricular roles as leader of a Sufi order and mystical sessions, adept at martial arts, or expert curer. Other status reinforcements are provided by claims to an illustrious intellectual genealogy traced to renowned *guru* elsewhere, to descent from the Prophet, or to visits to the Middle East for pilgrimage or study. Modern teachers and university lecturers share many of the same characteristics and teaching techniques, and even enhance their personal reputations in the manner of the traditional *guru,* deriving some of their authority from this analogy. Modern *guru* are also important vehicles of socialization and transmitters of values and ideas, and their personal influence — whether through formal instruction or informal interaction — can be powerful.

In secular society, the aura of royalty retains its influence among many Malays. Although much of their real political power has been abrogated by the postcolonial parliamentary-style government, the sultan of each state still retains residual powers as head of religion and Malay custom in his own domain.[8] In religious matters, the sultan, in conjunction with the state religious council, can resist any interference or religious pronouncements by federal and other secular government authorities; indeed, in religious affairs is found one of the last bastions of royal authority. Each state religious council has the right to issue *fatwas* (religio-legal interpretations) in its own territory.[9]

Some of the old halo-effect of royalty and a residue of what some local scholars call a "feudal mentality"[10] have been transferred to modern parliamentary political leaders. Even legitimate (political party) opposition to their authority is perceived as disloyalty to the ruler, or treason. However, for all their traditionalism in matters of legitimacy, modern Malay political leaders are basically of the technocratic mold, oriented toward Western-style economic development and modernization. Sympathetic to foreign investment and multinational corporations, they have been open to accusations of compromise in such Islamic precepts as the condoning of interest in financial institutions and in certain aspects of their personal lifestyles. To be fair, however, trends in the government of Prime Minister Mahathir suggest a growing sensitivity to Islamic values, although without sacrificing the goals of "development." The results of the election of August 1986 appear to reaffirm these general trends, managing as they did to maintain a precarious balance between antithetical interests.

Within the Malay ethnic community, Malay opposition parties are treated as "enemies in the blanket" — as traitors not only to their rulers but also to their "race" and "people." The Malay political party currently in power is the United Malays National Organization (UMNO). Its principal opposition comes partly from the ethnic-based parties of the non-Malays, particularly the Malaysian Chinese Association (MCA) and the Malaysian Indian Congress (MIC). The intra-Malay opposition is channelled largely through a religious party, PAS (Partai Se-Islam Malaysia). Because the principal opposition is fundamental Islamic, and since Islam itself is immune from attack, resistance by the incumbent party must take the more oblique strategy of questioning their opponents' interpretation of Islam and implying that the latter's claims to religious authority are illegitimate. In fact, more of the PAS support is centered in strongly Malay rural areas, and its leadership is drawn extensively from the ranks of the religious specialists, religious *guru,* and Sufi masters, some of whose practices and beliefs are labeled by UMNO as "deviant." The political struggle thus becomes a struggle to present oneself as the better Muslim.

Most electoral campaigns are fought under the banner of Islam, with each political group accusing the other of misusing the faith "like an infidel." Each party attempts to discredit the *imam* (leader) of the other, challenging the right of the other leader to perform religious functions in vituperative interchanges known locally as "mutual accusations of being an infidel." The practical outcome at the village level is often a situation in which, for example, UMNO Malays regard a marriage solemnized by a PAS functionary as invalid, or meat slaughtered by the "other side" as polluted. The two factions may refuse to pray in the same mosque. Islam can thus simultaneously unite and divide the Malays: unity comes from their common, constitutionally backed faith and identity vis-à-vis the majority of non-Malays; the disunity emerges from their different interpretation and political use of the faith.

One consequence of the overall demographic situation sketched above is the high degree of ethnic polarization in Malaysia. At its most basic level, this polarization is expressed as a Malay/non-Malay dichotomy now often symbolized as one between Muslim and non-Muslim. At this level, Malays and Muslims are one, their unity affirmed by religion. Internally, however, religious diversity is articulated not only in the two political styles mentioned but also through the distinction between the "born again" Muslim, or revivalist, and the "mainstream" Muslim.

A number of significant developments in modern Malay life bear upon changing religious values and practices. As a result of a series of five year plans partly designed to assist the Malays to catch up with the non-Malays economically, rural Malays have been increasingly settled in or have migrated to urban areas, and are also flooding into new, modern educational institutions away from home. Others are relocated in professsional or military quarters, or are sent overseas for special training. These changes create new environments and experiences for the Malays so affected (although many older attitudes and patterns of social groups, status rank, and authority persist). One of the striking features of the modern scene, then, is the rapidly burgeoning Malay intelligentsia in educational institutions, and a new Malay middle class of civil servants, professionals, and bourgeoisie. For this first-generation middle class (many of whom were born in rural areas), the professional roles they are expected to fill in return for their scholarship and prolonged education have no precedents in their own experience, and a crisis of identity and role performance may emerge. Others become confused by conflicts within the educational process itself. Exposure to the "hard" empirical and aggressively competitive Western variety of study sometimes has a brutal impact on those sent for education overseas, particularly where the home *guru* tradition has not emphasized challenging, questioning, or academic innovation. In the natural and social sciences, the issues that bewilder the student are in those areas where theories of genetics, Marxism, and structuralism appear incompatible with being a good Muslim. One reaction to this foreign intellectual assault is an attempt to substitute a more meaningful, directed approach to learning, one rooted firmly in a clearly defined foundation of religious morality (as opposed to the Western bias toward a "value-free" science). Inspirational knowledge through revelation is elevated to a status equal to that of the "empirical." The whole question of the ideal character of a Muslim scholar then becomes as central as the academic problems themselves.

Another constituency seeking a firmer anchorage in a clearly defined set of values (again, partly under the impact of Western styles), is that of the artist. Several well-known Malay writers in particular have undergone a much-publicized *angst* in their search for an "Islamic literature" and Islamic themes and ideas. They have sometimes explicitly renounced earlier (and successful) works in which these were not evident. (The principal writers' association is split over such questions.) Many artists have had wide foreign exposure and are particularly sensitive to the ideological conflict between the two styles. This common thread of foreign exposure and the resulting ideological conflict links the two sets of intellectuals. These intellectuals suffer most visibly from the crisis of conscience; by contrast, traditional rural religious specialists and teachers seem more secure in their own constituencies. While they, too, are involved in the religious resurgence, they are less personally vulnerable to the Western dilemma.

The Religious Revival

I turn now to the form of the religious revival itself. In contemporary Malaysia, any form of heightened religious consciousness and commitment, whether personal or in a private or public group, is known as *dakwah*. Whereas in many other Muslim societies the term *dakwah* means a general "call to the Faith" and is theoretically incumbent on all practicing Muslims, its popular use in Malaysia is the rather idiosyncratic reference only to the new tide of religious resurgence. *Dakwah* may be highly visible in matters of dress (half-purdah for women, "Arab" robes and turbans for men), as well as in rituals, prayer, and attention to food taboos. This visibility has reinforced its public impact in Malaysia on Muslims and non-Muslims alike. In the public mind, *dakwah* is associated largely with a number of named religious organizations, of which three are nationally prominent. These organizations are of varying degees of formality and structural tightness, with slightly different sources of authority. Leadership of the two best-known organizations, ABIM (Islamic Youth League of Malaysia) and Darul Arqam, is drawn mainly from the ranks of university graduates and lecturers, many of them educated overseas. ABIM actually grew out of an earlier Malay-language student association with an articulate and highly visible leadership. Darul Arqam has among its leaders Western-educated intellectuals as well as some more traditional religious school–style teachers. A third organization, Jemaat Tabligh, incorporates a more traditional style of Islamic leadership in the form of peripatetic religious specialists and missionaries, while some government-sponsored *dakwah* organizations try to draw on the force of their official status for their religious legitimacy.

Of all the organizations, Darul Arqam is the most reclusive. It has developed its own residential commune just outside the capital, Kuala Lumpur, although by no means do all of its members or sympathizers live there. It tries to create, as far as possible, its own counter-society and shadow economy based on cottage-industry–style manufacture and sale of food (noodles, chili sauce) and other basic products processed according to Islamic principles rather than by unclean non-Muslims, whether native Chinese or foreigners. Arqam also sponsors an extensive trading network, distributing its products throughout the country to other Malay/Muslim entrepreneurs. The Arqam commune and its enterprise operate through a series of Islamic committees, financed by a public purse drawn from religious taxes, by the voluntary contributions of supporters, and from its sales. Darul Arqam also runs a medical clinic where the treatment combines Malay folk medicine with selected Western techniques supplied by university-trained specialists. The commune and its services function in an environment controlled for religious purity, bodily and moral propriety, and prayer.

Both Darul Arqam and ABIM have developed a network of their own schools combining religious subjects and the Arabic of the older religious school with a selection of more secular or modern subjects. Although ABIM encourages its pupils to sit for the national promotional examinations, failure in the secular world is presented to the unsuccessful candidate as having compensations in the spiritual world, and is rationalized as part of God's plans for the candidate. Darul Arqam chooses secular subjects more in line with its own special needs, placing particular emphasis on medical arts and the practical electrical and mechanical skills suitable for the operation of its own enterprises.

Tabligh, whose origin goes back to a spiritual renewal in the 1920s in India (where its headquarters are still located), was initially introduced into Malaysia via the urban Indian Muslim community and was thus tinged with an ethnic (that is, non-Malay) character. Of late, however, with the recent revival, Tabligh has found new followers in the more monolithically Malay rural areas, including some traditional religious specialists who are attracted by the lack of any explicit leadership to threaten their own authority. In Tabligh organization, ideas move from group to group by personal contact and word of mouth via traveling missionaries without a strong local base. Tabligh's distinctiveness lies in its greater attempt to mix Malay and non-Malay (Indian) Muslims, whereas ABIM and Darul Arqam are conspicuous for their exclusive concentration on Malays and are perceived by outsiders to be as much ethnic as religious organizations. Darul Arqam and ABIM further divide the Malay ethnic community into "born" and "born again" Muslims, while Tabligh unites born again Muslims across the ethnic divide.

Politically, ABIM—with its sophisticated, articulate, university-based leadership—has always been seen by government as a potential challenge. In the past, ABIM was even regarded as sympathetic to PAS, although its own legitimacy was derived more from its own independent standards of Islamic rectitude and reinforced by the less traditional academic credentials of the *guru* and intellectual. Early in 1982, ABIM's longtime president, Anwar, once the epitome of the organization and of much that the religious revival stood for, stunned Malaysia by suddenly joining UMNO and running for political office with the cooperation of the prime minister. This in itself may be an indication that, in the present religious climate, even UMNO elites can now muster sufficient moral force and credibility to satisfy erstwhile critics, or that the political ambitions of the revivalists cannot be satisfied from their position on the sidelines. (The rising success of Anwar's political career within UMNO as of mid-1986 is testimony to the continuing strength of this policy.) Predictably, the government has spawned a number of *dakwah* organizations and programs of its own to defend its own religious image and to deflect attention away from the voluntary religious associations described. Darul Arqam and Tabligh are avowedly non-political in a formal sense, although their very withdrawal and—in Arqam's case—the creation of a shadow economy and society and refusal to cooperate with the government, may be seen as forms of political comment.

All of the organizations above, in their own way, favor the establishment of a full Islamic state and legal system based on the *Sharia* (Islamic Law). Beyond the level of generalities, however, there is little consensus as to what an Islamic state entails—for example, in matters of economic practices, the nature of leadership, social inequality, treatment of non-Muslim citizens, and so on. Iran and Libya have been the most popular state role models for Malaysian *dakwah* followers to date, while in many personal daily activities— for example, styles of eating, dress, and greeting—Arabic models are self-consciously adopted.

The revival of Islam in the Malaysian setting seems to have seeped into some of the cracks and more vulnerable areas of local society. It has come to represent, at different levels, a more general Western/non-Western dichotomy; a cleavage between Muslims and non-Muslims; the ethnic opposition between Malays and non-Malays; and, finally, a distinction between born again and mainstream Malay-Muslims that in turn finds its expression in the formal political life of the Malay community.

I now return to the original question of the relative importance of religious ideology or theology vis-à-vis the social matrix in which it can develop and thrive—the medium and the message. The remarks above should provide some sense of the broader social, ethnic, and political composition of Malaysia as a whole, as well as suggest how some issues are framed ideologically. What they do not explain, however, is why the new ideas appeal to certain individuals or constituencies. Nor do they throw any light on how the ideas are transmitted and interpreted, or to what extent they depend on the existence of already established social networks (rather than creating new networks for their own purposes).

In practice, the kinds of fundamentalist religious ideas now current in *dakwah* movements have often been acquired initially through contact with fellow Muslims by Malay students overseas, although these ideas have now gathered momentum at home. The original catalyst was frequently communication with Pakistani, Saudi Arabian, Libyan, Iranian, and/or Indonesian colleagues, even in such infidel countries as the United Kingdom, United States, and Australia. In other words, the networks and cliques of equal-status, same-generation peers, where residential propinquity and social interaction exert strong pressures toward acceptance and conformity, formed the foundation of information sharing and discussion. The influence of such interaction was reinforced by further cultural and social encapsulation common in foreign student communities. On their return home, many of these graduates have found jobs in Malaysian universities and schools and in the civil service, where they assume the mantle of *guru* and mentor to their students and subordinates in a vertical authority relationship. Here, they combine some of the authority of the traditional *guru* with a new legitimacy derived from Western academic credentials. Some teachers even continue the old-style form of one-way instruction, allowing little challenge or questioning from below, while others combine a more personal appeal with leadership, as in the role of some dormitory counselors.

Likewise, although to a lesser extent, university-educated civil servants (and also some military and police officers who have accepted *dakwah* ideas) use their status in their respective domains to introduce the new religious views. Emulation of leaders by the rank and file (and also of leaders' wives by wives of the rank and file) seems to be partly a function of the halo-effect of high office as much as the content of the ideas themselves.

Once an idea has been planted, it requires a suitable network of social support for its nurturing and further propagation. It is here that the strength of the horizontal peer groups comes into play. These groups are generally most effective within the limited social span of face-to-face personal cliques (not exceeding ten to fifteen persons) characterized by overlapping social ties and high role transparency — that is, where everyone in the group knows everyone else, and where there is substantial investment in the social relationships involved. At this level, social sanctions are most effective and pressures to conform are strongest, since individuals can maintain surveillance over one another and monitor group norms. Such clusters are most commonly found in schools and universities, where they are known as *usrah* (families) and provide the mutual support, discussion, learning, and assistance crucial in the decisions of young people to adopt *dakwah* behaviors: for example, rigid observance of religious and ritual obligations, food taboos, appropriate dress, and forbearance from many forms of entertainment. Usually, friends first discuss the pros and cons of various degrees of *dakwah* commitment and may even encourage a trial or preparatory period, such as wearing just a headscarf before adopting a full veil or making a vow to commit themselves to *dakwah* upon passing an important exam or finding the solution to some medical or other personal problem. The *usrah,* or family, is often the forum for analysis of personal and moral dilemmas, and appropriate religious solutions may also be sought to such questions as how a good Muslim can conscientiously accept modern science, or even some social science ideas, such as structuralism or Marxism. Humanities students may try to devise modes of incorporating Islamic themes into literature, whether through the cultivation of moralistic themes or of a more Arabic-derived vocabulary or by eliminating non-Islamic, pagan elements — Hindu, Christian, Western, or other. Even personal antagonisms may be played out in terms of identification with certain *dakwah* cliques or *usrah* in opposition to non-*dakwah* students, especially those in the "immoral" fields of drama and sculpture.

Internal solidarity of the *usrah* or family is intensified by such mechanisms as sharing of the dawn prayer and lecture, praying together in each others' rooms, and eating and studying together. All *usrah* members are of the same gender, and members exert strong pressure on each other to maintain a good reputation through circumspect relations with the opposite sex. For females in particular, the pressure from their *usrah* colleagues to preserve their reputations in the eyes of male students exerts a powerful sanction on their behavior. Social investment in *usrah* relationships is often great. Female students are therefore extremely reluctant to lose the approval of the *usrah* community through improper behavior with the opposite sex.

Once committed to an *usrah* withdrawal is difficult, short of leaving the community altogether. Most young people seem to make the decision to become religious in accordance with the tendencies of hostel-mates and siblings or cousins, and here residence factors reinforce the peer group. In general, parental influence in such matters appears to be minimal; in fact, many parents are ambivalent at best or even discouraging, for fear of possible consequences on marriage prospects in a traditional home village, or of negative impact on future careers. They are also apprehensive of the problems attending attempts to maintain rigid dress and other behavioral codes in the open rural village setting where they are less appropriate to agricultural activities.

Similar peer-group formations of *dakwah*-minded enthusiasts emerge among other constituencies of unmarried urban youth. In some cases, the commitment creates for them a new sense of purpose, and arrests what might otherwise be a drift into the aimless world of drugs and coffee-shop existence. Instead, they trade their jeans for Arab-style robes and the coffee-shop for the mosque, where their solidarity is fostered by various religious rituals and retreats involving commensality and the sharing of personal problems. Whereas many of the college youth are drawn to ABIM, a more intellectually inclined organization, working youth frequently prefer Tabligh with its greater emphasis on retreats. Comparable cliques and peer-group divisions are sometimes found in youth clubs where a *dakwah* segment will maintain a self-righteously separate existence from those members identified as "into drugs" or too fond of dancing and movies. The *dakwah* sections frequently assume an assortment of voluntary tasks, such as tutoring primary schoolchildren (with a predictably heavy emphasis on religion), and by playing the *guru* role may influence a future generation of *dakwah* recruits.

The *usrah* pattern of much *dakwah* activity may be compared to cells of secret societies, whose linkages to one another are often unstructured and idiosyncratic unless formally mediated by lectures, meetings, and conferences by their leaders. As a result, considerable differences in interpretation and practice sometimes emerge between cells (and may in turn differ from the public views of the leadership). Thus, it happens that the leaders of ABIM officially deplore racism as un-Islamic, whereas many of the "cells" operate on a more chauvinistic principle of Islam as being exclusively for the Malays, and are reluctant even to admit Chinese Muslims to the fold. Some *usrahs* may stress a more withdrawn kind of "spiritual" development, while others pay greater attention to more outward, visible ritualistic behaviors, as manifested in dress, for example.

The isolation of *usrah* cells, however, is tempered by the existence of a variety of mediating horizontal linkages that permit more faithful transmission of ideas from one cell to another, although again, replication may be imperfect and result in a distortion of the message. Among these linkages are the ever-active circuits of rotating lecturers, either university students or teachers, who create a dense network of reinforcing ties and distribute the books and tracts seen on every follower's bookshelf. Another linkage is created by a program of adoption, whereby university students "adopt" high school protégés and invite them to campus for familiarization visits, where they stay in the hostels and participate in religious activities. A variant of this practice is the "awareness campaign," in which students spend their vacations on village-improvement projects, especially the tutoring of children, thus helping to carry *dakwah* ideas to rural areas. Other graduates of *dakwah* persuasion become teachers in private rehabilitation schools specializing in cram courses for students who have failed government exams; here, they may have a freer hand in spreading their views by virtue of their authority as teachers. Finally, the simple event of students returning to their home village carries the winds of change to siblings and peers (although, as mentioned above, somewhat less smoothly to their parents and the older generation). Some of the latter are critical of the puristic objections of *dakwah* youth to such traditional albeit non-Islamic practices as wedding *bersanding*[11] and other rites of passage so crucial to the social life of the village and to the social integration of their elders. Sometimes, too, traditional rural religious leaders sense a threat from this unexpected source of self-proclaimed religious authority that reverses the old vertical status distinctions between generations and introduces a role conflict between old and new types of *guru*.

Other spearheads of *dakwah* penetration into such areas as government land schemes are also achieved initially through personal (old-school) connections of the missionaries with land-scheme administrators. In some government offices, however, there are attempts to control the influence of *dakwah* for fear of its impact on official authority. Government *dakwah* programs draw on their political status as a source of legitimacy for their own representatives, in opposition to that of the outsiders. Thus, it happens that many nongovernment *dakwah* sympathizers (that is, followers of ABIM or Arqam) in the civil service operate more as loners, and spread their message in the course of their interaction with villagers as much by deed as by word—for example, in placing more stress on spiritual than on material development in the implementation of government schemes. Linkages between the cells of the *dakwah* movements may be likened to a cadre system, probably resembling the underlying pattern of many types of social movement. Cadres provide critical links in the chain or network and help to ensure some measure of quality control, but permit sufficient local independence of thought and action to maintain a broad appeal. They have not yet reached the stage of rigid sectarian closure, although in any given cell or clique their methods are remarkably similar. Without the cadres, social movements would dissolve into the less evolved state of their constituent cells, and would cease to be movements at all; yet the cadres are the catalyst of ideas that can be planted and flower only in a nurturing social environment.

In the *dakwah* situation, then, two kinds of relationship appear to rest at the foundation of the movement: the horizontal, equal-status peer group, and the continuing importance of the authority derived from the superior status of such individuals as teachers. Generally, the latter provides the initial source of legitimacy (and some of these teachers may begin as cadres). On the peer or residential group, however, depends the continued dissemination, reinforcement, and—sometimes—reinterpretation of ideas.

Without intending to reduce *dakwah* or any other religious or ideological commitment to a totally dependent variable or to a social structure alone, the point of the account above should be apparent: While awareness of certain theological issues does play a role in the contemporary reflowering of Islam in Malaysia, receptivity to the new ideas and their dissemination are heavily influenced by the social base. Further, the pressures of immediate social interaction and personal connection can substantially modify or sanction those ideas.

Conclusion

Dakwah, or the religious revival in present-day Malaysia, is a manifestation of a body of Islamic ideas that have been selected and developed in particular directions according to the special conditions prevailing on the local scene. Recognition of the modifying influence of local conditions on the revival is neither surprising nor novel. More instructive is the route by which these ideas percolate through the system along lines of informal, preexisting social ties, as much between as within formal religious or other institutions. Awareness of certain theological issues does play a role in the contemporary reflowering of Islam in Malaysia, but evidence supports the view that the acceptability and spread of these new ideas is in part socially determined. Further, the pressures of immediate social interaction and personal connection can substantially modify or sanction these ideas. Without necessarily emptying *dakwah* of all of its theological content or belittling the commitment of some of its participants, it can nevertheless be argued that the pressures of the social environment have a power of their own. The persistence of a number of ties and obligations grounded in traditional Malay social structure — generation sets, neighborhood ties, respect for authority, and the role of the *guru* — is reflected in many modern institutions and situations, including the response to the religious revival. Again, the message depends in part upon the medium.

Closer examination of a religious or social movement from the bottom up, rather than from the leadership down, shows that it is often structurally difficult to identify the boundaries of membership, or to isolate or define concretely the central ideological core. Despite apparent unity, solidarity, and distinctiveness from an outside perspective, a closer inspection sees these features dissolve into amorphousness — into the loosely integrated series of cells and nodes of a discontinuous network such as marks the Islamic revival movement of modern Malaysia.

Notes

1. Normative change refers to changes in ideas regarding expected behavior. A norm is a statement that can be elicited from an informant about what ought to or should occur in relation to a particular institution, such as marriage, politics, or religion. Normative consensus is agreement on what behavior ought to occur. Victor Turner defines *communitas* as "society as an unstructured or rudimentarily structured and relatively undifferentiated *comitatus*, community, or even communion of equal individuals who submit together to the general authority of the ritual elders." Victor Turner, *The Ritual Process: Structure and Anti-Structure* (Chicago: Aldine Press, 1969), p. 96.

2. Edward Shils, *Center and Periphery: Essays in Macrosociology* (Chicago: University of Chicago Press, 1975).

3. K. D. Jackson, *Traditional Authority, Islam and Rebellion: A Study of Indonesian Political Behavior* (Berkeley, Los Angeles, and London: University of California Press, 1980).

4. Herbert Blumer, "Social Movements," in Barry McLaughlin, ed., *Studies in Social Movements: A Social-Psychological Perspective* (New York: Free Press, 1969); K. O. L. Burridge, *New Heaven, New Earth: A Study of Millenarian Activities* (Toronto: Copp Clark, 1969); and Anthony Wallace, "Revitalization Movements," *American Anthropologist* 58 (1956): 264–81.

5. Several provisions in the constitution ensure that a quota of 75 percent of Division 1 civil service posts, a high proportion of university scholarships, and many land privileges are reserved for Malays. It is also the rule that the prime minister of Malaysia and the chief minister of each state be a Malay.

6. Innumerable institutions and statutory bodies, including several banks, trading com-

panies, an urban development authority, federal land schemes (FELDA), and small business agencies, have been established exclusively for assistance to Malays.

7. Endogamy refers to marriage within rather than outside a group or category—here, marriage within the local community, the village.—ED.

8. Of the eleven states of West Malaysia, nine still retain the traditional royal house and sultan or rajah. Every five years, the title of King of Malaysia is rotated among the nine as a *primus inter pares*.

9. The religious councils for the states are the supreme arbiters of Islamic justice (through the *Sharia* court) and administrators of religious law in that state. No federal religious authority has the power to override their judgments, save within a small "neutral" zone around the capital known as the Federal Territory.

10. Chandra Muzaffar, *Protector?* (Penang: Aliran, 1979).

11. *Bersanding* is a ceremony in which the principals in any ritual (that is, a rite of passage, such as a wedding or a circumcision) are made the focus of attention. Its origins are Hindu, not Islamic.

III

CATALYSTS OF
THE CURRENT RESURGENCE

6

Islamic Renewal
and the "Failure of the West"

JOHN O. VOLL

The contemporary resurgence of Islam involves a dramatic reevaluation of the West. In the final quarter of the twentieth century, many Muslims believe that the West has failed, not just in spiritual terms but in material terms as well. This attitude represents a new stage in the long interaction between Western and Muslim societies. The evolution of Muslim evaluations of the Western experience is one dimension in the framework of Islamic thought in the modern era.

The concept of the "failure of the West" changes the orientation of reformist thought. As a concept, it plays an important role in the logic of Islamic revivalist thinking in the contemporary era. It makes it possible to ignore or reject Western models while clearing the way for a strong affirmation of the validity of the authentic Islamic message in the context of the modern world.

The modern and contemporary Islamic experience has many dimensions. A number of factors influence the developing modes of expression and the forms of Muslim life. The belief that the West has failed is only one of many aspects of the complex and multidimensional phenomena involved in the resurgence and renewal of Islam. However, it is worth examining this aspect in more detail, keeping in mind that it is only one part of a much larger context. Such an analysis can provide a basis for understanding some of the specific forms and ideas involved in the current phase of Islamic renewal. And while it is important to have sociological profiles of "resurgent Muslims" and quantitative data on the social composition of various movements, it is useful to attempt to understand the conceptual framework and intellectual content as well.

The concept of the failure of the West has a role in the logic of the Islamic revival. For some, it provides a reason for the return to Islam, while for others it helps to provide confirmation for the affirmation of Islam. However, no movement of Islamic renewal in the modern era ignores the West. Reformers may view the West in a positive fashion and others may call for a rejection

127

of Western ideas, but the context of modern world history makes it impossible to avoid making some evaluation of the West.

Islamic renewal has a long history within the Muslim experience. In principle, *tajdid* (renewal) does not depend upon the existence of a challenge from the Western world; it has occurred in many times and places before the expansion of the West.[1] However, in the modern situation, Western influences have a global impact. If Islamic renewers are to change their social orders, they must present an evaluation of the role of the West and of the nature of modern Western civilization. Such an evaluation is not the only aspect of *tajdid* in the modern world, however; the positive content of the ideology of Islamic renewal remains based, as it has always been, on the Quran and the Sunnah (tradition and practice) of the Prophet. Nevertheless, the application of the basic Islamic principles does not take place in a vacuum. As Abul Ala Maududi notes, the first step in the program of Islamic revival must be the "diagnosis of the current ailments: to examine thoroughly the circumstances and conditions of the time."[2]

Evolution of Muslim Attitudes toward the West

During the modern era, the attitudes of reformers, renewers, and revolutionaries in the Muslim world have changed in terms of their evaluations of the nature of modern Western civilization.[3] Within the framework of a dynamic variety of approaches, certain themes gained prominence at various times. A broad spectrum of views regarding the West is always present, but at different times certain views set the tone for the dominant evaluation of the Western experience in the Islamic context.

During the past two centuries, despite wide diversities due to local conditions, it is possible to see a gradual evolution of the dominant tone of Islamic renewal and its reaction to the West. In the eighteenth century, *the West* as a concept or conceptual entity played little or no role in the thinking of the leaders of major movements of renewal. The basic context was described in terms of the interaction of belief and unbelief, or of true Islam and corrupted Muslim practice. In areas where contact with the West was limited, such a position remained possible well into the modern era. "Modernity" and Western ideas were not consciously seen as challenges, and — if they were considered at all — were treated in a traditional manner as simply different manifestations of the old enemies, unbelief and unacceptable innovation. This eighteenth century tradition of renewal was replaced with varying rates of speed, again depending upon local conditions, by movements of reform and revival clearly conscious of the West.

In the nineteenth century, the major feature of this consciousness was that somehow the West had succeeded — and this success was frequently compared to the apparent weaknesses of the Muslim world. In many areas, major efforts were made to reform and reshape institutions of society and intellectual formulations in accord with this positive evaluation of the Western experience. By the end of the nineteenth century, the great movements of Islamic modernism were emerging as the dominant force in Muslim intellectual life. Islam, in this context, was increasingly defined as in accord with modernity and basic Western ideas. The process of the development of Islamic modernism and the adaptation to the new situation, in the context of a favorable evaluation of the West, has been described in detail by a number of scholars. The general tone of this development is seen in Albert Hourani's discussion of Muhammad Abduh's major concerns: Abduh "was not concerned, as Khayr al-Din had been in a previous generation, to ask whether devout Muslims could accept the institutions and ideas of the modern world; they had come to stay, and so much the worse for anyone who did not accept them. He asked the opposite question, whether someone who lived in the modern world could still be a devout Muslim."[4] In the movements of the late nineteenth century, there is a spirit of renewal which has ties to earlier efforts. However, this *tajdid* took place within the framework of a sense of the success of the West, not its failure.

While some Muslim intellectuals were relatively uncritical in their positive evaluation of Western civilization, total cultural assimilation was neither practically feasible nor ultimately desirable for most Muslims. Clearly, Western society was not perfect, and neither naive observers nor Western ethnocentric propaganda could make it so. As a result, by the beginning of the twentieth century, the positive evaluation of the West began to be tempered by a view that discriminated between positive and negative aspects of modernity and Western civilization. In the Arab world, for example, the intellectuals of the nineteenth century "Awakening" believed that they were proclaiming the dawn of a new age. In the serious thinking before World War I, the intellectuals "were primarily reacting to the challenge of European civilization. They perceived the West as a model from which one was to borrow the good and reject the bad."[5]

A very common theme in this era of positive evaluation of the West was to see the material culture of the West as desirable while rejecting aspects of Western morality. Among many thinkers the distinction is clearly presented between the materially successful West and the morally superior East. A pragmatic summary of this type of position was given by King Abdal-Aziz to an American ambassador: "We Muslims have the one, true faith, but Allah gave you the iron which is inanimate, amoral, neither prohibited nor mentioned in the Quran. We will use your iron, but leave our faith alone."[6] A view such as this recognizes the success of the West, at least in the material sphere. This is at least implied in the reference to "your" iron.

The positive evaluation of Western civilization remains clearly visible throughout much of the twentieth century. One of the most outspoken intellectuals in this regard is Taha Husayn, who has been described as "the writer who has given the final statement of the system of ideas which underlay social thought and political action in Arab countries for three generations."[7] In *The Future of Culture in Egypt*, he stated: "In order to become equal partners in civilization with the Europeans, we must literally forthrightly do everything that they do; we must share with them the present civilization, with all its pleasant and unpleasant sides. . . . My advocacy of contact with and imitation of the way of life that has brought progress and pre-eminence to the Europeans does not mean that I approve of their evils. . . . Obviously then I am pleading for a selective approach to European culture, not wholesale and indiscriminate borrowing."[8]

Following World War II there was a growing awareness of the imperfections of the Western model. "The Islamic intelligentsia became aware that within the Western world itself there were profound criticisms of that civilization and that the Western model which so many Muslims had tried to emulate was itself breaking down."[9] In many ways, however, this new awareness of the problems of Western civilization continued to be a form of accepting the success of at least part of the Western experience. This is visible in the fact that much of the new awareness was expressed in terms strongly affected by "successful" Western self-criticism rather than in more authentically Islamic terms. Emerging new literature in the Arab world, for example, was profoundly influenced by the works of such authors as T. S. Eliot. In the political and ideological realm, the failure of the West was most frequently described in the terms of Western-influenced radicalism or Western-stimulated nationalism. The established political elites were frequently displaced in the years following World War II, and the older intellectuals, who had been profoundly influenced by Western liberalism, gave way to new generations of thinkers. However, the new generations of the 1950s and 1960s differed from the older ones, not in replacing the older sense of the "success" of the West by a sense of the "failure" of the West, so much as by accepting different aspects of Western civilization as models or inspiration. From the perspective of global history, communism is as much a Western model as liberalism and capitalism, and Lenin as much a product of the West as Woodrow Wilson.

In the period since World War II, the continuing interaction between Islam and the West can be seen as an overlapping series of disassociations. A key element is a growing redefinition of the West and the elements of Western civilization that can be judged as failures. Ultimately, this has led to a major reorientation of the fundamental questions involved in the dialogue between the West and Islam. The evolution of the early questions which Albert Hourani suggested as basic involved the change from "Can a devout Muslim be 'modern'?" to Abduh's issue of whether or not a modern person could still be Muslim; in both cases there is an assumption that the West provides the most effective model of the modern. However, in the second half of the twentieth century, this assumption is being seriously challenged, both within the West and in areas such as the Muslim world. In many ways, one of the basic questions now is whether or not any Western model is effective for survival in the modern world. An important conceptual element in the Islamic resurgence of recent years is the realization that it is a legitimate question to ask: "Can *the West* survive in the modern world?"

The sequence of perceived failures of the West provides part of the foundation for the new Islamic awareness. This sequence has been described in many ways. The two world wars raised basic doubts about the ability of the West to survive, after which the ineffectiveness of programs that "borrowed the good" from the West continued the process. Liberal constitutionalism, various forms of capitalist economic systems, and party-parliamentary systems all exhibited severe weaknesses in the context of Muslim countries. The revolutions and movements of the 1950s and 1960s represent a rejection of these systems and, in many ways, reflect a belief in the failure of those aspects of Western civilization. However, the new radicalism was strongly influenced by other Western models. Socialism, communism, and various forms of Marxist analysis played an important role in the emerging consciousness. By the end of the 1960s, many Muslim intellectuals were willing to judge even these aspects of the West as failures. Both the various programs of radical socialism, such as Nasser's in Egypt, and the monarchically forced programs of Westernizing modernization, such as the shah of Iran's so-called White Revolution, failed to meet the needs of Muslim societies. Strong critiques developed within the Islamic community.

These new critiques were not always clearly Islamic in sentiment, but they were profoundly anti-Western in a relatively new way, in that they portrayed the Western models as dangerous because of their own inherent weakness. Some of the most articulate of these new critics of the late 1960s were Iranian. Jalal Al-e Ahmad coined a new term in naming the disease of early generations of reformers who blindly copied the West as *gharbzadegi* ("Weststruckness"). Ali Shariati wrote more broadly ranging critiques and provided important intellectual foundations for the later revolutionary movement in Iran.[10]

Early in the 1970s, some of the last elements of the perceived Western successes were undermined. For a long time, non-Western intellectuals had been willing to admit that at least in terms of material advancement and power, Western civilization was successful. These last spheres came to be seen in a very different light during the 1970s.

In terms of sheer military power, the prestige of the West was undermined in the years following World War II. The abortive Anglo-French invasion of Egypt in 1956 and the French defeat in Algeria, along with the dismantling of the old European empires, showed that the old imperialists had lost their positions of military dominance. Then, the defeat of the United States in Viet Nam pointed up the military weaknesses of even the superpowers. During the 1970s, this vision was reinforced. All of the Westernized military might of the shah could not prevent the Islamic revolution in Iran, while the Arab-Israeli War of 1973 did away with the illusion of the invincibility of Israel—another Westernized military power. Even the Russians were not able to subdue completely their small and militarily weak neighbor, Afghanistan. In the spring of 1986, the United States appeared to feel the need for the largest possible American battle fleet to mount a small bombing raid on the capital of Libya. The vision of Western military success created in the days of imperial expansion was now clouded, and in this military area as well one could now perceive a failure of the West.

Similarly, the material riches of the West and the strength of its economic systems had been widely accepted as demonstrating the success of the Western models, but the growing economic difficulties of the major developed economies tarnished that image. The revolution of global economics created by the transformation of the world oil market intensified this disillusionment. While much of the non-Western world remained economically weak, the tremendous transfer of wealth to oil-exporting countries, many of which are Muslim, changed the economic perception of the world: "The oil boom has shown the vulnerability of the West more dramatically than anything in the past five centuries. By confirming Islam in the eyes of many, it prepared the way for the Islamic movements of the 1970s."[11] The drop in world oil prices in the mid-1980s did not change the image of the vulnerability of the Western economies, since the leadership of the United States seemed at least as concerned by falling oil prices as the leaders of the major oil-exporting countries. Economics became another area in which there was a perceived failure of the West.

Finally, one of the fundamental ideals behind the process of Westernization—the idea of "development"—was being questioned in a variety of ways throughout the globe. The concern about the destruction of the natural environment that followed development in Western societies, the growing belief that underdevelopment in non-Western societies was related not to inherent backwardness but to the very process of development itself, and a questioning of the social and human consequences of the processes of industrialization and urbanization are examples of the profound issues raised by the contemporary situation in the West. For observers both within and outside of the West, it has become possible to ask whether or not development, as it has been understood in the past, is a legitimate strategy for survival in the modern world. This doubt about development has become a dimension in the question of whether or not the West can survive modernity.

Within this broad historical context, the theme of the failure of the West is a part of many of the major intellectual movements of recent years. Within the West as well as in other parts of the world, the concept of the failure of the West has shaped the logic of intellectual formulations and reformist hopes. Within the Islamic world, the concept is part of the logic and vocabulary of movements of resurgence and renewal. Again, to emphasize the point, this is not the only element of Islamic revivalist ideology, and is only one aspect of the current Islamic resurgence; however, it is an element that has influenced the possible forms of expression and logic of current manifestations of Islamic renewal. Utilization of the concept of the failure of the West marks a significant change in the logic of reformist thought in the Islamic world.

Implications of the Idea of the Failure of the West

The concept of the failure of the West makes it possible to distinguish certain aspects of the current mood of Islamic renewal from earlier modern Muslim reform and renewal efforts. The concept has provided a kind of liberation in a number of ways. The content of the message of Islam remains constant, but the form and mood of *tajdid* and the modes of expression are freed from certain limitations that had bound the terminology and style of earlier modern Muslim reformers.

The first area where the impact of the idea of the failure of the West is visible is in terms of the changing nature of the target audience, or effective partners in the dialogue involved in Islamic renewal. Earlier reformers tended to operate within the limitations imposed by "hoping to obtain a favorable verdict from the invisible jury of the West."[12] Frequently, this jury was not so invisible. Early modernist thinkers such as Muhammad Abduh and Jamal al-Din al-Afghani argued directly with Western critics of Islam. Many of the important works of such reformers were clearly in the genre of the defense of Islam, trying to persuade this invisible jury that Islam could meet intellectual and practical standards set by Western concepts. Instead of the Islamic tradition itself giving rise to the basic ideas of reform, Western ideas tended to define the areas of concern.

The failure of the West, however, liberates contemporary Muslim thinkers from many of these constraints. Such failure makes it possible to see the judgments of Westerners as less relevant. Instead of having to accept the basic analytical framework of Western thought as the definition of the ground rules for the dialogue, the failure of the West makes it possible to disagree with even that basic conceptual framework. While earlier reformers, for example, felt a responsibility to persuade those Western scholars who studied Islam of Islam's virtues, the conceptual framework of orientalism itself can now be criticized on the basis of more authentically Islamic values. The work of the traditional Western orientalists is increasingly seen as a reflection of Western ethnocentric values. [13]

Starting from the Islamic concept of *tawhid* (the absolute one-ness of God), contemporary Muslim scholars have worked to redefine basic academic disciplines in terms of moral obligation and value-laden scholarship. They argue, for example, that older Western ideas of value-free or objective analysis in the social sciences are not only impossible but undesirable. In this way, a more clearly Islamic orientation for social science scholarship is possible. Such scholars, convinced of the intellectual failure of the West, are not as sensitive as their predecessors to criticisms from the West based on Western assumptions. The concept of the failure of the West has liberated Muslim intellectuals from constraints imposed by the intellectual formulations of an outside "jury," and the way is thus opened for a positive rather than a defensive orientation in the presentation of Islamic values. This change has had an impact upon the mode of Islamic expression during the current resurgence.

Under these new conditions, the most important partner in dialogue has become other Muslims. The failure of the West has changed at least some of the terms of the dialogue of reform among Muslims. By liberating intellectuals and political leaders from the pressure to persuade Westerners, the concept opened the way for discussion in which the Islamic tradition could play a more significant role. This was in turn reinforced by the achievement of political independence and the resulting necessity for creating independent policy. It was already apparent to some observers in the mid 1960s that the basic dialogue for the new leaders, intellectuals, and policy makers "is not with the West; it is with their fellow citizens. They are judged internally by their performance and in the light of a shared ideology. . . . It is becoming evident that the Arab-Muslim intelligentsia feel and argue that an Islamic

meaning to modern society is feasible, that Islamic solutions to objective contemporary problems are possible."[14]

The discussions of the Western-oriented modernists were elite phenomena
that by the late 1960s could be described as symptoms of "Weststruckness."
However, as has long been noted, when concern for renewal is more broadly
inclusive of the Muslim masses, the terms of the dialogue become more clearly
Islamic. Concerning the development of nationalism, for example, in the 1950s
Wilfred Cantwell Smith pointed out that "the driving force of nationalism
has become more and more religious the more the movement has penetrated
the masses. Even where the leaders and the form and the ideas of movement
have been nationalist on a more or less Western pattern, the followers and
the substance and the emotions were significantly Islamic."[15] When the Western pattern itself is seen as a failure even the elite can move, as they have
in recent years, to transform the form and ideas into a more clearly Islamic
pattern. This modification in the attitude of the elite opens the way for a
more significant and meaningful interaction between the educated classes and
the majority of the population.

The movement toward more authentically Islamic solutions to major social
problems and to the needs for renewal is thus strengthened by the ability
of the educated elite to go beyond the concepts and goals set by the old intellectual domination by the West. One of the basic problems in implementing the ideas of the old modernists was that they assumed "as the final objective an ideal determined by considerations external to their own society."[16]
The perception of the failure of the West makes it possible to define basic
ideals and solutions in ways that may not coincide with Western solutions,
but which are more appropriate and authentically Islamic. It also makes it
possible to judge the progress toward those goals by standards other than those
set by Western ethnocentric observers.

The second general area of the impact of the concept of the failure of the
West follows from this discussion: the concept frees Muslim thinkers from
the domination of certain specifically Western concepts involved in interpreting modernity. *Secularism* is the most significant of these concepts. Because
of the specific conditions of the emergence of modern society in the West,
secularism was believed to be a critical element in the process of modernization. It was widely believed that "the secularization of the polity is in many
respects a prerequisite for significant social change."[17] The specific implications of this view for traditional religions was usually clearly spelled out: "The
secularization of the polity, like the secularization of culture and society, is
a process which has moved inexorably since the breakup of the traditional
religio-political system. . . . While religion, a mass phenomenon in traditional

societies, can play a useful role in transitional societies in making politics meaningful to the apolitical masses, the general forces of secularization of culture and society will in the long run erode its political effectiveness also."[18]

Within the Islamic world, secularism was an important part of the adjustments to the modern context. Albert Hourani has noted the importance of a positive evaluation of secularism in reformist thought in Syria and Lebanon during the first half of the twentieth century. The movement of secularization in that area, he has pointed out, "springs from the belief of many Arab thinkers that the superior strength and stability of Western society is due to the limitations which have been imposed upon the action and influence of religion."[19]

The adaptation of political organization was carried farthest in Turkey, where an officially secular state was established after World War I. In the program of the Republican People's Party adopted in 1935, the secularist rationale is clearly spelled out: "As the conception of religion is a matter of conscience, the Party considers it to be one of the chief factors of the success of our nation in contemporary progress, to separate ideas of religion from politics, and from the affairs of the world and of the State."[20]

While few other states were as explicitly secularized as Turkey, secularist thinking was important elsewhere, and few modernizing states became rigorously Islamic in the first half of the twentieth century. In the years following World War II, avowedly secularist although not antireligious ideas were popular and influential among the educated elites. A relatively extreme but widely read expression of this perspective was presented by Khalid Muhammad Khalid, who concluded that one "should remember that the faith should continue as its Lord wishes—with prophecy not kingship, with guidance not government, with preaching rather than the whip. Its separation from politics and its soaring above politics is the best agent for maintaining its purity and its perfection."[21]

Muslims have been liberated from the persuasiveness of this line of argument by the conviction that the West has failed. One dimension of the revival of the 1970s is the substantial decline in the pervasiveness of the idea that secularism is necessary for the modernization of Muslim states. In the experience of Middle Eastern countries, progress toward the goals of modernization is not inevitably accompanied by secularization.[22]

Contemporary discussions follow at least two lines—one attacking the idea of secularism as contrary to the Islamic sense of unity, and another advocating the virtues of a society in which faith is not separated from other aspects of life. Both of these are, not unexpectedly, part of the presentations of clearly fundamentalist thinkers who throughout the twentieth century have maintained a tradition of opposition to secularism. However, in addition to the traditional fundamentalists, most major Muslim intellectuals with thoroughly modern educations have abandoned or at least substantially modified their advocacy of secularism. One concrete example of the new mood is the change in the views of Khalid Muhammad Khalid, a major spokesman for secularism in the years following World War II. In 1981, he showed a significant change in his views, publishing a book advocating state implementation of Islamic law. The only clearly identifiable groups maintaining explicitly secularist positions are those that still accept the success of some type of Western conceptual model. Such cases are usually found among the openly Marxist secularists and communists.

The spectrum of backgrounds and positions of those who have been liberated from the domination of the ideas of secularism and who affirm the nonsecularist Islamic tradition is very broad. There is, however, remarkable unanimity on this issue among contemporary Islamic thinkers who disagree vigorously on a wide range of other subjects. The key element in this is a renewed emphasis on the concept of *tawhid*—the one-ness of God—and the implications of this one-ness for all of life.

A brief sampling of positions from a variety of people illustrates the nonsecularist unanimity among contemporary Muslims with significantly modern experience and education who might, in previous years, have been relatively secularist in their approach. The shift away from the secularist positions is most dramatic among what might be termed the radical segment of the spectrum of thought in the Islamic world. In previous years, positions of social and intellectual radicalism were most likely to include secularist views.

A significant element of contemporary radicalism in Iran is vigorously Islamic and presents a *tawhidi* rather than a secularist viewpoint. One of the leading formulators of this view was Ali Shariati. He rejected the separation of various realms of human life as exploitative and opposed to Islam: "The very structure of *tawhid* cannot accept contradiction or disharmony in the world. . . . Contradiction between nature and metanature . . . science and religion, metaphysics and nature, working for men and working for God, politics and religion . . . all these forms of contradiction are reconcilable only with the worldview of *shirk*—dualism, trinitarianism or polytheism—but not with *tawhid*—monotheism."[23] Similarly, the activist Islamic radical organization, the Mujahidin, bases its program on a *tawhidi* understanding of life. Mujahidin authors frequently reject implicit secularism as not only anti-Islamic but also ineffectively modern. In a discussion of how to study the Quran, the Mujahidin say: "We realize that there is a conventional view that religion is purely a matter of individual conscience and does not relate to social concerns, in fact, standing apart from social issues. We, on the other hand, take a very different view, namely, that religion is inextricably involved with the social plane of existence. It is not our concern here to refute the foregoing unscientific point of view."[24]

Similar positions can be seen in the emerging intellectual radicalism in the Arab world. Again, before the belief in the failure of the West many of these thinkers might have been expected to adopt a more secularist position as a part of their intellectual radicalism. For example, while the Egyptian philosopher, Hassan Hanafi, is thoroughly familiar with Western philosophy and objects to the "ritualism" of many traditional Muslim fundamentalists, his philosophical position is basically *tawhidi* rather than secularist. This position provides the basis for a "revolutionary theology." According to Hanafi, "A reactionary theology divides Man into two parts: body and soul as it divided the World into two parts: temporal and eternal. . . . [However, in a revolutionary theology] there is one World, one action and one life. . . . The only world is this world where Man exists. The spiritual is the temporal and the temporal is the spiritual. . . . A revolutionary religion does not have any cults. Devotion to God is expressed by devotion to Man. Cult is not symbolic but every act in the daily life is a cult."[25]

An affirmation of basic Islamic positions is in these positions. *Tawhid* is a fundamental Islamic concept that has always been a part of *tajdid,* or Islamic renewal. However, one dimension of this affirmation of *tawhid* is that the secularist model, as it has been defined by Western experience, is seen as having failed. In this way, the concept of the failure of the West provides an important reinforcement for the reassertion of Islamic themes. The perception of the failure of the West makes it possible to argue that the Western model has failed and that *tawhid* provides the foundation for a more effective way of coping with the challenges of modern history. This is true, as has been seen, not only in traditional fundamentalist thought but also in some of the significant contemporary radical Muslim formulations. Secularism can be labeled not only as unbelief, but also as reactionary and as unscientific.

It then becomes possible to identify a third area in which Islamic thought is liberated by the concept of the failure of the West. The concept makes it possible to divorce modernity from Western models and precedents. Non-Western modernity becomes both intellectually conceivable and practically possible. Western ideas and systems are still important in the dialogue, but they are now conceivable as simply one among a number of competing models of potentially equal efficiency. The old debate over whether or not a modern person could still be a devout Muslim tended to assume that the modern person was basically Westernized, there being an implicit equation between modern and Western. The perceived failure of the West makes it possible to break that old assumed identity, and the basic issue becomes reformulated in terms of which models provide the most effective form of modernity. Now

Islamic modernity competes with Western modernity, and the concept of the failure of the West strengthens the affirmation of Islam as the more effective model for modernity.

This has a number of implications for the forms taken by the current Islamic renewal. One of the most important of these is a vindication of the fundamentalist style of Islamic experience. Although there is often disagreement about using the term *fundamentalist*, and although fundamentalism has taken a variety of forms, the style of Islam often called fundamentalist has in recent years clearly experienced a significant revival. At least part of the reason for the revival is that this style of Islam is the one least affected in the modern period by the idea of the success of the West. As a result, in the context of an awareness of the failure of the West, Muslim fundamentalists have the most coherent and fully developed models currently available.

For many years, many educated Muslims rejected the fundamentalist models as reactionary. As long as the West was viewed as the major successful model of modernity, most specifically Muslim reformist efforts were aimed at showing the compatibility between Islamic and modern Western ideas. Any perspective that rejected these assumptions, such as the fundamentalist viewpoint, could be viewed as an obstacle to progress. However, when Islamic and Western models came to be seen as competitive formats for modernity, and when it could be argued that the West had failed, the Islamic fundamentalist perspective gained popularity. This can be seen in the fortunes of the Muslim Brotherhood in Egypt and other such groups. In the past decade, fundamentalist-style views have become popular among college students and younger educated classes. In the Sudan, for example, the Muslim Brotherhood won all of the special parliamentary seats elected by graduates in special nonterritorial constituencies in the 1986 elections. A survey of Moroccan university students in 1984 showed widespread sympathy for the fundamentalist message.[26]

The fundamentalist format of much of the contemporary resurgence of Islam should not be taken for granted as the only possible alternative. *Tajdid* has taken many forms in Islamic history. A history of *tajdid* written by a contemporary Muslim fundamentalist describes a number of leaders of renewal who are not clearly fundamentalist in style, such as al-Ghazali, the great medieval mystic. Renewal has come through the efforts of synthesizers and adaptationists, and individualist charismatic leaders as well as fundamentalists. However, in the contemporary Islamic world, the major reform and revival style utilizing methods of adaptation and synthesis is associated with Westernizing modernization. As a result, it would appear that such a style of renewal, for the moment at least, has reduced appeal in a context where the concept of the failure of the West is widely held.

The fundamentalist style of *tajdid* is the least affected by the discrediting of Western models. It represents a clear and untainted alternative to earlier modern reform efforts. In this the importance of the eighteenth century heritage is visible. During the eighteenth century, fundamentalist reformism was defined without reference to the West. This legacy has provided an important foundation for continuity with significant past experiences, paving the way for more broadly based support in the present. The clearest example of this is the Wahhabi experience in Saudi Arabia.

In the process of transition from an Islamic modernism that accepts the success of the West to a more fundamentalist Islam that perceives the failure of the West, there has been a reinterpretation of the actual meaning of Islamic fundamentalism. When adaptationist Islamic modernism was clearly in the ascendancy, fundamentalism was regarded as an anachronism. At best, it was considered an unrealistic attempt to recreate the conditions of the seventh century; at worst, it was claimed that the aims of the fundamentalists were "to arrest development and progress and to deprive the people of their hard-won gains, acting as agents of imperialism and reaction. . . . It has gone even further and attempted to make religion seem to contradict science, knowledge and progress."[27] Such a rejection of fundamentalism was strengthened by the assumption that modernization involved at least some significant aspects of Westernization and by a simple definition, often inaccurate, of fundamentalism as a rejection of all elements of modernity. In a context where secularism was a powerful force, the reaffirmation of the traditional religion was assumed to be inherently antimodern. Once Westernization and modernization came to be seen as two separate (if related) phenomena, Muslims were free to examine the fundamentalist positions in a new light.

The attempt to picture modern Muslim fundamentalists as simple-minded utopians who want to restore the conditions of the seventh century is inaccurate. For those who were willing to take the teachings of twentieth century fundamentalists seriously, this has long been apparent. In his analysis of the ideology of the Muslim Brotherhood, Richard Mitchell, for example, notes that the Ikhwan issued "a call to return to Islamic principles and not a literal return to the seventh century; those who say this are confusing [in the words of Sayyid Qutb] 'the historical beginning of Islam with the system of Islam itself.'"[28] This type of approach is clearly appealing in the contemporary context of defining an authentically Islamic modernity.

By liberating Muslims from the belief in secularism as a necessary part of modernization, and by making possible a distinction between Westernization and modernization, the concept of the failure of the West has strengthened the appeal of fundamentalist Islam. It is possible to challenge Westernization measures on the basis of Islamic principles without automatically being considered antimodern. Such challenges are now being made in the context of the contemporary competition among the various models of modernity.

Under these conditions, the writings of such older fundamentalists as Hasan al-Banna and Abul Ala Maududi are increasingly popular. Fundamentalist ideas are now put into practice in many areas. One of the best examples is in the area of economic activities. Fundamentalists have long argued against the payment of interest but the dispute remained largely in the realm of theory. However, in recent years a number of Islamic banks have been established. The debate over alternative models of economic modernity is now based on actual experience, rather than on comparison of theories alone.[29] In this way, fundamentalism is providing one basis for an Islamic model of modernity. In the context of the failure of the West, the renewed popularity of the fundamentalist style stems from contemporary perceptions rather than from traditional reasons alone. In the long run, the fundamentalist mood may be replaced by a more adaptationist style of Islam. However, the new adaptationism will continue to recognize the failure of the West, and will be far removed from the simple borrowing of the good from the West that was a crucial part of early Muslim modernism.

Conclusion

The evaluation of the experience of the West is an important dimension of the modern Islamic experience. Many of the major movements of modern Islamic thought were based on an assumption of the success of the West, at least in certain key aspects of human life. However, by the beginning of the fifteenth Islamic century, the concept of the failure of the West emerged as an important assumption. The perception of the West's failure liberated Muslim intellectuals from certain limitations that had bound earlier Muslim modernists. Although this factor does not fully explain the nature of the current resurgence of Islam, it is one dimension of the contemporary situation. It is not a measurable factor, such as class origin or age of participants in movements; it is, however, an important part of the logical framework and intellectual context of contemporary Islamic renewal.

The concept of the failure of the West has helped to liberate Muslims from concern about the invisible jury of foreigners watching events in the Islamic world. It has opened the way for a significant dialogue within the Islamic world, among Muslims, as to the authentic nature of Islam. In a second area of liberation, this Islamic discussion is no longer hindered by constraints imposed by the concept of secularism as a necessary part of modernization. In this way, affirmation of religious positions was no longer seen as being reactionary by definition. A third aspect of liberation is that the perceived failure of the West makes it possible to distinguish between Western and modern and, in this way, opens the door for the creation of an authentically Islamic modernity.

Muslims are not the only people to perceive a failure of the traditional Western models of modernity. There is a great global effort to achieve liberation from at least some aspects of the consequences of Western-dominated and Western-oriented modernization. This effort can be seen within the West itself. The postmodern theology described by the Christian theologian Harvey Cox, for example, is a clear statement concerning the end of the old Western-dominated styles of "modernity."[30]

The rethinking of the present era is an important part of a new phase of interaction between the global Islamic community and the West. It is to be hoped that this new phase of interaction will be a constructive development in the long history of that great dialogue. In many areas, the Western and Islamic traditions have contributed constructively to each other's development. The opportunity is again at hand for thinkers working on shared problems to inspire each other. For this to happen, the mutual insensitivities and competitive parochialisms of the past need to be overcome. Every Islamic revival need not be seen as threatening the West, and every Western disagreement with a Muslim need not be seen as an attempt to reestablish imperialist control.

The concept of the failure of the West has provided some dimensions of intellectual liberation for many people, but it can also open the way for a new set of stereotypes about the West. It is to be hoped that the dominating concepts in the coming years will place less emphasis on such ideas as the success or failure of the West, or the success or failure of Islam, and instead give higher priority to the concept and aim of the success of humanity.

Notes

1. John O. Voll, "Renewal and Reform in Islamic History: *Tajdid* and *Islah*," in *Voices of Resurgent Islam*, ed. John L. Esposito (New York: Oxford University Press, 1983), pp. 32–47.

2. Abul A'la Maududi, *A Short History of the Revivalist Movement in Islam*, trans. al-Ash'ari (Lahore: Islamic Publications Limited, 1976), p. 38.

3. See, for example, Hamid Enayat, "The Resurgence of Islam, 1: The Background," *History Today* 30 (February 1980).

4. Albert Hourani, *Arabic Thought in the Liberal Age, 1798-1939* (London: Oxford University Press, 1962), p. 139.

5. Hisham Sharabi, "Islam, Democracy and Socialism in the Arab World," in *The Arab Future: Crucial Issues,* ed. Michael C. Hudson (Washington: Center for Contemporary Arab Studies, Georgetown University, 1979), p. 96.

6. William A. Eddy, "King Ibn Sa'ud: 'Our Faith and Your Iron'," *The Middle East Journal* 17, no. 3 (Summer 1963): 257.

7. Hourani, *Arabic Thought,* p. 326.

8. Taha Hussein, *The Future of Culture in Egypt,* trans. Sidney Glazer (Washington: American Council of Learned Societies, 1954), pp. 15, 17.

9. Seyyed Hossein Nasr, "Islam in the Islamic World, an Overview," in *Islam in the Contemporary World,* ed. Cyriac K. Pullapilly (Notre Dame, Ind.: Cross Roads Books, 1980), p. 8.

10. See, for example, Jalal Al-e Ahmad, *Gharbzadegi [Weststruckness],* trans. John Green and Ahmad Alizadeh (Lexington, Ky.: Mazda, 1982); Ali Shari'ati, *Marxism and Other Western Fallacies, An Islamic Critique,* trans. R. Campbell (Berkeley, Calif.: Mizan Press, 1980); and Seyyed Hossein Nasr, "The Western World and Its Challenges to Islam," in *Islam – Its Meaning and Message,* ed. Khurshid Ahmad (London: Islamic Council of Europe, 1976), pp. 222-25.

11. Daniel Pipes, "'This World is Political!!' The Islamic Revival of the Seventies," *Orbis* 24, no. 1 (Spring 1980): 22.

12. Ibrahim Abu-Lughod, "Retreat from the Secular Path? Islamic Dilemmas of Arab Politics," *The Review of Politics* 28 (1966): 475.

13. See, for example, the comprehensive analysis of this issue in Edward Said, *Orientalism* (New York: Vintage Books, 1979). The methodology of this study remains, however, within the tradition of Western scholarly methods of analysis. A more rigorously Islamically based analysis can be found in Maryam Jameelah, *Islam and Orientalism* (Lahore: Mohammad Yusuf Khan, 1971).

14. Abu-Lughod, "Retreat from the Secular," p. 475.

15. Wilfred Cantwell Smith, *Islam in Modern History* (Princeton, N.J.: Princeton University Press, 1957), p. 75. This phenomenon was also noted in the 1940s by H. A. R. Gibb. See Gibb, *Modern Trends in Islam* (Chicago: University of Chicago Press, 1947), p. 119.

16. Gibb, *Modern Trends,* p. 104.

17. Donald Eugene Smith, *Religion, Politics, and Social Change in the Third World* (New York: The Free Press, 1971), p. 3.

18. Ibid., pp. 3-4.

19. A. H. Hourani, *Syria and Lebanon, A Political Essay* (London: Oxford University Press, 1946), p. 81.

20. Quoted in Smith, *Religion, Politics,* p. 66.

21. Khalid Muhammad Khalid, *Min Huna Nabda'* (Cairo: Mu'assisah al-Khanji, 1963), p. 184.

22. See, for example, Bruce M. Borthwick, "Religion and Politics in Israel and Egypt," *The Middle East Journal* 33, no. 2 (Spring 1979): 145-63.

23. Ali Shari'ati, *On the Sociology of Islam,* trans. Hamid Algar (Berkeley, Calif.: Mizan Press, 1979), p. 86.

24. "How to Study the Qoran," *Mojahed* 1, no. 4 (April 1980): 42.

25. Hassan Hanafi, *Religious Dialogue and Revolution* (Cairo: The Anglo-Egyptian Bookshop, 1977), pp. 207-9.

26. Henry Munson, Jr., "The Social Base of Islamic Militancy in Morocco," *The Middle East Journal* 40, no. 2 (Spring 1986): 272-75.

27. "Report by the Legislative Committee of the U.A.R. National Assembly on the Republi-

can Law Regarding the Moslem Brotherhood," *Arab Political Documents 1965* (Beirut: American University of Beirut, n.d.), p. 453.

28. Richard P. Mitchell, *The Society of the Muslim Brothers* (London: Oxford University Press, 1969), p. 234.

29. See, for example, Mahmoud Abu Saud, "Islamic Banking—The Dubai Case," *Outlines of Islamic Economics, Proceedings of the First Symposium on the Economics of Islam in North America* (Indianapolis, Ind.: Association of Muslim Social Scientists, 1977), pp. 128–35, and Ahmed A. El-Naggar, "Islamic Banks: A Model and the Challenge," in *The Challenge of Islam,* ed. Altaf Gauhar (London: Islamic Council of Europe, 1978), pp. 220–34.

30. Harvey Cox, *Religion in the Secular City, Toward a Postmodern Theology* (New York: Simon and Schuster, 1984).

7

Religion against the State

A Political Economy of Religious Radicalism in Egypt and Israel

ERIC DAVIS

Introduction

The recent rise of militant religio-political movements in the Middle East was unpredicted by Western social scientists. In the view of the dominant paradigm, orthodox development theory, secularism was assumed to be ascendant in the so-called developing countries. The rise of radical religio-political or religious nationalist movements in the Middle East during the past decade and a half has proved this prediction false. The West was shocked and perplexed by the fall of the secular, pro-Western government of the shah of Iran, and its replacement by a radical Islamic Republic committed not only to completely restructuring Iranian society but also to overthrowing neighboring "infidel" regimes. The perception of an Islamic revival sweeping the Arab world was enhanced by the seizure of the Grand Mosque of Mecca in 1980 and the assassination of Anwar al-Sadat by Islamic militants in 1981. In Lebanon, attacks upon American and Israeli troops and the taking of American hostages by a shadowy group known as *al-Jihad* (Islamic Holy War) was seen as yet another indication of an Islamic revival.

Israel has also witnessed the emergence of a powerful religio-political movement. In the realm of foreign affairs, groups in this movement have argued that the whole of Jerusalem as well as the occupied territories belong to Israel by divine right; in domestic politics, they have increasingly tried to enforce public policy defined in religious terms. In its more extreme variants, Jewish radicalism has called for curtailing the rights of the non-Jewish citizenry of Israel, the Arabs, and even expelling them along with the Arabs of the occupied territories if they do not agree to an Israeli state defined in strictly Jewish terms.

No scholars have raised the question of whether or not the factors that have led to the rise of Islamic radicalism are also responsible for the rise of Jewish radicalism. Through an examination of the most powerful Islamic move-

145

ment in the Middle East, the Society of Muslim Brothers (or Muslim Brother-hood) in Egypt, and the most powerful religio-political movement in Israel, the Gush Emunim, as well as their more radical splinter groups, this study offers such a comparative analysis. Five sets of questions are posed. First, what is the ideological perspective of each of these groups? What is their funda-mental critique of society, and what are the social and political changes they seek to bring about? Second, what factors have stimulated the growth of these movements? Does their growth reflect a rise in religiosity in Egypt and Israel, or must additional explanatory factors be drawn upon to understand their expanded influence? Third, what are the social bases of the respective move-ments? What social strata support these movements, and why did they come to support them at a particular point in time? Fourth, what types of predic-tions can be made about the future political influence of these movements? What are their prospects for implementing their ideological objectives and perhaps even seizing political power and gaining control of the state? Fifth and finally, to what extent are the causal factors giving rise to those two move-ments similar, and to what extent are they different? Which social science models best explain these movements?

Models of Religious Radicalism

The dominant explanation of the genesis of and political support for re-ligious radical movements has been centered around the concept of political culture. The rise of radical religio-political movements is seen as a response to changes in the core values of the dominant political culture of the two countries in question. These changes are in turn seen as reactions to two criti-cal events—the Arab-Israeli war of June 1967 and that of October 1973—events that led to major shifts in public opinion and political attitudes.

The ahistoricism of models based upon political culture leads to several theoretical shortcomings. In avoiding historical analysis, these models treat religious radicalism as largely isolated from the dominant societal ideology, the state, and the socioeconomic environment. According to an alternative perspective, an explanation of the rise to prominence of radical religio-political movements in Egypt and Israel requires a historical and structural analysis incorporating three basic elements. First, these movements need to be seen as one of a number of possible logical responses to the breakdown of the cor-poratism inherent in Arab nationalism and Zionism, both of which have tra-ditionally aimed at integrating secular and religious symbols. Second, these movements should be viewed as responses to changes in the world market, the endogenous class structure, and the state apparatus, all of which have undermined the traditional corporate unity of Arab nationalism and Zionism. Finally, it is necessary to incorporate the impact of specific catalysts, such as the June 1967 and October 1973 wars, since such catalysts tended to accelerate the crystallization of new and emerging countervailing political coalitions and new symbol structures resulting from transformations in the class bases of Arab nationalism and Zionism as political movements. In this latter model, informed by the political economy tradition, the rise of radical religiopolitical movements can be seen as the unraveling of Arab nationalism and Zionism as movements. This unraveling has been the result of demographic changes, changes in the world market, and the behavior of dominant political elites and bourgeoisies in both Egypt and Israel. Because of such factors, Arab nationalism and Zionism no longer speak to basic social needs or reflect the changing class, political, and cultural base of Egyptian and Israeli societies, respectively.

The rise of religious radicalism must be understood as much as a failure of leftist and secular ideologies as a resurgence of interest in religion.[1] Traditionally, dominant elites are unable to sustain ideological fervor in the face of such external pressures as the world market and such internal pressures as changes in the domestic social structure and the dominant ideology. Religious radicalism—or what some have referred to as religious nationalism—is not supported by all strata of society, but largely by members of the middle and lower middle classes, particularly those who are upwardly mobile (or aspire to upward mobility). Historically, these groups have largely been excluded from political participation. They reject the dominant social ideology. In formulating a religiously based ideology, these groups seek to restructure the state and civil society according to their own hegemonic vision.

Ideological Perspectives: The Two Movements Compared

The religious radical or religious nationalist movements in Egypt and Israel share many similarities. First, each seeks to restructure society along more overtly religious lines. Second, both agree that the laws embodied in the Torah and the Quran, respectively, are absolute and indivisible, and therefore cannot be subject to human debate. An authoritarian tendency is implicit in each movement's worldview: both movements claim to possess the "true" understanding of God's dictates, and to know how they should be interpreted and applied. As a result, there is little room for compromise and bargaining between these movements and the secular state. Third, both believe that society cannot hope to maintain a sense of mission and purpose if organized on a purely secular basis. Both movements therefore resort to an antirational and mystical interpretation of religious affairs as they relate to social organization and political legitimacy. Since the reasoning behind divine prescriptions can only be known to God and not to mortal men, Islam and Judaism are ultimately comprehended in a mystical or intuitive manner.

Both Islamic and Jewish religious radical organizations seek to promote the use of religious texts as the basic elements in the determination of public policy. Legal codes and personal conduct or morality in Israel should conform to the dictates of the Torah, while in Egypt they should follow the dictates of the Quran. Adherents of both movements feel that the distinctive character of Egyptian and of Israeli society is to be found in their respective religions. Islam and Judaism are conceived as more than narrow doctrines of faith reserved for the Friday prayer, the Sabbath, or religious holidays; rather, Islam and Judaism are comprehensive belief systems that provide the individual believer with everything needed to pursue a moral and religiously correct life.

Religious radicalism holds the opposite attitude toward alien values— particularly, those values emanating from the West and from the socialist countries. The worst characteristic of these countries is thought to be their promotion of secularism. Secularism in the West is associated with materialism and an individualistic perspective on life. These values are seen as the cause of the erosion of social solidarity in Western society. The moral decay, the breakdown of the family, and the isolation of individuals observed in Western industrialized societies are beginning to corrupt Egyptian and Israeli society as well. At the political level, the corrosive effect of imported and alien values are reflected in extensive corruption in public life. Socialism is even more violently condemned, since it explicitly rejects religion and seeks to substitute materialism for spiritualism. As a result, no basis for societal morality exists.

One of the most obvious characteristics of radical religio-political ideology is the linking of the personal and the public spheres. Great emphasis is placed upon strengthening the family, particularly upon strengthening the position of the male while confining the female to such traditional roles as the socialization of children. Given a social environment seen as hostile to core religious values, the family becomes the central institution for protecting and promoting such values. In the process of strengthening the family, both Muslim and Jewish women find restrictions on their ability to control their futures.

These ideological orientations of the two movements are paralleled by a distaste for party politics. Both the Muslim Brotherhood and the Gush Emunim have refused to constitute themselves as political parties, reflecting their aversion to what they see as the corrupt nature of secular political life. In order to hold themselves above the rest of society, these two groups do not want to stoop to the level of their adversaries. Putting their policies to a vote by the public would imply that the dictates of God can be judged by the populace at large. This is an unacceptable notion: absolutes are eternal and cannot be judged by mankind.

Structural Determinants of Religious Radicalism in Egypt and Israel

In addition to sharing similar ideologies, the Muslim Brotherhood and the Gush Emunim are the outgrowths of similar, long-term structural changes in Egyptian and Israeli society. The wars of 1967 and 1973 are only catalysts that accelerated ongoing processes of social change. The development of nationalism among the Arabs and the Jews underwent two historical phases: liberalism and corporatism. For the Arabs, liberal nationalism was largely centered in individual Arab countries like Egypt and Iraq, where it sought to achieve political independence from colonial rule but eschewed any attempts to restructure the social and economic bases of society. Zionism also began with a liberal phase under the leadership of Theodor Herzl. Primarily concerned with the "problem of the Jews"—namely, the establishment of a nation-state to provide a haven from antisemitism—Herzl and the political Zionists offered little in the way of a socioeconomic program for the new Jewish state.

Historically, both Arab nationalism and Zionism have had very specific class bases.[2] Although both nationalist movements did derive some support, especially in their early phases, from sectors of the upper class, the initial social base of the two ideologies drew largely upon the middle and lower middle classes. As with many forms of nationalism, Arabism and Zionism represent political ideologies that attempted to synthesize religious and nationalist symbols.

Zionism and Arab Nationalism in Their Historical Contexts

Between 1880 and the early 1930s, Zionist settlers were largely drawn from the lower middle class—particularly, the small traders, artisans, and petty merchants.[3] The Zionists wished to escape their socioeconomic status in Eastern Europe and Russia; they were determined to become landowners, and thereby join the "natural"—as opposed to the market—economy. In many respects, their ideology was Utopian socialist in character. Class struggle within the Jewish community tended to be deemphasized in favor of the corporate unity of all Jews.[4] In secular terms, they aimed to become farmers in Palestine and implement their variant of socialism through collective ownership of the means of production. This process would "normalize" the Jews—that is, make them like everyone else. For these settlers, rural life reflected their intense rejection of the stereotype of the passive urban Jew who sought to avoid conflict with Gentile society through accommodation or assimilation. In religious terms, they would establish communion with God through tilling the soil of Palestine. Indeed, the notion of the "ascent," or the journey to Palestine, represents one of the most important convergences of secular and religious symbols. The emphasis on labor was both a religious obligation linking Jews to their traditional homeland and a mode of promoting a collective ideology. In nationalist terms, the ultimate objective of Zionist settlement in Palestine was to recreate the ancient Land of Israel. The link to socialism came through the emphasis on labor as the road to salvation. Yet, ontologically, this socialism had little in common with Marxism. Class struggle was played down in favor of the need for unity in the Jewish and Zionist community. History was not seen as shaped by material forces but by the free will of men. In its corporatist, ahistorical, and idealist construction, Zionism resembled the utopian Christian communities founded in early nineteenth century America more than the dictatorship of the proleteriat envisioned by Marx and his successors.

Arab nationalism gained its earliest support in the Arab East which, prior to the nineteenth century, maintained the strongest ties with Arabic culture. This area included Greater Syria, Palestine, the Hijaz, and northern Iraq. Egypt also developed a nationalist movement during the nineteenth century. However, this nationalism, apart from a competing indigenous pan-Islamic movement, emphasized an Egyptian rather than an Arab identity. In its own struggle against European colonialism, the Maghrib or North Africa drew upon Islam more than Arabism. With the defeat of the Ottoman Empire in 1918 and the subsequent abolition of the caliphate, pan-Islamism as a movement was discredited. While Egyptian nationalism was largely supported by members of the agrarian bourgeiosie linked to cotton cultivation, pan-Arab nationalism received relatively little support from the Arab upper classes.

Following the First World War, increased problems of development throughout the Arab world gave an even greater impetus to support for Arab nationalist thought. At the same time, these problems led to the formation of the Muslim Brotherhood in Egypt in 1928 supported largely by members of the lower middle class.⁵ The period following the Second World War found the Arab world caught between two competing ideologies, religious and secular. The latter was a more powerful, secularly oriented Arab nationalism that shed much of Western liberalism for a corporatism that attacked reactionary Arab bourgeoisies and Western colonialism and called for land reform and the nationalization of industry—especially industry under Western control. As with Zionism, this corporate Arab nationalism was extremely hostile to Marxism and the latter's emphasis on class struggle, despite a self-conscious reference to itself as socialist. Reflecting its middle and lower middle-class social base, corporatist Arab nationalism resented the Arab bourgeoisies for their monopoly of wealth, their corruption, and their cooperation with foreign capital. Yet supporters of corporatist Arab nationalism reserved their deepest hostility for Marxists and Arab communist parties, whom they accused of furthering social disintegration through their emphasis on class struggle. As economic conditions deteriorated, the middle and lower middle classes increasingly feared proletarianization.

Despite open hostility to the Muslim Brotherhood and other Islamic radical organizations, the most prominent variants of corporate Arab nationalism, Nasserism and Baathism, never really addressed the question of the status of Islam. Although the concept of Arabism was inextricably tied up with the rise of Islam and the achievements of the Ummayyid and Abbasid empires, a satisfactory synthesis of secular Western notions of nationalism and the notion of Islam as a core ingredient of the identity of Arab society was never achieved. Instead, an uneasy accommodation was developed between what were essentially secular governments and the Islamic hierarchy. Islam was declared to be the state religion, and religious leaders were made employees of the state and given a limited amount of power in the judicial realm —particularly, that of personal-status law and public education.

Labor Zionism faced a similarly contradictory relationship to the religious community. Although the Zionist movement had to fight a rear-guard battle with the orthodox community, which claimed that the return to Zion could not be accomplished through human agency but only through divine intervention, Zionism found that other sectors of the religious community accepted its goals and its attempted synthesis of nationalist and religious symbols (although they were often hostile to the secular and economic dimensions of its socialist symbolism). Rabbi Avraham Isaac Kook, chief rabbi of Jerusalem, argued, for example, that the coming of the Messiah and Redemption for the Jewish people could be accelerated through human agency. Even though Kook disagreed with some of the overtly socialist aspects of Labor Zionism, he saw the movement as one that had unintended consequences for Judaism and the Jewish Diaspora: in his view, Zionist settlers who rejected Judaism in religious terms were, in settling Palestine, regarded as unintentionally carrying out God's will by bringing the Jews back to the holy land of Eretz Israel.[6]

The powerful (religious) Mizrahi movement also cooperated pragmatically with the dominant secular Zionist movement during the 1930s. Considerable accommodation existed, therefore, between secular Labor Zionism and the religious community in the Jewish community in Palestine prior to 1948. In spite of this uneasy cooperation, conflict between the corporatist and secular, and more overtly religious definition of Zionism was already manifest. The tension between the two competing definitions of Zionism continued after the founding of Israel, when the religious Zionists were able to prevent the adoption of a constitution during the early 1950s that they considered to be too secularly oriented.[7]

The overriding theme in Labor (as opposed to political)[8] Zionism, as well as in the thought of the religious Zionism of Rav Kook, is the theme of wholeness and unity; the world is fragmented and unstable, and must be made whole again. Both mainstream Labor Zionism and religious Zionist thinking stressed corporatism. The Jewish people were a unity and should not be thought of in either class or regional terms. The antimaterialist, mystical, anticapitalist, and anti-Marxist quality of mainstream Labor Zionist ideology reflected in large measure its middle-class base. In this sense, Zionism paralleled Arab nationalism, which likewise stressed the unity of the Arabs and the Arab nation, arguing that the disunity of the Arab world was an artificial creation of colonialism.

Although professing a socialist ideology, Labor Zionism attempted to synthesize secular and religious symbols drawn from Utopian socialism, Western nationalism, and Judaism. At the turn of the century, the Utopian socialist symbols appealed to the lower middle-class social stratum of Jews in that it promised to eliminate their marginal status in society. Jews would develop a concrete relationship to the means of production like that enjoyed by Gentile society through becoming landowners and farming the land. The nationalist component of labor Zionist ideology offered to "normalize" Jews in yet another way: by situating them in a specified territory, Palestine. Thus Jews would be able to take their place among the family of nations in the same manner as other peoples of Central and Eastern Europe who were in the process of forming nation-states. The third aspect of Labor Zionism implicitly revised the orthodox understanding of Judaism by in effect arguing that, not only did the settlement in Palestine make one's life more virtuous through tilling the holy soil of Palestine, but also that the Redemption of the Jewish people could be accelerated through human agency.

The Decline of Labor Zionist and Corporatist Arab Nationalist Hegemony

The dominance of Labor Zionist ideology following the creation of the state of Israel was a natural result of its dominance of the socioeconomic and political life of the Jewish community, or *yishuv.* Labor Zionism deemphasized the class nature of Jewish society. To a certain degree such an ideological position was understandable, since the Jews of the ghettos and the villages of Poland and Russia where Zionism first took root were not highly socially stratified. This situation continued throughout the early period of Zionist settlement in Palestine, from the first migration in 1882 until the early 1930s. Once nazism took hold in Germany and was paralleled by fascist movements throughout Europe, Jewish emigration from Europe — particularly from Germany — took a dramatic upturn. Often of relatively well-to-do backgrounds and very individualistic, the German Jews possessed little desire to participate in a collectivist society centered around the kibbutz. A small but significant portion of Eastern European Jewish immigrants to Palestine were turning to a new, militaristic variant of Zionism, namely Revisionism. Revisionism, as articulated by Vladimir Jabotinsky and his followers (including Menachem Begin), held little sympathy for socialism. With fascism on the rise in Europe, and the conflict between Arabs and Zionist settlers intensifying in Palestine, Revisionist thinking emphasized political power and the military might needed to acquire such power.

Following World War II (but especially after 1948), the newly created state of Israel witnessed the influx of a large number of Arab Jews from surrounding Arab countries and from North Africa. The influx of German settlers, East European Revisionists, and ultimately large numbers of Arab Jews created a political stratum that did not wield political power in proportion to their numbers. This was due to the headstart of early Zionist settlers in institutionalizing their position by developing such institutions as the *Histadrut,* or Jewish labor federation, which also came to own and operate a wide variety of economic enterprises. German settlers, the Revisionists, and the Arab Jews possessed little of this collectivist tradition. Thus they were disadvantaged in two respects. This diverse grouping possessed neither the institutional network of the Labor Zionists nor an organizational tradition for mobilizing to challenge it. The heterogeneity of their social and cultural backgrounds was perhaps the greatest barrier of all to effective collective political action.

With the advent of independence, Labor Zionists in the Israeli parliament (Knesset) were able to further consolidate their power through transforming the economic institutions of the *yishuv* into state enterprises. This process institutionalized the labor party both as a political and economic elite.[9] The Labor party was further strengthened by the significant influx of foreign

capital during the post-1948 period, including American foreign aid, contributions from Western Jewry (particularly from the United States), and repa-
rations payments from West Germany. World sales of Israeli bonds alone ac-
counted for $4.3 billion in funds between 1951 and 1978.[10] Further economic
benefit resulted from the large amounts of cheap labor in the form of Arab
Jews, especially those of Moroccan origin and the Palestinian Arabs who now
found themselves living in the Israeli state. With the tremendous boom in
construction occasioned by the need for housing and infrastructural development, the Israeli economy experienced an annual growth rate of roughly ten
percent between 1950 and 1967. Only Japan, South Korea, and Taiwan achieved
a comparable growth during the same period of time.[11]

The development of state enterprises institutionalized the social welfare
policies of the Jewish community. The state became the employer of a large
sector of the labor force in a carryover of the responsibility fulfilled by Zionist
organizations in providing for Jewish settlers prior to the formation of the
state. As in Egypt, the result of this policy was the creation of a large number
of protected but inefficient state enterprises. Following the 1973 war, only
25% of the Israeli labor force was employed in industry, while over half was
employed in state enterprises or in the service sector.[12] Perhaps most critical
for the economy was the institutionalization of the system of wage-price indexing, whereby a worker's wages rose as fast as the rate of inflation. This
policy was an outcome of the corporatist character of Labor Zionist ideology.
While enhancing social solidarity and labor peace, it placed severe constraints
on the Israeli economy once it entered a period of severe inflation. This represented the contradiction of an ideology that tried to achieve class harmony
through both denying class differences and attempting to give all classes a
significant portion of the national economic pie. Hyperinflation made clear
the class nature of Israeli society, since the bourgeoisie found itself tied to
policies that prevented it from shifting the costs of economic change onto
the working class. As one official stated, "Nobody suffers much from inflation,
so it is hard for us to argue the need for restraint."[13] The notion of indexing,
which had become part of the hegemonic ideology promoted for over half
a century by Labor Zionism, could not be readily undone without strong protest from the working class as well as from white-collar workers employed by
the state.

Politically, the Labor party concluded a tacit agreement with the religious
parties. In return for their acquiescence to Labor party hegemony in economic,
defense, and foreign policy, the religious parties were given control of the
religious affairs and education ministries. Although professing socialist values,
the Labor party was giving significant power over the socialization of the next
generation of Israelis to sociopolitical forces that articulated an ideology op-

posed to secular values. This decision should be seen not only as a necessary response but also as a decline in commitment to socialist ideology among Labor party members themselves. The fact that they now constituted the dominant political and economic elite led to a tempering of this commitment. During the 1950s and 1960s, the type of corruption that was later to be exposed began to develop as some Labor party members used their positions within the state public sector to advance their own economic interests.[14] Although many Israelis were benefitting from economic policies fostered by the state, the sense of struggle and communal solidarity that had characterized the *yishuv* was on the wane. The sense of social solidarity that had existed prior to 1948 was less in evidence as economic prosperity accentuated an individualistic and materialist ethic. The ethnic homogeneity of Israeli society based upon Eastern European Ashkenezic dominance changed with the influx of Arab, and to a lesser extent American and Russian, Jews. At the same time, due to rates of population growth, the Arab Jewish population—the so-called Orientals—was increasing in number. Likewise, a second generation of leaders from the religious parties and the Revisionist movement—groups that were not committed to the collectivist ethic of Labor Zionism—was coming of age. In many instances, these individuals were either upwardly mobile or aspirants to upward mobility who resented the domination of the socioeconomic system by the Labor party elite. For them, as for many Israelis, the concept of socialism became increasingly meaningless in ideological terms. Indeed the term assumed a pejorative meaning as it came to be associated with the domination of the political and economic system by an Eastern European Jewish elite that still drew its ideological legitimacy from the *yishuv.*

Ideological Vacuum and Growth of the Right

We can now point to the conditions leading to the rise of religious radicalism in Israel. First, the emergence of the Gush Emunim resulted not so much from religious resurgence as from a much more complex conjuncture of structural changes and events. The rightward drift of Israeli politics since 1967 came as much from a failure of the left as from a strengthening of the right. After years in power, the Labor party began to take its control of the state for granted, allowing the development of a power vacuum within which other political parties could then operate.[15] Second, the Labor party was not sufficiently attuned to the changing demographics of Israeli society. The growing Oriental community was largely ignored and viewed in a patronizing and condescending manner. A third factor concerns changing economic conditions. By the mid-1960s, the development boom of the 1950s and 1960s was coming to a close. Given the already tense situation in the country resulting from the hostility of the Arab world and Palestinian resentment at the loss of their land, a weakened economy only added to the sense of insecurity.

Still another significant structural change consisted of the socioeconomic and ideological changes taking place among Diaspora Jewry, especially Jews in the United States. For the latter, Israel assumed nationalist, religious, and cultural significance. Given the experience of the Holocaust, Israel represented a place of material and psychological comfort. The heavy involvement and support of American Jews have served to make Israel responsive to the views of these benefactors.[16] As a significant section of American Jewry has become upwardly mobile throughout the twentieth century, it has also become politically more conservative. A group of Jewish intellectuals has increasingly viewed Israel as a crucial element in preventing Soviet expansionism in the Middle East. Such a perspective assumed even greater importance after the precipitous rise in oil prices during the early 1970s. This conceptualization of Israel corresponded with the dominant view of successive United States governments. Due to external pressures, the tendency was to play down the leftist character of the Israeli state. Clearly, the large amount of United States aid served to temper the ideological commitment of socialism. During Israel's early years, the United States provided high levels of aid. After 1967, United States and Israeli interests began to coincide more closely. The United States was Israel's sole supplier of arms after 1967, and between 1972 and 1978 supplied Israel with over $7 billion in aid—four times more than had been provided prior to 1967. This process of escalation of aid was exacerbated by the increased international isolation experienced by Israel after 1967.[17]

In addition to generating large amounts of funds and urging Israel to assume an anti-Soviet posture in the Middle East, American Jewry has exerted pressure on Israel even more directly. Emigration to Israel has become a means of avoiding the problem of intermarriage and assimilation, an issue of growing concern among American Jews, especially orthodox Jews. For many younger Jews, particularly the more religious and conservative, emigration to Israel has provided a way of escaping the rampant materialism of American life. Thus, in recent years, Israel has witnessed an upsurge in emigration of politically and religiously conservative Jews. A significant proportion of these emigrants have become politically active once in Israel—particularly within the ranks of the Gush Emunim.[18]

The situation in Egypt is contextually very different from that of Israel; however, many of the structural conditions are quite similar. Throughout the 1920s and 1930s, nationalist intellectuals and religious figures fiercely debated the question of the direction Egyptian society should take. Since secular nationalism was supported by the army, it was ultimately victorious. The Free Officer Group led by Jamal Abd el-Nasir (Nasser) that came to power in 1952 was, by the late 1960s, perceived by the populace to be a leftist government (like the Labor government in Israel). This perception derived not only from Egyptian foreign policy, which was antiimperialist, nonaligned, and supportive of third world liberation movements, but also from the nationalization of British, French, and Jewish industry after the Tripartite invasion of 1956 and the more widescale nationalization of foreign and domestic industry between 1961 and 1964. The creation of a single-party system that centered around the Arab Socialist Union, extensive trade with the socialist bloc, and the influx of large numbers of Soviet military and technical advisers only served to reinforce this perception.

As in Israel, the state's commitment to socialism came to be viewed very cynically by the populace at large. Paralleling Israeli Labor party practice, public sector sinecures tended to be awarded to those who were loyal to the regime. Whereas in Israel this meant those who had dominated the politics of the *yishuv*, in Egypt this meant those who had ties to the Free Officer group responsible for the 1952 revolution. Thus, socialism in both countries came to be identified with elitism and ultimately with corruption.

While never very strong after World War II, the Egyptian economy derived some benefit from the nationalizations of 1956 and the early 1960s. However, by 1965 the policies of state economic control followed by the Nasser government had already begun to experience economic stagnation. In response, state economic policy began to move to the right, anticipating the "open door policy" that was to become so important under the Sadat government. During this period, Egypt also witnessed the beginnings of the emergence of a new bourgeoisie within the state public sector and in the many small private-sector firms developing economically lucrative and corrupt relationships with public-sector firms.[19] Rightist forces were able to make gains in this economic space. The open door policy was not the creation of Anwar Sadat, for there had been a significant move in this direction since the mid-1960s.

This historical analysis demonstrates a number of points. First, socialism as an ideology was undermined in both Israel and Egypt during the 1960s. A significant segment of both Israeli and Egyptian society was committed to the social-welfare benefits to be derived from this system. As an ideology, however, socialism meant little to the vast bulk of the populace of either society. Second, both societies were experiencing a sense of drift prior to the 1967 war. In Israel, this stemmed from the decline in the commitment to building a model society that had given so much impetus to the Zionist movement in pre-1948 Palestine. In Egypt, on the eve of the 1967 war, the expectations raised by Nasserism had not been met: the general standard of living had not shown any appreciable rise, Egypt was involved in a disastrous war in the Yemen, corruption was perceived to be widespread, and political dissent was severely curtailed.[20] The religious revival in both countries was as much a response to the political vacuum created by the weakness of the left as it was to the inherent strength of the religious right.

The June 1967 War exerted a significant but differing impact on Egyptian and Israeli society. In Egypt, the war accelerated the dissatisfaction with Nasserite policies, despite the ability of Nasser himself to avoid much of the blame for Egypt's stunning defeat. With the closing of the Suez Canal, Egypt's economy was severely curtailed; not only were canal revenues lost, but hundreds of thousands of Egyptians had to be relocated from the urban areas along the canal to Cairo, Alexandria, and cities and towns within the Egyptian delta. These economic pressures created an extensive dependence on the conservative oil monarchies of the Arabian peninsula, such as Saudi Arabia and Kuwait. Given their emphasis on Islam as the basis of political legitimacy, the increased power of these states in Arab affairs provided moral as well as financial support for radical religious organizations. Together with the subsequent withdrawal of Egyptian forces from the Yemen, the 1967 defeat dramatically diminished Egypt's role as an aspirant to pan-Arab leadership.

For the Islamic radical movement, the June war demonstrated conclusively that Egypt's decline was a result of a massive deviation from Islamic principles. In its view, as a secular atheistic doctrine Arab socialism was not an authentic element of the Egyptian character. Rather than increasing Egypt's economic and political independence, it had made the country even more dependent upon a foreign power: the Soviet Union.

For Israel, the June 1967 war proved to be a mixed blessing. Politically, the nation received a tremendous uplift from the devastating defeat inflicted upon the Egyptian, Syrian, and Jordanian armies. In addition, the conquest of East Jerusalem served to place all of Jerusalem under Israeli control. The religious forces took the outcome of the war as a divine statement that God wanted the Jews to control the newly occupied territories. The war also gave a tremendous ideological and political boost to those forces seeking to create more indigenously authentic politics. Few observers at the time paid close attention to the economic ramifications of the war. Military expenditures increased from 11.7% of gross national product to 24.1% in 1972, while the increase in imports of military hardware increased from $116 to $800 million.[21] In the process, the Israeli goal of achieving economic self-sufficiency was suddenly out of reach.

In a sense, the October 1973 war represented a reversal of the process that had taken place in 1967. In terms of defense, the war destroyed much of Israel's military capacity, necessitating a massive and costly new arms buildup. (Military expenditures had reached more than $2 billion by 1975.)[22] Just when Israel began to drastically increase its defense spending, it was struck by the global inflation of 1974–75, resulting largely from the rise in oil prices. The 1973 war also frightened foreign investors, causing such investment to trickle to a halt. Although Israel ultimately prevailed over the Egyptian and Syrian armies, the coordinated attack by these two Arab states and the destruction of the myth of Israeli invincibility resulting from the impressive Arab military gains were profoundly sobering to the large majority of the Israeli populace. The religious right interpreted the 1973 war as yet another divine intervention, but in this instance a negative one: Israeli society had strayed from Jewish values and was being punished. The obvious solution was to renounce the secular and materialist values dominating Israeli society. Not surprisingly, the actual political coalescence of the religious nationalist forces growing since the 1960s took place shortly after the 1973 war with the founding of the Gush Emunim at Kfar Etzion in 1974.[23]

In Egypt, the war had an effect similar to that which the 1967 victory had had upon the Israeli populace. Many Egyptians felt a restoration of national pride. The religious forces in particular saw the war as a vindication of the move away from Nasserism pursued by the Sadat regime since 1971. As the war was instrumental in consolidating Sadat's political power, it became possible for him to move Egypt even deeper into the Western political and economic orbit. At this point, tensions between the Islamic movement and the Sadat regime began to develop. Having expected Egypt to move toward a more Islamic definition of society, Islamic radicals instead found a dramatic expansion of Western influence and Egypt entering into negotiations with Israel.

The major impact of the October 1973 war was to increase the power of the religious right in both Egypt and Israel. However, in the Egyptian case, the war was both a catalyst — further strengthening the morale of those seeking to Islamize Egyptian society — and the beginning of a process ultimately leading to the assassination of Anwar Sadat in October 1981. In the Israeli case, the war led to profound dissatisfaction with the Labor government of Golda Meir. Rather than increasing tension between Jewish radicals and the state, however, the period following the October 1973 war served to draw the state and the religious radicals closer together, as government financial assistance to the settler movement began to grow. At the same time, the Gush Emunim through its settlements began to build a state within a state on the West Bank and in the Sinai Peninsula.

Anatomy of the Gush Emunim and the Muslim Brotherhood

The social bases of the Islamic and Jewish radical movements shed further light upon the nature of the changes affecting Israeli and Egyptian society. An analysis of the membership of the Muslim Brotherhood and the Gush Emunim shows them both to be largely comprised of upwardly mobile lower middle-class elements.[24] In per capita income terms, members of the Gush Emunim are much more prosperous than those of the Muslim Brotherhood, but these groups occupy the same structural position in their respective societies. Both organizations represent groups that considered themselves marginal to both the dominant power structure and the dominant ideology. Additionally, their own ideology is reflected in an apparent contradiction. On the one hand, they seek to better their material status, as evidenced in their efforts to acquire higher education and enter professional employment; on the other hand, they reject the rampant materialism characteristic of both Egyptian and Israeli society. Indeed, they argue that a "return to religion" is a necessary antidote to the spread of this materialism.[25]

The emphasis on a traditional interpretation of religion reflects an effort to reconstruct a counter-ideology to replace Labor Zionism and corporatist Arab nationalism. The type of ideology created is especially congruent with the material conditions of its adherents. In the case of the Gush Emunim, the call for settlement on the West Bank is purposed to be a return to the original pioneering spirit of Zionism. A close look at these settlements, however, indicates that they do not resemble the *kibbutzim* of the early Zionist settlers. In many instances, these settlements are commuter communities: most of their inhabitants travel to Tel Aviv or Jerusalem to work in white-collar employment. Other Gush Emunim settlements provide the location for small business and industry, such as the development of computer software.[26] There is little of the commitment to agriculture or the collective ownership of property that characterized the *kibbutz*.

The upwardly mobile middle-class character of the Gush Emunim movement represents a key variable in explaining its ideology. Gush Emunim members have been fearful of societal fragmentation as represented by the decay and rigidification of orthodox Labor Zionism, the emigration of many educated Israelis seeking better material conditions to the West, the incidence of intermarriage among Jews and non-Jews in the West, and the increasing materialistic character of Israeli society. Despite these dissatisfactions, Gush Emunim members have not successfully reconciled their radical interpretation of Judaism with their desire for material prosperity. Settlement on the West Bank has been very lucrative for most settlers: land, mortgages for houses, and the residential infrastructure have been subsidized by the Israeli government.[27]

While still a distinct minority, a significant phenomenon is the considerable number of Oriental and American Jews among the Gush Emunim settlers. The attempt by radical religious elements to recast Zionist ideology is, in large measure, the result of major demographic changes in Israeli society. As such, the gradual shift in political power away from the Eastern European Ashkenazic to the Oriental community is indeed only the "tip of the iceberg." The ideology of Gush Emunim is symptomatic of a much larger ideological change in Israeli society as a whole.[28] This demographic change also represents a major restructuring of Israeli class structure. Many Oriental and American Jews, especially those who have been upwardly mobile, have opted for a rightist religious or Revisionist interpretation of Zionism, rather than the traditional left-of-center Labor Zionism. These subgroups have begun to appear in the ranks of the Gush Emunim.[29] More upwardly mobile, middle-class Oriental and American Jews will likely be recruited to the ranks of the movement in the future.

In Egypt, the social base of the religious radical movement continues to grow as the economy deteriorates and the gap in income and consumption patterns continue to widen among the very rich and the middle and lower classes. Whereas the Muslim Brotherhood once represented the core of religious radicalism, during the past two decades more radical offshoots of the Brotherhood have begun to assume powerful positions within the movement. The Society of Muslims, al-Jihad, and the Islamic Liberation party are the most prominent groups, but other radical organizations have also been identified.[30] The appearance of these more radical groups signifies the increasing desperation felt by large numbers of Egyptian youth. No longer feeling any hope of finding meaningful employment, they are venting their resentment at the Western-oriented Egyptian bourgeoisie that has promoted a materialist and consumerist culture, especially since the initiation of Sadat's open door policy.

These splinter groups from the Muslim Brotherhood find their analogue in Israel in the form of the Kach organization of Rabbi Meyer Kahane. As a recent study indicates, members of the Kach organization tend to be drawn from those strata of Israeli society that are not economically marginal but which feel threatened by the continued influx of the cheap Arab labor sought by Israeli industry in an effort to depress overall wage levels.[31] As economic conditions deteriorate for increasingly larger sectors of Egyptian and Israeli society, the appeal of more radical and violence-prone religious-nationalist organizations will likely increase. This appeal will no doubt be more pronounced in Egypt, which has a much more fragile economy than Israel. Never-theless, we can also expect the appeal to grow in Israel, where economic ex-pectations are higher and where the government has only been able to bring down a highly destructive inflation rate through elimination of employment in the state bureaucracy and in the state-controlled public sector, and through eroding the traditional system of indexing wages to inflation — a policy part of the corporatist consensus originally rated by the Labor Zionist ideology.[32]

Conclusion: Religion against the State

This essay has sought to provide a comparative analysis of religious radi-calism in Egypt and Israel. It has attempted to move the discourse on re-ligious radicalism, with its attendant focus upon revival, resurgence, and fundamentalism, away from a narrow cultural to a broader socioeconomic analysis. The significance of culture is not eschewed; quite the opposite, the reconstruction of Islam and Judaism by religious radicals in a more explicitly and *modern* political manner demonstrates the centrality of culture.

The phenomenon of religious radicalism has been analyzed in a dynamic fashion that allows us both to understand its genesis and evolution and to make some predictions about its future course of development. The type of cultural approach that has dominated the analysis of religious radicalism to date is too static. It fails to explain why religious radicalism has become so salient for Egyptians and Israelis at this particular point in time as well as for so many other citizens in developing as well as in Western countries.[33]

The discourse on Islamic and Jewish radicalism needs to be broadened tem-porally to encompass a historical focus. Such an approach is intended as an antidote to the tendency to reify religion — to see the strength of religious radicalism largely in terms of religion itself. Rather, any theory of the rise to prominence of such groups as the Muslim Brotherhood, the Gush Emunim, and their more radical offshoots must situate their strength in the weakness of the forces with which they are struggling as much as the inherent strength of religion cast as a political ideology. The ideological weakness of corporatist Arab nationalism (Nasserism, for example) and Labor Zionism lies in their inability to provide either an effective model of societal organization or a sym-bolic nexus to meaningfully interpret social reality for large segments of the populace. As a result, a political space was opened for religious nationalism to offer itself as a competing ideology.

These ideologies have not appealed in any significant way to either the upper or lower classes. They have addressed themselves primarily to the concerns of the upwardly mobile lower middle classes in both Egypt and Israel. As economic conditions in both societies have deteriorated (due to the inability of political elites to protect these classes from the negative impact of world-market forces), religious nationalism has begun to appeal to elements of the lower classes that feel increasingly despondent about their ability to achieve upward mobility. In Egypt, these lower-class recruits are in actuality often downwardly mobile lower middle-class youth who have dropped out of the university and given up hope of achieving a meaningful career.[34] In Israel, the movement has taken a more virulent and violent tone among sectors of the working class that feel threatened by Arab labor. Religious nationalism appears to have broadened its appeal to the lower classes, and in the process become more radical. In Egypt, however, the "lower classes" seem in fact to be downwardly mobile lower middle-class youth, while in Israel the workers who support the Kach movement come from the "aristocracy of labor" — namely, those Oriental Jews who seek to retain their material and psychological advantage over the even poorer strata of Arab workers. Those who avoid a class analysis of religious radicalism fail to explain why the movement appeals only to certain strata of society and not to others.

Despite the cooperation between the state and the religious radical movement at various periods, such as during the early years of the Sadat and Begin regimes, these movements ultimately seek to impose their own vision on society in opposition to the state. While the Muslim Brotherhood is but a shell of itself when compared to the large business, educational, and health infrastructure that it possessed prior to being disbanded in 1954, the attempt to create a society within a society has fallen to more radical groups of youths, such as the Society of Muslims and al-Jihad. The establishment of urban and desert communes as well as the use of the mosque in lower middle-class quarters of Cairo and other urban areas represent the start of what Gramsci referred to as the "war of position." Reinterpretations of Islam by such thinkers as Sulaymen Faraj and Shaykh Kishk and the extensive use of the writings of Sayyid Qutb form the core of a counter-ideology to the symbolically diluted state ideology synthesizing in an unimaginative way remnants of Nasserism, Western liberalism, and reformist (i.e., modernized) Islam.[35]

In Israel, the efforts to create a new, alternative society have gone even farther. In the West Bank in particular, the Gush Emunim has fashioned a ministate complete with municipal administration, educational system, and paramilitary organization, and a religious intelligentsia that provides a counter-ideology to both Labor Zionism and the orthodox religion of the chief rabbinate.[36] As the efforts to remove the Sinai settlement of Yamit demonstrated, any attempt by the state to dismantle Gush Emunim settlements in the West Bank will face fierce opposition. Indeed, it would lead to civil war, many Gush

Emunim members have asserted. Despite the distaste of many members of the movement for violence, Gush Emunim efforts to blow up the Mosque of Omar in Jerusalem and the uncovering of a terrorist underground linked to the movement indicate that violence is an important component of the Gush's strategy to ultimately control the state.[37]

Unless the left in both Egypt and Israel is able to develop more organizational strength (which is very doubtful given their inability to date to generate viable public policies to confront development problems), the religious nationalist movement will continue to expand its influence. A central question is whether or not an "Iranian option" is a possibility. Given their relatively narrow class base and their lack of control of the armed forces, the coming to power of the Muslim Brotherhood or the Gush Emunim or any of their splinter groups within the near future seems highly unlikely. Rather, the growth of these movements symbolizes the expansion of increasingly chauvinist, xenophobic, parochial, and obscurantist politics in both Egypt and Israel. In the short term, such policies will benefit the Egyptian and Israeli bourgeoisies, who will be able to exploit this trend to thwart efforts at social and economic reforms by progressive groups. Perhaps more sobering, the growth of religious radicalism bodes ill for any meaningful solution to the Palestinian problem in the near future as well as for the continuation of peace between Egypt and Israel. Continued increase in tension between the state and the religious radical movements can be predicted as each seeks to manipulate the other in order to expand its influence within society at large.

Notes

I would like to thank the National Fellows Program of the Hoover Institution on War, Revolution and Peace at Stanford University for a twelve-month fellowship during 1981 and 1982 that allowed me to conduct much of the research for this study.

1. For a critique of the recent literature on Islamic revival, see Eric Davis, "The Concept of Revival and the Study of Islam and Politics," in Barbara Stowasser, ed., *New Directions in the Study of Islam and Politics* (New York and London: Croom Helm, forthcoming).

2. The class bases of Arab nationalism are discussed in Samir Amin, *The Arab Nation* (London: Zed Press, 1978). On the Zionist movement, see Allon Gal, *Socialist Zionism* (New Brunswick, N.J.: Transaction Press, 1973).

3. Gal, *Socialist Zionism*, pp. 98–113.

4. This emphasis is clear in the writings of the foremost Labor Zionist thinker, A. D. Gordon: "Nor must we tie ourselves to the world proletariat, the International, whose activities and whose methods are basically opposed to ours. . . . I believe that we should not even combine

with Jewish workers in the Diaspora specifically as workers, much as we respect labor; they should be our allies as Jews, just like any other Jews in the Diaspora who share our aspirations, no more and no less. We must draw our inspiration from our land, from life on our own soil, from the labor we are engaged in, and must be on guard against allowing too many influences from outside to affect us." Gordon, "Our Tasks Ahead," in Arthur Hertzberg, ed., *The Zionist Idea* (New York: Atheneum, 1982), p. 382.

5. Richard Mitchell, *The Society of the Muslim Brothers* (London and New York: Oxford University Press, 1969), p. 7.

6. Abraham Isaac Kook, *The Lights of Penitence, Lights of Holiness, Moral Principles, Essays, Letters and Poems* (New York; Ramsey, N.Y.; Toronto: Paulist Press, 1978), pp. 126–28.

7. Steven Heydemann, "The Origins and Development of Maximalist Religious Politics in Israel" (B.A. thesis, University of Michigan, 1982), pp. 28, 36–37.

8. Political (or liberal) Zionism, as articulated in the thought of such thinkers as Theodor Herzl, Max Nordau, and Leon Pinsker, dominated the Zionist movement for only a relatively short period of time. It was a movement that reflected the concerns of the more assimilated middle and upper middle-class Jews of Germany and Western Europe. As is well known, its primary concern was the "problem of the Jews"—specifically, their safety from the pogroms and persecution in Eastern Europe. Unable to speak to the more socioeconomic and spiritual needs of lower middle and lower-class Jews, it was soon swept away by Labor Zionism.

9. Rael Jean Isaac, *Party and Politics in Israel: Three Visions of the Jewish State* (New York and London: Longman, 1981), pp. 97–99.

10. Ann Crittenden, "Israel's Economic Plight," *Foreign Affairs* 57 (Summer 1979): 1013.

11. Ibid., p. 1006.

12. Ibid., p. 1009.

13. Ibid., p. 1010.

14. On corruption in the Labor party, see William Frankel, *Israel Observed: Anatomy of a State* (New York: Thames and Hudson, 1980), p. 29.

15. Myron J. Aronoff, "The Decline of the Israeli Labor Party," in H. R. Penniman, ed., *Israel at the Polls: The Knesset Elections of 1977* (Washington, D.C.: American Enterprise Institute for Public Policy Research, 1979), pp. 123ff.

16. Nadav Safran, *Israel the Embattled Ally* (Cambridge, Mass.: The Belknap Press of Harvard University Press, 1978), pp. 573–74.

17. Ibid., p. 577.

18. Kevin Avruch, "American Immigrants in Israel: Social Identity and Change" (Doctoral diss., Department of Anthropology, University of California at San Diego, 1978), pp. 355–60; Chaim I. Waxman, "Political and Social Attitudes of Americans Among the Settlers in the Territories," in D. Newman, ed., *The Impact of Gush Emunim: Politics and Settlement in the West Bank* (New York: St. Martin's Press, 1985), pp. 200–20; and David Newman, "The Role of Gush Emunim and the Yishuv Kehillati in the West Bank, 1974–1980" (Doctoral diss., Department of Geography, University of Durham [N.C.] 1981), p. 311.

19. John Waterbury, *The Egypt of Nasser and Sadat: A Political Economy of Two Regimes* (Princeton, N.J.: Princeton University Press, 1983), pp. 255–60, 347–49.

20. Leonard Binder, *In a Moment of Enthusiasm* (Chicago: University of Chicago Press, 1979), pp. 329, 341–47, 349.

21. Ann Crittenden, "Israel's Economic Plight," *Foreign Affairs* 57 (Summer 1979), p. 1007.

22. Ibid.

23. Actually, the founding of the Gush Emunim can be seen as the outgrowth of an earlier prototype: the Land of Greater Israel Movement. This movement, founded after the June 1967 war, was highly significant in that it represented the first time that fundamental ideological cleavages in Israeli society were transcended. Thus the movement attracted *kibbutznika* who sought

to recapture the Zionist ethos of pioneering, as well as religious nationalists who considered set-tlement in the occupied territories their divinely ordained "duty." On the Land of Greater Israel Movement, see Rael Jean Isaac, *Israel Divided* (Baltimore, Md.: Johns Hopkins Press, 1976), pp. 45–72.

24. On the social bases of the Gush Emunim, see the references cited in n. 18, above. On the more radical splinter of the Gush Emunim, the Kach organization, see Yoav Peled and Ger-shon Shafir, "Thorns in Your Eyes: The Socio-Economic Basis of the Kach Vote," mimeographed (n.p., n.d.); Ehud Sprinzak, "Kach and Meir Kahane: The Emergence of Jewish Quasi Fascism," *Patterns of Prejudice* 19, nos. 3, 4 (1985) (reprinted by the American Jewish Committee); and Leon Wieseltier, "The Demons of the Jews," *New Republic* no. 3,695 (11 November 1985): 15–25. On violent activities, particularly against the Arab population of the occupied territories by both the Gush Emunim and the Kach organization, see Robert I. Friedman, "In the Realm of Perfect Faith: Israel's Jewish Terrorists," *Village Voice* (12 November 1985): 16–22. On the social bases of the Muslim Brotherhood and more radical Islamic organizations, see Eric Davis, "Ideol-ogy, Social Class and Islamic Radicalism in Modern Egypt," in S. Arjomand, ed., *From National-ism to Revolutionary Islam* (London: Macmillan Press, 1984), pp. 140–45, and Giles Keppel, *The Prophet and the Pharaoh: Muslim Extremism in Egypt* (London: Al-Saqi Books, 1985).

25. A comment by an American emigrant to Israel is indicative of the attitude toward a global materialist culture expressed often by Israelis and Egyptians who provide the recruitment base for Islamic and Jewish radicalism: "In the States the constant fighting for the buck . . . it's bad for the kids and it's bad for their parents. . . . They are *suffering*, in a way my son, somewhere on the Golan, will never suffer. Those kids are choking on America's affluence. They have no values." Avruch, "American Immigrants," p. 195.

26. Newman, "Role of Gush Emunim," pp. 286, 300–2, 303, 307, 311, 313–15, and Meron Benvinisti, *The West Bank Data Project* (Washington, D.C.: The American Enterprise Institute for Public Policy Research, 1984), pp. 54, 57–58.

27. Benvinisti, *West Bank*, pp. 59–60.

28. Ehud Sprinzak, "Gush Emunim: The Tip of the Iceberg," *Jerusalem Quarterly*, no. 21 (Fall 1981): 39–46.

29. See Avruch, "American Immigrants"; Newman, "Role of Gush Emunim"; and Waxman, "Political and Social Attitudes."

30. Keppel, *Prophet and the Pharaoh*, esp. pp. 70–102, 191–218, and Israel Altman, "Is-lamic Movements in Egypt," *Jerusalem Quarterly*, no. 10 (Winter 1979): 87–105.

31. See Peled and Shafir, "Thorns in Your Eyes," pp. 5, 7–9, 20–23.

32. Shlomo Frankel, "Israel's Economic Crisis," *MERIP Reports*, nos. 136/137 (October–December 1985), pp. 20–23, and Leonard Silk, *New York Times*, 28 May 1986.

33. That the rise of religious radicalism and religious nationalism is not limited to the Mid-dle East but has also affected the advanced capitalist countries of the West should be obvious. In the West, the failure of a "left" alternative such as New Deal liberalism to provide economic and social security is very apparent. On religious radicalism in the United States, see Robert C. Liebman and Robert Wuthnow, eds., *The New Christian Right* (New York: Aldine Publishing Company, 1983).

34. Davis, "Ideology," p. 155.

35. Keppel, *Prophet and the Pharaoh*, pp. 172–90.

36. See Newman, "Role of Gush Emunim," and Ehud Sprinzak, *Gush Emunim: The Politics of Zionist Fundamentalism in Israel* (New York: The American Jewish Committee, 1986), pp. 18–22.

37. See Friedman, "In the Realm," for a discussion of the violent activities of some Gush Emunim members.

IV

RELIGIOUS RESURGENCE
AND POLITICAL SYSTEMS

8

Religion and Political Dissent in Israel
The Case of Gush Emunim

David J. Schnall

Introduction

Religion and politics have always maintained a complex and confusing relationship in Israel. As Israel is a Jewish state whose ideology requires the "ingathering of the exiles" from their millennial Diaspora, it is no surprise to find religion established as a part of the fabric of life. Nevertheless, much of Zionist theory has been married to liberal nationalism and evolutionary socialism, two ideologies that are devoid of or hostile to religious content. The majority of Israeli citizens profess little taste for religious orthodoxy, and their degree of traditionalism tends to decrease with greater integration into Israeli life.

Nevertheless, the religious community and its traditions appear to wield power out of proportion to their numbers. Marriages and divorces are performed according to Jewish ritual, and intermarriage is officially forbidden. With limited exception, pigs may not be raised nor may pork be sold. The designation of personal status, carrying with it immediate citizenship, is set within religious dicta. (The "Who is a Jew?" controversy is a direct result of this proposition.) In parliamentary terms as well, religious elements have played an important role, buttressing their hold on much legislation. The National Religious Party has participated in almost all of Israel's coalition governments, holding a virtual monopoly on certain ministries and areas of government activity. Further, this party has often received significant support from the Arab minority, who fall under the jurisdiction of their own respective religious establishments, as under the Turkish *millet* system.[1]

Thus, organized religion has generally operated within the mainstream of Israeli life, albeit often under stress and with internal tension. Nevertheless, dissent has also been motivated by religious belief, and movements of religious radicalism have not been unknown. In particular, Gush Emunim — the Bloc of the Faithful — has gained considerable visibility, both in Israel and abroad. Stemming originally from the National Religious Party and the Rav Kook Center, the movement has won adherence from a broad cross-section of Israelis as well as sympathy from among Israel's supporters elsewhere. The intention of this paper is to describe the historical development and ideology of this movement since its emergence roughly a decade ago.[2]

The Early Period

Though its formal establishment dates only from the spring of 1974, the earliest roots of Gush Emunim may be traced to the period immediately following the 1967 war and the activity of the Land of Israel movement. Composed of intellectuals, demobilized soldiers and kibbutz members, this group demanded the immediate annexation of conquered territories and their mass settlement. Among them, religious elements were the first to populate the Hebron and Ezion regions. Many had been driven from homes in that area prior to 1948; some would later join the Gush and help to form its leadership.[3]

Meanwhile, contemporaneous rumblings were felt within the National Religious Party (NRP). With its historic participation in the political establishment, the NRP saw as its primary goal the bringing under religious control of as many aspects of daily life as possible. In return for this hegemony, the party was traditionally docile in matters of foreign affairs, military security, and domestic economics, and supported the policies of its senior coalition partner, the Labor Alignment.

At the same time, however, a generation of religious Zionists was being raised within the youth movements of the NRP and its religious schools. The political machinations and compromises of their elders notwithstanding, these students were much imbued with the spirit of activism and a fierce love for the land. Religion and nationalism were here united in a singular sense of purpose, and the result was a maximalist politic unbridled by the moderating effects of practical politics.

The nature of the growing generational conflict within the NRP is best exemplified by the very incident that brought the issue to a head. On the eve of Israel Independence Day in 1967, Rabbi Zvi Yehuda Kook addressed his students. He recalled the sins of the nation in abandoning Hebron and Bethlehem to Arab jurisdiction. Seen in light of the victories some four weeks later, his words appeared prophetic and nurtured an annexationist spirit with an emphasis upon settlement not easily denied.

For the bulk of the Party's veterans, such ideology was an anomaly—perhaps even a bit naive. Only a last-minute decision to adopt a strong territorial resolution prevented the youth faction from pulling out and breaking up the NRP's 1967 convention. Many party leaders, trained in the very practical world

of Israeli politics, continued to take issue with their young colleagues on religious, social, and strategic grounds.

Perhaps the greatest impetus for the formation of Gush Emunim was the
1973 war, which left a state of demoralization and self-doubt in its wake that
was readily apparent during the national election that immediately followed.
Though still only a faction within the NRP, settlement activists seemed to
exhibit a spiritual appeal sorely lacking during those gray times. For most
of the party faithful, however, their ideology was of little use in the hard
world of protracted coalition negotiations following the 1973 election. Clearly,
limitation with the NRP was no asset to these dissidents.[4] The appeal of settlement transcended party lines. Perhaps as a surprise to the dissidents themselves, both secular Israelis and those little interested in formal politics were
attracted to the cause of pioneering in the conquered territories. An independent organization was imperative.

The formal founding of the movement may be traced to February 1974,
when a conference of students, members of the armed forces, and other activists was held at Kfar Ezion. Here the movement adopted its name and loose
organizational structure, at the same time severing its official links with the
NRP. No formal membership cards were to be issued; that way, the movement could claim a large number of supporters without the necessity of
showing hard evidence. Further, sympathizers could support specific activities without having to accept the movement's broad platform.[5]

From its founding to the first election of the Likud government in the spring
of 1977, Gush Emunim concentrated its activities in three broad areas. The
first consisted of civil protests against the so-called shuttle diplomacy of Henry
Kissinger, aimed at forging interim agreements among Israel, Syria, and Egypt
following the 1973 war. These protests continued for almost two years, and
included rallies, obstruction of traffic, picketing, and the circulation of peti-
tions. The second level of Gush activity was centered about a series of projects
whose goal was to popularize the strategic, historic, and religious importance
of Judea and Samaria, lest the dynamic created by the Kissinger negotiations
be directed toward territorial compromise. Candle-lighting ceremonies,
marches, and marathons were undertaken throughout Judea and Samaria,
and established as annual events. Tens of thousands of Israelis participated
in these projects, including then opposition leaders Menachim Begin and Yigal
Hurvits. Indeed, the Herut faction of the Likud bloc held its 1975 convention
at Kiryat Arba, the newly founded Jewish Quarter outside of Hebron.

Finally, the movement undertook actual settlement at strategic locations,
often in close proximity to large Arab population centers. Kiryat Arba was
the prime example in Judea, while the most famous and most stubborn attempt in Samaria was the Elon Moreh group which settled just outside the
city of Nablus after some eight previous attempts.[6]

Under the Begin Administration

Gush leaders rejoiced at the shift in government following the Likud victory in 1977. Never committed per se to extralegal protests and demonstration as a strategy for social change, they looked with great anticipation toward Menachim Begin as one who would legitimate their stand and fulfill their dream of mass settlement in Judea and Samaria. His electoral promise —"There will be many more Elon Morehs"— confirmed that hope, as did the appointment of then Agriculture Minister Ariel Sharon to head a joint ministerial commission on settlement.[7]

Perhaps because its expectations were unrealistic from the first, the movement soon grew disenchanted with Mr. Begin's stance. Though far more amenable than its predecessor, the Likud Government, they felt, moved too slowly in approving settlements and too hesitantly in providing the necessary supplies and subsidies. The cabinet was less accessible than had been anticipated, and the confusing diplomatic initiatives being undertaken appeared to run counter to Begin's avowed political position.

If these tendencies led to a certain ambivalence toward the new government, the following events spawned outright hostility and shock. In quick succession, President Sadat visited Jerusalem and Mr. Begin flew to Cairo. Israel then signed the Camp David Accords, committed itself to Palestinian autonomy on the conquered territories, and pledged to return the Sinai. The effect was overwhelming for the Gush.[8]

The movement was not alone, however, in its negative assessment of these events. There were many who mistrusted Anwar Sadat, and who chafed under American pressure. These included members of Begin's own party, distinguished academics such as Yuval Neimen, and such Knesset members as Geula Cohen and Moshe Shamir. Together they founded the Tehiya Party, which would become the political successor to the ideology of settlement. The party won three seats in the 1981 election, and it has worked together with others of similar sentiment in the parliament, such as Chaim Druckman, a settlement activist representing the National Religious Party. Tehiya was drawn into the government coalition in the summer of 1982 by Prime Minister Begin.

Perhaps the most important result of their disenchantment with the Begin administration was the realization among Gush activists that, no matter how friendly, the government could not be sufficiently resolute in pursuing an acceptable program of settlement. Consequently, the hope of relinquishing an extralegal program was abandoned; if the government would not take the initiative, the movement would.

By 1978, a sufficient number of settlements had been established for the movement to undertake a major administrative change. Without relinquishing the title Gush Emunim as a catchall, it created Amana — an alliance of settlements with clearly defined relationships and structures for joint action, as well as procedures for the appointment of personnel and the pursuit of common political and social goals. While utilizing Gush offices and serving generally as a front for its activities, Amana has also served as the basis for the Council of Settlements in Judea and Samaria, which includes settlements not formally aligned with Gush Emunim. With the establishment of a political party and an administrative council to further its objectives, the Gush completed its metamorphosis from a small splinter group with some emotional appeal to a legitimate participant in the Israeli political system — and all this within the short space of a decade.[9]

Ideology

The ideology of Gush Emunim derives from several elements that tend to overlap and reinforce each other, and which span the intellectual gamut from sacred to secular. Indeed, it is often this breadth of scope that confounds those who attempt to categorize its thinking simplistically or unidimensionally. It is this same breadth which has allowed it to appeal to a large segment of the Israeli population, despite profound religious, social, political, cultural, and generational cleavages. Nevertheless, in comparing its constellation of values, the religio-mystical elements clearly take precedence over all others in the thinking of its leadership.

There are few distinctions between theory and action in Gush thinking. The concept of West Bank settlement, which informs much of the world view held by adherents, is not merely an ideal to be justified and defended; it is rather the course of action undertaken by most of its leaders and activists and planned by its youth cadres and overseas supporters. Though some of the reasoning may be romantic, the resultant concerns — for schools, roads, housing, and employment — are mundane. This is as it must be for a group that prides itself on "creating facts."[10]

Strategic Considerations

Matters of defense strategy and military security are important props to the ideological position of Gush Emunim; nevertheless, they are essentially peripheral to its ideology. The Jewish claim to Judea and Samaria runs far deeper than the needs of military tacticians, and cannot be erased by international guarantees, hollow promises, or foreign peace-keeping missions. Still, the argument of the military necessity of adequate defense has its value, if only in attracting those who have little taste for the more ephemeral elements of the ideology. (The defense argument is also useful in representing the movement overseas.)

Its essence is quite simple. Pre-1967 Israel was no more than ten miles wide at its most narrow point. It was constantly subject to terrorist infiltration, and its major population centers were within hailing distance of advancing enemy forces. The territories provide Israel with sorely needed strategic depth for the first time in history. A familiarity with the topography and geography of the region lends credence to this argument, the Gush claims. The very "spine" of the region is a mountain range running through the territories from Jenin in northern Samaria to Hebron in southern Judea. One who holds a position on these hills commands easy access to Tel Aviv and the coastal plain in one direction and Jerusalem in the other.

The upshot of the argument, however, is not merely the need to hold these territories, but to populate them with civilian settlements that might also serve as first lines of defense and as front-line lookouts. Those familiar with the history of Jewish settlement in Palestine can attest to the rich precedent of such use for civilian outposts. In this regard, Gush Emunim sees itself as performing an important security function. That individual military leaders have concurred only strengthens their position.[11]

Political Considerations

Like strategic issues, the political assessments influencing the thinking of Gush Emunim fly in the face of the irrational, romantic image by which they are generally portrayed, and, like these strategic issues, political assessments are not central to Gush ideology. Nevertheless, they play an important role in justifying and explaining the movement's position to those on the outside. In the broadest sense, these political evaluations reflect a jaundiced view of the Arab world. For example, the primary raison d'etre for the Arab States, according to Rabbi Moshe Levinger, a leading Gush spokesman and activist, is to destroy the state of Israel in its entirety. The call for a Palestinian national entity on the West Bank is merely a step, an opening gambit, in a game whose ultimate objective is to create an Arab state where Israel presently stands. To think otherwise, Rabbi Levinger argues, is romantic and naive, and in this sense the settlers of Gush Emunim are the true realists.[12]

Peace initiatives must be viewed as cynical and manipulative. Since Arab leaders have learned that they will not win on the battlefield, it is their hope to regain by the pen what they have lost by the sword. Can decades of enmity and animosity be brushed aside by kind words and solemn assurances? Or might even the most dramatic of moves, Gush Emunim suggests, be little more than another ploy? And even if negotiation offers are sincere, what is the value of assurances vulnerable to eradication by a well-aimed assassin's bullet? Those who view the peace process from a liberal-Western stance are simply ignorant of political history in the Middle East, where violence and religious fundamentalism can negate parliamentary process. The assassination that followed the peace initiatives undertaken by Anwar Sadat has buttressed this view. Once more, the Gush hopes to portray itself as the realist.

Consequently, Gush Emunim rejects the Camp David Accords as a political sham in which the state of Israel was required to make concrete concessions in return for hollow promises. It opposed the dismantling of Yamit, the major town in the Sinai, as well as the return of that territory. It further pledged to reject any territorial compromise on the West Bank in the most militant manner. Broad civilian settlement in the region is considered to be the best prevention of such an eventuality.

Finally, the settlement of Judea and Samaria has important sociopolitical value. The development of independent political structures by West Bank Arabs since 1967 has been an unfortunate consequence of the government's hesitation to settle the area. Isolation from the Israeli civilian population has contributed to the exaggerated influence of the PLO, and the general fear expressed by potentially moderate leaders. If any peaceful settlement is to emerge, it will be necessary to reduce the physical isolation between Arabs and Israelis. The movement maintains that its settlers are on the forefront, forging realistic day-to-day relations in the very heart of the conflict. New Israeli homes are being built by Arab contractors and laborers, and the development of new settlements is helping to create jobs and markets for local goods and services.

In this regard, the movement attempts to portray itself in humanistic terms hearkening back to the binationalism of Socialist Zionist thinking of the thirties and forties. Of course, there is never the least doubt that the social and political goal of this economic activity is far more clearly the permanent integration of the region into the general fabric of Israeli life.[13]

The Lessons of Jewish History

As one moves from these more contemporary questions to those of history, nationalism, and religion, one moves also from concerns peripheral to the movement toward those more central to its ideology. In the final analysis, strategic considerations can be debated and mitigated without weakening the legitimacy of the Jewish claim to the area. Just as Haifa and Tel Aviv are legitimately Israeli by historical and national right irrespective of strategic considerations, so too does the Jewish claim to Judea and Samaria transcend its importance as a security link. Indeed, drawing from biblical history, the movement argues that the legitimacy of the latter might be even more defensible. From a craggy hilltop outside of Elon Moreh, for example, the visitor is given a cursory tour of the terrain, complete with scriptural commentary. There stands Shechem, now the Arab city of Nablus, where Genesis records Jacob's wanderings and the violation of his daughter Dinah. There are the twin peaks of Mount Eval and Mount Gerizim, where Deuteronomy prescribes the blessings and admonitions to be meted out to the people of Israel by their tribal leaders.

A similar view is available to one standing outside of Kiryat Arba to the South. From here it is but a brief walk to the burial places of Abraham, Isaac, and Jacob and their wives, and only a short ride northward to the tomb of Rachel. Could the Gush ask Jewish settlers to forego their claim to this territory or to forget their claim merely because of strategic assurances and international border patrols?

Lessons of recent history inform the thinking of Gush members and leave them with a sense of isolation and a profound need for self-sufficient independence. The events of Jewish history—particularly, the evidence of the Holocaust—have taught that allies and friends among the world's well-meaning nations are neither to be trusted nor relied upon for security. The peoples of the world have learned how to mourn for Jews, it is claimed, but not yet how to live with them. In the final analysis, the Jewish people and their vanguard in the state of Israel must rely upon their own initiative and the benevolence of their Lord.

Their sense of history leads the Gush to claim that the call for settlement is not merely a demand to populate areas of ancient Jewish settlement. On the contrary, many West Bank sites were the homes of Jewish populations in the very recent past. Some were the result of Zionist settlement during the last century, while others, hundreds of years old, were brutally uprooted during Arab nationalist disturbances of the twenties and thirties. Much is made, for example, of the old Jewish Quarter in Hebron, where residents were massacred in 1929. In this sense, the movement argues, its call is not so much to settlement as to return.[14]

Zionism-Nationalism

At the very core of its ideology, the movement leans upon the twin pillars of Zionism and Jewish religious tradition. It is devoid of the socialism that marked the thinking of many Zionist founders, but displays a prominent strain of militant nationalism. Its religious bent emphasizes the mystical link between the Jew and his land, as well as the fulfillment of the messianic prophesies. In this regard, the movement looks toward the work of the late chief rabbi Abraham Kook for its inspiration—a point to be discussed below.

The two elements of Zionism and Jewish religious traditions, though distinct, are not always easily separable or distinguishable. For purposes of analysis, Zionism here will include those more secular aspects of the movement's ideology that closely adhere to Jewish nationalist sentiment of the past century. The religious elements of its ideology, covered in the section to follow, will include the theological and mystical foundations upon which much of its thinking is based. (Conceptual overlap must be expected.)

In many respects, Gush Emunim seeks to portray itself as well within the traditional Zionist mainstream. Its members aspire to be like the Zionist pioneers of the turn of the century—that is, founders and builders of a renewed Jewish presence in the Middle East on the back of a messianic dream. They seek to define their settlements as the Tel Avivs and Beershebas of the eighties, and thus cloak themselves with the mantle of Zionism. The great social experiment that was the Jewish renaissance in Palestine has soured, they claim. Israeli life has turned from its idealistic beginnings toward a crass materialism presided over by an overextended bureaucracy lacking in resolve. There is no longer the vision of national renewal for which the state was created, and for which it should ever be an instrument.[15]

The most obvious symptom of this psychosocial malaise is the trend of outward migration that has marked Israeli society for at least a decade; it is estimated that some 300,000 Israelis presently reside in North America, for example. Parallel to this is the movement of those newly liberated Soviet Jews who forego the opportunity to settle in the ancestral homeland, though ostensibly it was for this purpose that they were granted exit visas by the USSR. The Gush views these developments with shock and alarm, and calls for a spirit of self-sacrifice to overcome these difficulties whose roots lie in the priority of the purely personal over that which is national. All too often, Jewish history and Zionist thinking have been taken lightly. The approach of recent governments has been pragmatic and devoid of ideological content. The fact that Zionist thinking appears radical and bizarre today is seen as evidence of the distance traversed by modern Israeli society from its original mooring.

This thinking has also led the movement to articulate a forceful position toward those Arabs who will necessarily be their neighbors. By history, natural right, and ultimately divine decree, the land of Israel belongs to the people of Israel, collectively. Sections of land may belong to individuals, but the land in its entirety must ever belong to the Jewish Folk. Consequently,

Arab residents can have no national rights or aspirations. They are welcome to live as a minority community, with all the respect and tolerance that ethics and justice demand, subject to their peaceful acceptance of Zionist primacy. However, "there is no such a thing as Arab territory in the Land of Israel."[16]

Finally, the movement views the structures of the present Israeli political system as legitimate and acceptable in themselves. Based on the analysis of others as well as on my own original qualitative research, the revolutionary imperative assigned to the Gush by some is not apparent.[17] On the contrary, leaders of the movement extend respect and honor to elected and appointed units of government and the military. Its members have served with distinction in Israel's army and have helped integrate the Gush into the religious lives of army personnel by popularizing a unique program of higher Jewish study and military service.[18]

The key appears to be the almost gnostic assessment of these institutions of state as means toward, rather than ends of, the higher Zionist goal: Jewish settlement and renewal. Opposition to legal remedy and the democratic process for conflict resolution is not generally encouraged. However, if the issue revolves about some aspect of settlement and the retention of territory, then such opposition becomes obligatory. Simply stated, democracy must be upheld so long as it operates within a Zionist framework. When, in the movement's evaluation, the two clash, then Zionism and the pioneering spirit must prevail. Action on behalf of Zionism may not be legal in the most formal and transitory sense; it is quite legitimate, however, in the ultimate and universal sense. Here Gush Emunim follows the rich heritage of civil disobedience that has marked protest movements and many organized interests of the recent past throughout the Western world.

Religious Imperatives

Religious aspects of the movement's ideology are directly derived from the thinking of Israel's first chief rabbi, Abraham I. Kook (as interpreted by his son, Rabbi Zvi Yehuda Kook). The latter, until his recent death, was headmaster of the religious academy that bore his father's name, and wherein most of the leaders and directors of Gush Emunim were trained. In every sense, Rabbi Abraham Kook was an original thinker, unique among his intellectual and religious peers. Both the religious breadth and the mystical nationalism expressed by him have left their mark upon the movement.[19]

Rabbi Kook assigned a sacred status to the state of Israel. He understood the return of the Jew to his land to be the beginning of the process of Redemption that would ultimately usher in the long-awaited messianic era. All who helped in furthering this process, no matter what their religious leanings or personal beliefs, were seen as performing a holy mission equal to the fulfillment of other religious precepts.

Gush Emunim has incorporated this perspective in evaluating more contemporary events; in particular, the War of 1967 was imbued with this spiritual aura. In a matter of days, against overwhelming odds and with little support from abroad, Israel regained major sites of religious and biblical significance. The reunification of Jerusalem was taken to symbolize the rejoining of the People with its heritage and birthright. To return any of this land would therefore be heretical. In addition, the spirit of religious tolerance in pursuit of the cause has allowed the movement to seek and gain supporters and followers outside of its immediate community. The issue is the Land of Israel and the process of Redemption. One's dietary practices or Sabbath observance, by contrast, are relatively unimportant. In the context of Israeli politics, this tolerance is both novel and explosive.

Religious ideals are strengthened by a mystical significance attributed to the land itself. In the words of one activist, "Every piece of our land is holy — a present from God." Yet its holiness is not only the result of divine largesse. It has also been sanctified by Jewish blood shed in its defense and by Jewish blood spilled during the millennial Diaspora. It is unthinkable that a Jewish authority should return the very heartland of Israel's national and religious heritage.

The singular conclusion and course of action demanded by such thinking is *hitnahalut*. Almost untranslatable, *hitnahalut* is a combination of settlement ideology and messianism requiring that Jews return to the land of their heritage out of religious obligation and cultural imperatives. This is no "right" they argue, to be bartered or forfeited; it is prerequisite to the Redemption. Thus, in the words of Rabbi Kook the Younger, redemption will be manifest by "the resettlement in the Land and the revival of Israel in it." In contemporary terms, however, the objective is directed specifically toward the lands of Judea and Samaria.[20]

The Impact of Gush Emunim

According to a typical definition, a group exerts political influence through its ability to move its targets to act on its behalf because they believe that they will suffer some deprivation or, what amounts to the same thing, fail to gain some reward. Consequently, to say that a group has political influence implies that (1) it has elicited a particular response from its target, usually, though not exclusively, in the form of some aspect of public policy; (2) the response would not have been undertaken by the target save for the influence of the group; and (3) the motivation for the response was the fear of reprisal in some form on the part of the group.[21]

The relationship between the group and its target is not necessarily a direct one, other theorists have pointed out. This is particularly the case with protest groups of limited political and social resources. Such groups may not have the wherewithal to confront government institutions directly, for example, and may therefore resort to extralegal means of high visibility to activate interested third parties on their behalf. Thus, a sit-in or rally would be of little direct consequence to an executive agency; however, the intercession of the media and the sympathetic demands of other constituents can serve as an important source of pressure to move otherwise indifferent policymakers and their staffs. Of course, such a strategy is not exclusive to protest movements or groups of limited resources.[22]

Based on such a definition, the difficulty of qualitatively assessing the impact of Gush Emunim upon the Israeli political system is apparent. It is by no means easy to tell which aspects of public policy may be attributed to its exclusive influences, upon which aspects it exerted partial influence (and if so, how much), and which would have been undertaken anyway. Further, to the extent that the given responses are attributable to the actions of the movement, it is not altogether clear whether these resulted from fear of reprisal or from latent sympathy and support from within the government itself. Finally, any assessment of the movement's impact would have to concern itself not only with its direct confrontation with government agencies but also with its appeal to such intermediary groups as the NRP, the religious public in Israel, and the spectrum of Israel's supporters abroad, particularly in the United States.

One further caveat needs yet to be added. Gush Emunim has had a profound influence upon the Israeli political system since its inception only a few years ago. As early as 1977, one Israeli analyst was moved to suggest: "Over the last three years no settlement with the Arabs could be developed without considering the possible reaction of Gush Emunim and its supporters."[23] Nevertheless, to limit the analysis purely to the specifics of government policy undertaken in response to Gush action or the intervention of its sympathizers elsewhere would be to miss a significant part of its impact. Gush Emunim has fundamentally influenced the fabric of Israeli society in ways that transcend the political marketplace and speak to the heart of Israeli life. In addition, its influence has been felt within Jewish and Zionist circles outside of Israel, and has gained visibility in the international media. It can no longer be seen as a fringe element in a political spectrum known for its factionalism.[24]

Ideological Impact

As important as is its impact on government policy, the main influence of Gush Emunim is upon the Israeli political ideology, Zionism. In many ways, its thinking has opened a national debate over issues long dormant. Indeed, its influence on Zionism has allowed the movement to reach beyond its immediate constituency and appeal for secular support in a way that other religious movements and organizations have not.

Zionism was the great state-building ideology of Jewish nationalism throughout the last century. Born in the hamlets of Eastern Europe, it spread to the West, where it served as an alternative to the millennial Diaspora to which Jewish life had accommodated itself. Its vitality was infused by pogroms and discrimination, and its agenda became a frantic appeal during the course of the Holocaust. Zionist leaders were generally secular, and their tactics and approach paralleled those of other budding nationalists demanding recognition. Yet in many ways, Zionism stemmed from traditional Jewish beliefs harkening back to the words of ancient prophets and the dreams of a messianic age. The very enterprise of Jewish national renewal had a biblical ring. The foundation of the state of Israel in the wake of the destruction of Europe's Jewish communities appeared to lend credence to this mystical aspect of the movement and to serve as fulfillment of its mission.

With the formation of the state, however, Zionism faced a dilemma. Its mission fulfilled, should it seek some other charge or, rather, should it simply recede? In fact, it did both. The movement, particularly through its organizational arm, the Jewish Agency, sought to focus its attention on the immigration of Jews throughout the world to the ancestral homeland. In part, the responsibility was thrust upon the Zionists by the forcible emigration of hundreds of thousands of Jews from the Middle East and North Africa during the first decade of Israel's existence. However, aside from these involuntary migrants, the idea of relocating in Israel was not generally appealing to Jews elsewhere — particularly those who resided in the West. In addition, the self-sacrificing and pioneering spirit of Zionism, which had been a hallmark during the prestate period, waned as Israel moved from its charismatic beginnings toward the establishment of rational-bureaucratic processes (to borrow Weberian terminology). The new generation of Israelis had little taste for ideology, but welcomed rather what one analyst has called the "routinization" of their lives.[25]

Many of Israel's leaders bemoaned this tendency. It was particularly troublesome to the Labor coalition, which had led Israel's government for its first three decades. This new nonideological generation had been educated in institutions created under Labor administration. For a party tracing its beginnings to the *kibbutzim* and worker's movement that helped found the State, the loss was quite disturbing. Nevertheless, little was done to overcome this malaise.

Gush Emunim has made its primary ideological impact in this context. Emerging from families of nationalist sentiment but of traditional religious observance, this new generation was far less influenced by the process of routinization mentioned above. They found little difficulty in applying religious dicta to political and national issues—a tendency always present in religious-Zionist thought, but less emphasized by their elders in return for coalition partnership. The sense of mission that may have dissipated in others with the founding of the state could not have been lost to those who later formed the Gush, for in their minds the ultimate mission—the messianic redemption—had not yet been accomplished.[26]

Yet, unlike other religious movements in Israel, the Gush had made virtually no demands regarding personal religious belief or practice. To the Gush, the issue was the fulfillment of Israel's national destiny and the security of its borders. Following the trail blazed by its spiritual mentors, any who subscribed to the cause were seen as fulfilling God's plan. A willingness to sacrifice, to settle the land, and to support those who do so was all that was necessary.

The call to pioneering settlement was not lost on other, less theological elements of the Israeli political and social spectrum. Members of the Labor Coalition, kibbutz leaders, right-wing Revisionists, and others found common ground with the Gush from the very start and expressed admiration for its activities.[27] Indeed, the support of official kibbutz organizations for the Gush was a point of considerable embarrassment to the Labor government between 1974 and 1977. The Ein Vered Circle, in which leading figures of the labor movement pledged their support and willingness to work for the Gush, institutionalized this ability to transcend the erstwhile barriers to secular-religious collaboration—a phenomenon unique in Israeli life. With the conquests of 1967, Gush Emunim reopened an ideological debate that had never been adequately resolved. The issue of settlement in Judea and Samaria has encouraged the discussion of Zionist goals and the proper attitude toward the Arab resident there. It has paved the way for a discussion of the role of religious belief in responding to these issues, and it has allowed for a renewal of those religious tendencies inherent in Zionist thinking from the first, despite its secular leadership.[28]

Finally—and paramountly in the context of this debate—Gush Emunim has been part of the socio-ideological backdrop within which a movement has developed to oppose its thinking. Peace Now calls for territorial compromise in return for security and "good neighborly relations" with the Arab world. It demands that the Israeli government be guided by security considerations only: "Historical and religious claims . . . must be denied." This is not to suggest that Peace Now is a direct result of the formation of Gush Emunim. It is to say, however, that much of the thinking of the former is overtly or covertly directed toward the activities of the latter. It is "the Government of Israel today which we see as legitimizing the actions of Gush Emunim," Peace Now declares. In sum, its creation is a manifestation of the intellectual and ideological impact of Gush Emunim.[29]

Social Influence

In addition to its ideological impact, Gush Emunim has also contributed to several forms of social change within Israeli life. Indeed, it is at times difficult to differentiate between that which is ideological and that which is social among its activities. This is perhaps a natural phenomenon in a movement whose ideology is action-oriented and whose leaders maintain their status through participation in the very programs of settlement that they advocate. However, some of these social effects have transcended the context from which they were spawned. One is the emergence of the knitted skullcap as a symbolic force in Israeli life. This small hat worn by members of Gush Emunim and others of similar life-style is meant to differentiate wearers from both the secular Israelis (whose heads are bare) and from the more traditionally Orthodox who generally wear black skullcaps or fur hats. Symbolically, the knitted skullcap has come to represent the activist and nationalist youth of Israel today. It has come to mean a willingness to sacrifice and a desire to live a life of uncompromising nationalist and religious values. The media has popularized the image by displaying such young men in uniform at prayer near their tanks, or holding religious study sessions at the front line.

The social image of the scholar-warrior has also been enhanced by the popularization of a program of study and military service. Yeshivat Hesder allows a recruit to spread his three years of conscription over six years, alternating between a semester of study at a religious academy and a semester in uniform. As noted above, Gush Emunim has encouraged participation in these and other institutions of government and state. In this sense, it attempts to project itself as merely the logical continuation of traditional Israeli life and the best of its contemporary manifestations.[30] In addition, the Gush has moved toward bridging the practical gap that exists between the religious and secular within Israeli society. Several of its new settlements are "mixed," including families of a variety of religious backgrounds and belief, thus demonstrating that the overriding demands of the cause can aid in overcoming the petty squabbling often characterizing such relationships in the cities.

These new settlements have also been portrayed as an excellent setting for new arrivals to Israel, particularly those from the West. The latter have had notable difficulty adjusting to life in Israel, given the alleged anonymity of big-city life, the impersonality of its bureaucratic structures, and the lack of community within its neighborhoods. The settlements are claimed to be most amenable to newcomers in that they are small and personal, provide a sense of belonging and equality in communal decision-making, and offer a respite from the noise and pollution of the cities. Indeed, Gush Emunim settlements have been strikingly successful in attracting new immigrants, and Americans appear to be disproportionately distributed among them. Americans have been attracted by the very nature of pioneerism and its ideology, some suggest. Apparently, one who emigrates to Israel from the West expects his standard of living to fall, and is often willing to make the trade in return for the spiritual gain which may have inspired the move. While such devotion may be lacking elsewhere in Israel, it is abundant in Gush Emunim settlements.[31]

The movement has sensed this impact and has responded in kind. Gush Emunim has undertaken a variety of missions abroad, both for purposes of solicitation of funds and for formation of seed groups. These latter are composed of individuals who declare their interest in moving to Israel and settling in an existing unit or helping to found a new one. Many recruits for Gush Emunim settlements have come to the movement in this manner.

Gush Emunim has left yet another imprint on the sociopolitical landscape in the form of internal government. One of its criticisms of Zionist activities concerns the latter's alleged preoccupation with social experimentation over basic settlement. While the first kibbutzim were formed with such aims, these kibbutzim were often too much socialist and too little Zionist, Gush argues.[32] And such enterprises likely would not succeed today. A large proportion of the religious youth who are the movement's natural constituency in Israel have little grounding in socialist theory and little taste for communal dining halls or child-rearing experimentation. Many are university graduates with professional aspirations that require commuting to the big cities according to their own schedules in their own vehicles—something impossible in a traditional kibbutz.

The issue is even more clearly evident when considering those who are likely recruits for settlement from abroad. Particularly among the Americans and other Westerners, the habit of owning one's own home and leading a private life is ingrained and nearly universal. While settlement on the West Bank may be appealing to them, social experimentation or corporatism would be unnecessary and discouraging. Consequently, Gush Emunim has introduced an internal structure elsewhere familiar but rather unique in Israel: the *yishuv kehilati* (community settlement). Roughly equivalent to a close-knit suburban community, such units allow each resident to live in his own house or apartment, work when and where he chooses, and generally carry out his personal affairs in most any manner he sees fit. For purposes of communal need, decisions are made by representative council. These elected and appointed units make decisions regarding cultural programs, education and child care needs, security, and the like. These settlements have taken the appearance of bedroom communities linked in a surburban ring around the large cities. Internally, there are frequent disparities of living arrangements and affluence, though only rarely of such dimension as to cause open conflict.[33]

Gush Emunim has helped influence the manner in which many Israelis perceive the conquered territories. As noted, to the movement these are not Arab lands, but rather an integral part of Israeli society and Jewish life. In projecting to other, less ideologically inclined Jews, however, the movement has portrayed the area as an attractive one for those seeking to improve the quality of their lives. Utilizing the very suburban attractions that appealed to urban dwellers in the United States after World War II, the movement offers residence in Judea and Samaria not so much as a political statement but rather as an alternative for those who live and work in the cities. This image, while controversial within the movement itself, has been met by a parallel government program of residential construction in the territories, to be discussed below.

Religious Contributions

If we differentiate religious from social and ideological factors for analytical purposes, we can note the important impact of Gush Emunim upon Jewish life in Israel. This impact can best be felt in the religious and theological thinking emerging in response. It can also be seen in more tangible changes that have occurred both within religious institutions and within Israel's politically sensitive religious establishments. In addition, its impact has not been limited to Israeli domestic life. Sharp response, both positive and negative, has been elicited from religious and social organizations abroad.

For the first two decades of the state's existence, the NRP concentrated its primary efforts on bringing various aspects of Israeli life under religious control. On matters of foreign policy, security, economics, and so forth, the Party was largely docile, following the lead of its senior cabinet partner, the Labor Coalition; little was done to submit such matters to comprehensive religious evaluation. The emergence of the party's new, more hawkish generation has necessitated important changes in that stance, however. Following the lead of Rabbi Kook, its spiritual mentor, the NRP has demanded precisely such a comprehensive religious assessment. Religious leaders are now expected to have serious opinions regarding the legitimacy of Jewish claims to the territories, the rights of non-Jews in a Jewish State, and the circumstances by which territory may or may not be relinquished.[34] The movement has not only prodded religious leaders to assume positions on matters both political and strategic, but has also insisted that such issues be grounded in classical Jewish sources. This demand requires an assessment of contemporary political issues in terms of traditional Jewish lore. It asks for an examination of the status of conquered territory in light of talmudic writ and medieval Jewish authority.

Jewish sources are replete with systematic analyses of essentially political and international issues written at a time when such discussion was largely moot. Further, the religious-Zionist movement has utilized such material from its inception. To Gush Emunim can be attributed a renewal of such intellectual activity, its popularization within the religious and educational establishment, and its application to the very specific and immediate issues surrounding the conquered territories and their settlement. And the result of such religious analysis has not always been a happy one for the Gush. Several leading Israeli religious thinkers have sharply criticized the movement and specifics of its program in light of classical Jewish sources. These have been joined by counterparts elsewhere, who, from positions of religious authority, question both the motives and the actions of the movement. In addition, a small but significant group of religious reservists have banded together under the banner Netivot Shalom (Pathways to Peace) in the wake of the 1982 Lebanese campaign and the massacres in the Sabra and Shatila refugee camps. This group has raised serious ethical concerns about the nature of a Jewish invasion force and its responsibilities as an occupying power.[35]

The movement has also influenced the Israeli religious establishment. Much of the criticism leveled at secular Zionism for its routinization, loss of charismatic appeal, and lack of purpose has also been directed at organized Judaism in Israel. Leaders of the NRP and its religious functionaries have been accused of an overwillingness to compromise in the name of political gain, status, and prestige. Corruption, patronage, and indifference have allegedly characterized the operations of both the party and the agencies under its control. The institutionalization of religion has left it devoid of personal and spiritual content, it is claimed, and therefore lacking in appeal to the new Israeli generation. Similarly, the NRP and its educational and cultural arms have frequently been under attack from the religious right for their willingness to compromise with secular authority and their supposed laxity with specifics of religious life. Though no less institutionalized and politically active, this sector of the religious public in Israel has been vociferous in its attacks, and has created a sense of insecurity regarding the legitimacy of more liberal religious beliefs and practices.

The thinking of Gush Emunim as well as its activities have served to revitalize religious belief among the children of the old guard within the NRP, and has offered a response to critics from the religious right. In contrast to the alleged routinization and impersonality of religious belief, it offers an activist and emotional program with immediate potential for results; in contrast to the institutionalization and compromise of organizational politics, it offers a loose and flexible social structure within the context of uncompromising principles; and finally, in contrast to the mechanics of religious practice, it offers one primary precept: settlement. When reinforced by nationalist and strategic considerations, the combination is formidable.

The movement faces the religious right with a sense of single-minded security. In demanding that religious thinkers apply Jewish law to issues of foreign policy, the Gush goes far beyond the theology of its attackers. In fulfilling the alleged religious requirements of settlement, it transcends their level of ritual practice. Once again, the combination is most appealing.[36]

This influence has been felt in practical terms as well. The NRP has moved progressively to the political right, and has undertaken increasingly militant positions regarding the status of the territories and the Palestinian issue. It has incorporated leading members of Gush Emunim and its supporters within its parliamentary delegation. One such, Yehuda Ben-Meir, served as deputy foreign minister, while a second, Rabbi Chaim Drukman, held the second position on its electoral list.

Finally, the Gush has utilized this spiritual appeal to gain supporters and recruits from abroad. Working in collaboration with American Jewish institutions, for example, summer tours have been arranged, speakers and lecture programs have been sponsored, and an experiment in settlement for American families has been undertaken. Of course, not all Jewish organizations have been receptive to the call. Several have attacked the Gush on political and historical grounds, and have objected to the use of religious symbolism as a mask for a militant foreign policy.

Political Impact

Much of what has been discussed thus far has important political overtones. Consequently, some overlap is to be expected here and in the unit to follow. The intent is to deal with those aspects of Gush influence most directly related to the secular electoral and parliamentary systems.

Most obvious is the rise in visibility of the opposition to territorial compromise and the creation of a political constituency for West Bank settlement. Until the advent and popularity of Gush Emunim, the conquered territories were viewed as bargaining chips to entice the Arab world into negotiation. Indeed, the late President Sadat's desire to regain the Sinai was undoubtedly an impetus for his peace initiatives and served as a model for this attitude. Gush Emunim has successfully competed with this reasoning. In particular, it has found ready friends among cabinet members and military officials, who fight its battles at the very center of government.

In this regard, some speculation about the direction of its influence may be in order. The administration may have utilized the presence of the movement to encourage settlement or land claims not so easily undertaken by the Government on its own. By winking at Gush activities, the administration may move toward territorial goals without direct involvement. Further, the presence of such a vociferous force on the political fringe may help the government slow negotiations for Palestinian autonomy or other diplomatic concessions. By claiming that its leverage is limited because of the support the Gush can muster, the Israeli government has a ready excuse for avoiding what it may have been hesitant to do in any case. These circumstances generally suit Gush Emunim, and it is prepared to be "used" in this regard. Its influence is thus reciprocal.

Aside from raising the visibility of the territorial issue, the movement has created a broad though by no means uncontested constituency for settlement. On a variety of occasions, for example, international attempts have been made to label its settlements illegal. However, the movement has capitalized on these attempts. No matter what their position on the wisdom of settlement, few Israelis can accept the idea that it is illegal for a Jew to reside anywhere he chooses, most especially on land with historic Jewish links. Thus, strategy has been traded for legitimacy.[37] Recognizing that the territories will be difficult to concede if they are well-populated by Israelis, the movement has undertaken to "create facts" in the region. There are now some 60,000 Israelis resident in Judea and Samaria in more than 100 settlements, Gush proudly proclaims. Many no longer live in tents or mobile homes, but have built permanent single-family units or moved into large apartment complexes. Their message is clear: populating the area will soon make territorial negotiation a moot issue.

In yet another vein, the movement has successfully tapped an element of support from a large constituency that would never consider settlement itself but is prepared to use the influence of both its numbers and position in support of the cause. The Gush has been characterized as the radical tip of a large and powerful iceberg, most of whose substantial base is below the surface of active politics but well-connected to its more visible apex. For this reason, the government cannot utilize sustained force in opposing the movement for fear of activating its supporters and forcing them to emerge from beneath the political surface. The iceberg image goes far in illustrating the nature of the relationship between the several Israeli administrations and support in the electorate at large.[38]

In organizational terms, Gush Emunim has exerted influence on the structure of Israeli politics and administration through its two new creations. The first, Amana, is essentially an administrative unit created to coordinate the activities of the various settlements and develop plans for the location and foundation of new ones. Through Amana, the movement speaks to the myriad of bureaucratic and quasi-governmental institutions comprising the immigration, settlement, interior, and housing agencies in Israel. Such a structure can represent the movement to the government without impinging on the freedom and flexibility necessary for the brand of politics associated with its parent body.

The more interesting and instructive incarnation is a new political party formed in 1980. Tehiya is an alliance between Gush Emunim and other, more secular, right-wing, and nationalist elements, many of whose members broke with the Begin government after Camp David. Tehiya stood for elections in 1981 and gained only three seats, one of which is held by Gush Emunim leader Hanan Porat. (It extended its support to five seats under a different name in 1984.) The initial lack of success of this electoral list, despite the popularity of the movement and its ideology, deserves some comment. Partisan ties run deep in Israel: most voters retain their political affiliations over time and pass them along to their children. Aside from political ideology and policy stance, the parties provide numerous social and welfare benefits, pension programs, and the like; these benefits tend to shore up voter loyalty (as does the threat of their loss). For Tehiya to expect that large numbers of voters would spring to answer its essentially ideological call was ill-advised and a bit naive; even its supporters generally returned to their electoral moorings within the Likud Bloc or the NRP. In addition, Gush Emunim support is issue-oriented and submerged within the general electorate. Support of Gush Emunim was generally insufficient to draw the voter to new candidates and an untried party list created but a year before the elections, especially in the face of the electoral appeal of Menachim Begin, the incumbent. Further, the decision to present an electoral list in 1981 was by no means a unanimous one within Gush Emunim; an important element of its appeal was based upon a claim to nonpartisanship. Its very call for a spiritual and nationalist revival was based upon a claim to organizational purity impugned by electoral participation. The move to create a party was seen as motivated as much from a desire for personal gain as from the best interests of the movement.

Finally, it was argued that the ability of the movement to appeal to a broad-based constituency stemmed from the fact that no deeper or more permanent demands would be made upon the supporter. The creation of a party and all that it implied might well frighten those who could offer only temporary allegiance, since it smacked of the very institutionalization that the movement was created to combat. Nevertheless, over time elections may witness a reversal in these trends.

Influence on Policy

The most visible impact of Gush Emunim was upon the implementation of the policies of the Likud government during the early 1980s. At the same time, this is also the area most difficult to accurately assess. One cannot categorically assume that many of these programs would not have been undertaken otherwise, or that Gush Emunim might only have hastened the inevitable. In addition, the reciprocal nature of its relationship with the government as discussed above also complicates the analysis.

Nevertheless, several aspects of Gush influence stand out. First was the general commitment of the Likud government to populate Judea and Samaria. The government program included massive civilian settlement in large suburban complexes, a multi-million dollar investment to improve the infrastructure surrounding these complexes, the administration of new towns and villages under Israeli law for judicial and budgetary purposes, and the projection of 100,000 Israelis on the West Bank by the end of the decade.[39] The government also undertook to make such residence attractive not only to the ideologically inclined but to the average Israeli as well. Given the existence of triple-digit inflation and the expense of home ownership, securing living quarters has been a traditional difficulty for the young in Israel. Utilizing both its own resources and funding from abroad, the Likud government began a massive subsidy program entitled Build Your Own Home. Through special loans, reduced interest mortgages, and outright grants, Israelis could build spacious single-family units reminiscent of American suburbia, although heretofore virtually unknown in Israel. Though unattached to Gush Emunim, the program is as full an acknowledgment of its demands as could possibly be expected. (It was largely curtailed with the accession to the premiership of Shimon Peres, leader of the Labor Alignment, in 1984.)

During the summer of 1982, Tehiya was included in the Begin coalition. Its leading member, Yuval Neiman, was named minister of science and technology; though not a Gush member, Neiman reflected its ideology clearly and was fully aware of his mandate. In addition, Gush Emunim was included in new programs designed to promote immigration, particularly from the West. Its representatives travel to Jewish communities abroad under the auspices of the Jewish Agency to meet with prospective immigrants, arrange pilot trips and summer programs, and generally publicize their religious/nationalist ideology. By all accounts, Gush Emunim has moved from the fringe of Israeli society to its mainstream. Its impact has been felt in support elicited from within the Israeli population, within its government, and abroad. It is also felt in the sharp opposition it has engendered and the controversies it has created.

Much remains yet to be said about Gush Emunim's long-range influence. Further analysis might discuss the future of the movement under an independent Labor government, the future of peace negotiations in the face of mass settlement, and the likelihood of a reverse in the process of settlement (and the fortune of the movement's relationship with the NRP should a new coalition be formed). The impact of those who have settled, their relations with local Arabs, and the generation that they raise might also be of interest. Clearly, these and other issues deserve future consideration.

Notes

1. The ideological and political role of Jewish tradition in Israel has been well covered elsewhere. See, for example, S. Z. Abramov, *Perpetual Dilemma: Jewish Religion in the Jewish State* (Rutherford, N.J.: Fairleigh Dickinson University, 1976); Daniel Elazar and Janet Avoad, "Religion and Politics in Israel: The Interplay of Judaism and Zionism," in Michael Curtis, *Religion and Politics in the Middle East* (New York: A.P.P.M.E., 1982); Emanuel Gutmann, "Religion and its Role in National Integration in Israel," *Middle East Review* (Fall 1979): 31–36; David J. Schnall "Religion, Ideology and Dissent in Contemporary Israeli Politics," *Tradition* (Summer 1979): 13–34; and Zvi Yaron, "Religion in Israel," *American Jewish Yearbook* (1976): 41–90.

2. Unless otherwise noted, the historical overview that follows was culled from Moshe Kohn, *Who's Afraid of Gush Emunim* (Jerusalem: Jerusalem Post, 1976); Zvi Raanan, *Gush Emunim* (Hebrew) (Tel Aviv: Poalim, 1980); Danny Rubinstein, *On the Lord's Side* (Hebrew) (Tel Aviv: Hakibbutz Hameuchad, 1982); Rafael Salasnik, "Gush Emunim: A Study of the Movement, 1974–8" (Senior thesis, Brunel University, October 1978); David Schnall, *Radical Dissent in Contemporary Israeli Politics* (New York: Praeger, 1979); Ehud Shprinzak, "Gush Emunim: The Tip of the Iceberg," *Jerusalem Quarterly* (Fall 1981): 28–47; David Schnall, *Beyond the Green Line* (New York: Praeger, 1984); and David Newman, *The Impact of Gush Emunim* (London: Croom, Helm, 1985).

3. Regarding the Land of Israel Movement, see Rael Jean Isaac, *Israel Divided: Ideological Politics in the Jewish State* (Baltimore: Johns Hopkins University, 1976), ch. 3.

4. Relations between the Gush and the NRP at this point are described in Rubinstein, *Lord's Side*, pp. 28–37, 46–50.

5. See Ehud Shprinzak, "Gush Emunim: The Iceberg Model of Extremist Politics" (Hebrew) (Paper presented to the Davis Institute of International Affairs, 1981), pp. 22–28.

6. On the founding of Kiryat Arba, see Yehuda Litani, "The Story of Kiryat Arba," *New Outlook* (October 1976): 12–14, and Yosef Goell, "Hebron's Faithful," *Jerusalem Post* (27 February 1981). Regarding Elon Moreh, see Yosef Goell, "The View From Jebel Kabir," *Jerusalem Post* (11 April 1980), and Yosef Goell, "Gush Country," *Jerusalem Post* (30 January 1981).

7. On the elections of 1977 and their implications for Gush Emunim, see Schnall, *Radical Dissent*, pp. 207–11.

8. Shprinzak, "Gush Emunim: Tip of the Iceberg," pp. 32–35.

9. On the creation of Tehiya and Amana, see Rubinstein, *Lord's Side*, pp. 152–57.

10. Ibid., pp. 51–57.

11. See, e.g., the quote from Israel defense force chief of staff Raphael Eytan in Mordechai Nisan, "Gush Emunim: A Rational Perspective," *Forum* (Fall 1979): 19.

12. Moshe Levinger et al., "Brief Answers to Timely Questions," *Gush Emunim* (Hebrew) (March 1976): 34.

13. Mordechai Nisan, "Gush Emunim and Israel's National Interest," *Jerusalem Letter: Viewpoints* (January 1980).

14. For a fuller development of these points, see David Schnall, "Strategic Theology," *America* (September 1980): 17–20.

15. Raanan, *Gush Emunim,* pp. 56–60.

16. Personal interview with Rabbi Yochanan Fried, then director of the Overseas Department of Gush Emunim, August 1976.

17. See, e.g., Janet O'Dea, "Gush Emunim: Roots and Ambiguities," *Forum* (Fall 1976): 39–50.

18. Shprinzak, "Gush Emunim: Tip of the Iceberg," p. 39.

19. See, e.g., the interview with Zvi Yaron, an authority on the writings of Rabbi Kook, in Moshe Kohn, "Redemption or Disaster," *Jerusalem Post* (30 July 1976).

20. Zvi Yehuda Kook, "Zionism and Biblical Prophecy," in Yosef Tirosh, ed., *Religious Zionism: An Anthology* (Jerusalem: World Zionist Organization, 1975).

21. Gabriel Almond and Sidney Verba, *The Civic Culture* (Princeton, N.J.: Princeton University, 1963), p. 180.

22. Michael Lipsky, *Protest in City Politics* (Chicago: Rand McNally, 1970), pp. 1–15, 163–205; and Michael Lipsky, "Protest as a Political Resource," *American Political Science Review* (December 1968): 1144–58.

23. Ehud Shprinzak, "Extreme Politics in Israel," *Jerusalem Quarterly* (Fall 1977): 42.

24. In developing the scheme for analyzing the impact of Gush, I have roughly followed a model suggested in T. R. Gurr, "On the Outcome of Violent Conflict," in T. R. Gurr, ed., *Handbook of Political Conflict* (New York: Free Press, 1980), pp. 238–94.

25. This analysis is suggested in Kevin Avruch, "Gush Emunim: Politics, Religion and Ideology in Israel," *Middle East Review* (Winter 1978–79): 28.

26. On the messianic ideal in Gush Emunim, see Raanan, *Gush Emunim,* pp. 60–74.

27. See, e.g., the interviews with kibbutz leaders in Moshe Kohn, "Redemption or Disaster," *Jerusalem Post* (July 26, 1976).

28. For a fair cross-section of this intellectual activity, see recent issues of *Forum,* published by the World Zionist Organization.

29. Janet Aviad, "Peace Now," *Jerusalem Letter: Viewpoints* (January 1980).

30. Rubinstein, *Lord's Side,* pp. 12–17.

31. The analysis was offered by Amiel Ungar of the political science department of Bar-Ilan University. Dr. Ungar is an American immigrant and the official spokesman for Tekoah, a West Bank settlement south of Jerusalem.

32. For an elaboration of this point, see Schnall, *Radical Dissent,* pp. 146–47.

33. On the internal governance of these settlements, see Sholom Reichman et al., *Jewish Non-Agricultural Settlement in Judea and Samaria* (Jerusalem: Hebrew University, 1981).

34. For some of the results of this demand, see Zvi Yehuda Kook, *Discussions of Rabbi Zvi Yehuda* (Hebrew) (Jerusalem: Rabbi Kook Center, 1980); Y. Filber, *Breath to the People on It* (Hebrew) (Jerusalem: Emunim, 1974); and Chaim Drukman, "The Bond Between the People of Israel and the Land of Israel" (Paper presented at the European Religious Youth Conference, April 1976).

35. See, e.g., David Dedein, "Genesis of an Israeli Religious Left," *New Outlook* (January 1976): 39–42; Uriel Tal, "The Nationalism of Gush Emunim in Historical Perspective," *Forum* (Fall/Winter 1979): 11–13; Moshe Kohn, "Orthodox Opponents of Gush Emunim," *Jerusalem Post* (3 August 1976); Uriel Simon, "Spiritual and Political Dangers of Politicized Religion," *New Outlook* (November 1976): 7–11; and Daniel Gavron, "A Fresh Voice," *Jerusalem Post* (15 October 1982).

36. The point is suggested in Lawrence Kaplan, "Education and Ideology in Religious Zionism Today," *Forum* (Fall/Winter 1979): 25–34.

37. The point was made in an interview with Hanan Porat MK (member of the Knesset)—a founder of Gush Emunim.

38. Shprinzak, "Gush Emunim: Tip of the Iceberg," pp. 43–46.

39. For an overview of the new Begin program, see Judy S. Itzkovich, "City on Seven Judean Hills," *Jerusalem Post* (26 September 1982), and Yosef Goell, "Settlement and Suburbia," *Jerusalem Post Magazine* (7 January 1983).

9

Islamic Revival
or Political and Cultural Revolution?

An Iranian Case Study

MARY ELAINE HEGLAND

It would be a serious mistake to imagine that the upsurge in Shiah Muslim religious activity, rhetoric, and interpretation in Iran is a manifestation of increased interest in religion per se.[1] During the years and months preceding the Iranian revolution, Iranians did not turn to religious figures, organizations, language and metaphors as a spiritual haven from alienation, anomie, disorientation, atomization, complications, or the psychological pressures of today's world. On the contrary, in uniting under the leadership of Ayatollah Khomaini and the progressive ideology of Dr. Ali Shariati, Iranians were taking self-assertive, constructive steps forward to deal with the political realities of today's world. As the most feasible and practical ideology and language available, Shiism served as a rallying point around which the Iranian population united to accomplish their political aims of ridding themselves of the shah and of American hegemony in Iran. Shiism provided a framework with which to organize a political interest group. It was all the more effective as a revolutionary ideology and ethos because it does not recognize a distinction between political and religious effort, nor does it regard politics as outside the realm of religious concern: Shiism is a political religion.

Because of political repression, Islam was the only unifying and organizing belief system available to voice the concerns and aims of the politically powerless. Abner Cohen's words concerning "retribalization" can quite appropriately be applied to the role of Shiism in the Iranian revolution:

> "Retribalization" is the socio-cultural manifestation of the formation of new political groupings . . . the outcome, not of conservatism, but of a dynamic socio-cultural change which is brought about by new cleavages and new alignments of power. It is a process by which a group from one ethnic category, whose members are involved in a struggle for power and privilege with members of a group from another ethnic category within the framework of a formal politi-

cal system, manipulate some customs, values, myths, symbols, and ceremonials from their cultural tradition in order to articulate an *informal* political organization which is used as a weapon in that struggle. . . . Ethnicity is thus basically a political . . . phenomenon, and it operates within contemporary political contexts and is not an archaic survival arrangement carried over into the present by conservative people.[2]

In Iran, of course, people did not organize merely to work *"within* the framework" of a political system, but — realizing that they could not hope to have a political voice within the current system — to *overthrow* that political system. Iran's "retribalization" also differed from Cohen's type case in that the aspect of cultural tradition utilized in organizing the informal political organization was religion rather than ethnicity; the competing political groups rallied around differing interpretations of Shiism, rather than differing ethnic identities. In addition, the oppositional organization consisted not only of persons from one religious group (the Shiites); other non-Shiite Iranians also joined the organization, since they shared the same political goals — the removal of the shah and American hegemony in Iran.

Due to the repression of other political organizations and the appeal of progressive Shiah ideology to both Shiites and non-Shiite activists, Iranians found Shiah ideology to be the most effective in organizing for revolution. Ayatollah Khomaini, because of his completely uncompromising stance and his obvious selflessness, was found to be the most effective leader. Thus organized, Iranians traversed a process of revolution, which included a transformation in their attitudes towards themselves, their fellow Iranians, and the Iranian nation. The experience of participating in a revolution coincided with the emergence of a new pride and confidence in themselves and their fellows, and a new spirit of cooperation and willingness to sacrifice personal interests and safety for the good of society.

Most Iranians were Shiites who placed faith and trust in their religion and used the Shiah worldview and ethos in dealing with many aspects of reality.[3] They saw the revolutionary experience and the transformational experience in Islamic terms, and described it to themselves and to others using the language of Shiism. The concerted and effective organizational and informational efforts of members of the Shiah religious hierarchy also contributed to the widespread use of Shiah terminology in discussing the process of revolution. For many Shiites, the revolutionary experience made their religion more immediate and meaningful; for others — non Shiites or less devout Shiites — the political direction advocated by Shiah leaders aroused in them a greater respect for religion and religious figures. Thus, one might say that a resurgence of Islam was apparent in Iran. However, this resurgence of Islamic activity, organization, and language was largely the result of political activity and dissidence, and the coincidence of the political aims of religious leaders with the aims of other Iranians.

This resurgence of Islam was not the result of any "return" to Islam on the part of the population; rather, there was a transformation in Shiism. Only after Shiism changed its message from one of acceptance of the conditions of dependency and inferiority to one of self-sufficiency and personal and national pride and self-confidence were more Iranians drawn to it. The resurgence of Islam in Iran was initiated, not by a return of Muslims to their old religion, but rather by a transformation in the religion that made it possible for the religion to respond to the current needs and concerns of Iranians. Any increase in the religiosity of Shiites was a function of their political participation in the revolution, and continued only as long as did their support for the revolution and the subsequent government.

In arguing that any resurgence of Islam in Iran was due in large part to its role as a cultural instrument in political struggle rather than to any revival of religious sentiment or fervor, I will first discuss a number of indications that the Iranian revolution—that is, the shah-Khomaini struggle—was primarily a political one, although fought in a religious idiom, utilizing religious organization, and bringing with it a resurgence of Shiism parallel to the escalation of struggle. In the second section of the paper, I will trace the process of cultural resistance and revolution centering around Shiism. Material for the article is drawn from eighteen months of research in Iran between June 1978 and December 1979. The research site was the village of "Aliabad," a settlement of some three to four thousand inhabitants located half an hour by bus from the outskirts of Shiraz, capital of the southwestern province of Fars.[4]

Political Aspects of the Iranian Revolution

During the course of the revolution, the language and ethos of Shiism served as a political idiom of protest and revolt. Many indications in Aliabad led to the perception of religion as an aspect of culture used to organize political revolution. The following eight are among these indications.

1. From almost the beginning of my stay in Aliabad—that is, from about the first of September 1978—political conditions and events were much more frequently a topic of conversation than religion. People complained bitterly and at length about the two landlords, the Askari brothers—Seyyid Ibn Ali, who had moved to Shiraz, and Seyyid Yakub, who lived right in the village.

These two men had cheated the villagers out of land during the land reform of the early 1960s, and since then had continued to take over for themselves land belonging to other villagers.[5] With the assistance of gendarmes and other governmental figures, the two brothers had also brutally suppressed revolts of the villagers against them.

The government was also a target of verbal abuse. Villagers faulted the government for backing and keeping in power the two Askari brothers and other members of the village political elite. Villagers also complained about the corruption and complete lack of dedication and concern on the part of officials. One man complained that the *korsi-neshin* ("the people who sit in chairs," or government employees) are the thieves of today: they steal much of the money that comes their way. People were angry at the government because of the 1961 land reform, as a result of which many had lost their land and agriculture had deteriorated markedly. Further, the government didn't help cultivators; the cost of raising wheat was therefore greater than what one got for it at market, villagers complained. Due to this kind of negligence, Iran was increasingly forced to turn to importation of food.

This agricultural policy was purposeful, villagers suspected. The shah planned the decline of Iranian agriculture, some said, in order to provide a market for the crops of his American masters. Thus, the United States government and Americans in general were also the object of adverse political comment. Americans working in Iran received twice the salary of their Iranian counterparts, people complained; they lived in separate compounds and didn't like to mix with the Iranians, whom they considered inferior. Iranians were hurt and insulted that Americans brought by their companies to work in Iran received "hardship" pay during their stay there.

In addition to the bitter attacks against the village political elite, the shah and his government, the United States government, and the perceived collusion between these two governments, during September and October of 1978 I often heard complaints about socioeconomic inequality in Iran. For example, one day I was standing with a man on the common roof between his own courtyard and that of Seyyid Yakub, his cousin. He pointed down into Seyyid Yakub's courtyard, commenting, "One family lives in that clean, tiled courtyard with a big garden full of fruit trees." Then, pointing toward his own courtyard, he said, "Ten families live in that dirty, broken-down courtyard." Another villager informed me that "all of Iran's problems today are because of the differences between the city people and the rural people, between the haves and the have-nots."

Only later did one hear religious idioms used to describe political and economic conditions and what should be done about them. People were aware of and resented disparities in political and economic power, and only later began to use religious language in discussing them. This occurred as individuals were exposed to information networks organized by religious figures who were successful in disseminating the religious idiom. However, people who did not become involved in the revolution did not use religious terminology in complaining about political and economic conditions; for example, the peasants of Aliabad, who did not become active in the revolution, did not use religious idioms.[6]

Even later, when use of the religious idiom became common among many village residents, reactions of anger and horror concerning acts of government violence were expressed first; only later in the conversation would the religious metaphor be applied. In other words, people first reacted to a situation, then later applied the religious label. People were dissatisfied and angry about political and economic conditions. Eventually, in large part because of the successful propagation of the religious idiom by religious networks, people tended more and more to communicate with each other about these events, conditions, and dissatisfactions using the language of religion.[7] For many people, religious metaphor became the means of interpreting political change and struggle, and of assessing what their own stance should be.

2. All of the observable increased religious activity of Aliabad villagers was related to political resistance. Some of the villagers who commuted to Shiraz to work joined religious study groups in that city; men from adjoining shops gathered periodically to study the Quran and discuss religious matters. However, there was also a political cast to these groups, and—as the government became aware of this—the groups were forbidden to meet.

During the last several years, increased attention had been given in Aliabad to the mourning practices commemorating the martyrdom of Imam Hosain, the most important figure in popular Shiism. But such manifestations of increased religiosity and devotion to Imam Hosain were not encouraged by the local political elite—traditionally, the sponsors of commemorative activities. Rather, the heightened mourning activity was brought about by persons opposed both to the central government and to the local political elite. Such members of the political opposition were responsible both for the greater numbers of persons participating in mourning practices and the greater intensity of the mourning symbolized by taking part in the more painful practice of beating the back with chains rather than beating the chest with one's fist.

For several years prior to the revolution, it had been customary for many men who had moved into Shiraz to come back to the village in one large group for the commemoration of Ashura, the anniversary of the martyrdom of Imam Hosain. Among these mourners for Hosain were individuals with a long history of opposition to both the central government and the village political elite. These visitors from the city revived a mourning ritual that had gone out of practice in Aliabad; instead of beating themselves on the chest with their fists during the mourning chants and processions, they beat themselves on the back with chains. The city dwellers were joined in this custom by other villagers who no longer worked in agriculture in the village, but rather commuted to the city to work in factories or at other jobs. As the latter became economically independent of the village landlord, Seyyid Yakub, and of the rest of the village's political elite, they also became politically independent to a great degree, and no longer felt obliged to support Seyyid Yakub. The custom of beating themselves with chains practiced by the city dwellers and the village opposition to Seyyid Yakub was a muted sign of resistance to the village political elite and to the government.

Another aspect of the increase in religious activity was the presence in Aliabad of a *mulla* (preacher) from Qom during three summer months of 1978. He rented a room in the courtyard of the person who had led the village opposition to the landlord. Both the preacher's choice of living accommodations and the fact that the people going to him to study the Quran were all from families connected with the opposition were indications of the preacher's stance of political dissidence. He and his principal associates in the village utilized religious activity and organization in the struggle against the central government. The preacher returned during the fall of 1978, and in his sermons and Quran classes (which I attended) he openly and consistently spoke against the government. He also assisted in organizing such antigovernment activities as the marches in Shiraz and political trips to surrounding villages. He maintained the same role in his sojourns to other towns in the area.

The activities of the preacher in Aliabad as well as the vigorous efforts of religious persons among the migrant poor in Tehran (as studied by Kazemi[8] and Bauer[9]) all appear to be for the promotion of Islam and Muslims against the power of the shah and the central government. The presence of the visiting preacher from Qom is a reminder that Islam was used for political purposes by at least two different types of political interest groups. First, the Shiah hierarchy used their own religious groups and networks to actively promote the political freedom of Shiah religious figures and organizations against the shah's government, which had attempted to break down their power and influence. One means by which the religious figures did this was by mobilizing the population against the shah and his government.

Second, the Iranian population as a whole, including persons professing both greater and less devotion to Shiism, found the ideological and organizational aspects of Shiism useful in their struggle for personal political freedom and expression as well as for their political goals of ridding the country of the shah and American domination. Some of these people were not at all concerned about increasing the political power of the Shiah hierarchy; how-

ever, they took advantage of Shiah figures, ideology, and organizational networks to attain their own political goals. Thus, each of these two political interest groups used the other for its own political purposes.

This was true in the village of Aliabad as elsewhere. The visiting preacher
worked to mobilize the village population in the revolutionary movement
against the shah. On the other hand, the village activists—many of whose
final aims and philosophies did not agree entirely with those of the preacher
or even of Ayatollah Khomaini—took advantage of the organizing activities
of the preacher and worked with him for the purpose of fulfilling their own
aims. But in no case during the months prior to the revolution were the religious activities organized by the preacher or by others without specific political content. Any apparent increase in religious activity or language was related to the growing resistance movement.

3. All of the people involved in the heightened religious activities and in
the revolutionary movement (especially in the earlier months of mobilization
and up until about November or December 1978) were persons with a history
of antigovernment—or at least anti–village political elite—activism. Among
the first to become involved were people who had been pro-Mossadeq—the
prime minister who had led the struggle against the shah—in the early 1950s.
These people had been severely punished for their political activities at that
time. They had been badly beaten, and at least one of them had been exiled
from the village for a number of years. After the return of the shah and their
subsequent punishment, they had refrained from open political activity but
had maintained a quiet, cautious resistance. The most important of these
leaders were teachers in the local school. As a matter of fact, all of the Aliabad
men who were teachers in the local school or elsewhere became supporters
of the revolution. Most of these men were not especially religious, and any
beliefs of a religious nature that *were* held by such persons tended to be rather
progressive.

Another category of people who became involved early on in revolutionary
activity was composed of those who had opposed the landlords in previous
village conflicts. These included some of the peasants and sons of peasants
who had lost land during land reform, and had then participated in the subsequent revolt against the landlords. These people, who had been forced to
find work outside of the village, had not forgotten their enmity toward the
landlords from the time of land reform and other conflicts.

Both of these groups—and there was some overlap between them—had
long resented the Askari brothers (the village landlords) and their backing
of the shah's government. Although forced to acquiesce to the power and force
of the village political elite, they were by no means satisfied with the *status
quo*. Taking advantage of the opportunity to express their long-standing dis-

content, they joined the political movement against the current political system.

4. The revolution was by no means a strictly Shiah phenomenon.[10] Many other religious groups in Iran were represented in the revolutionary movement. Christians, Jews, and Zoroastrians were active, and Sunnis took part as well. The Sunni Kurds of the Mahabad region, for example, were very active. Government forces in Mahabad were defeated by revolutionaries even before the victory of the revolution in Tehran. In Shiraz, the Qashqai—nominal Shiites but not known for their religiosity—took part in marches and demonstrations.

On the other hand, many Shiites did not participate in the revolution at all—in fact, many were active in opposing revolutionary tendencies. For example, Aliabad peasants stayed out of the fray entirely. Members of the political elite, opium smugglers, and policemen attempted to quell the movement, often in brutal fashion. Yet all of these people considered themselves to be Muslims in just as good standing (if not better) than those taking part in the revolution.

Shiite ideology was by no means the only ideology prompting revolutionary action. People of a variety of political persuasions were active in the revolution. The following incident is an example of a non-Shiite ideology prompting revolutionary activity. Because of terrible fights with his father over revolutionary activities, a friend, Mohammad, temporarily left his father's home to stay with his married sister. One day in late fall of 1978, Mohammad's mother received word of his participation in yet another demonstration in Shiraz. She rushed to her daughter's home and proceeded to scream at her son that he shouldn't take part—that it was dangerous, that he would be killed. Mohammad finally moved into another room and closed the door, to escape her tirade. The daughter prepared a herbal tea to soothe her mother's nerves and attempted to calm her, while in the other room Mohammad was quiet for a few minutes. Finally, he said: "I *have* to keep on going to demonstrations. Do you know why?" And he proceeded to tell the story of "The Little Black Fish" by Semad Behrangi, an activist Iranian author.[11] Mohammad explained his determination to continue his revolutionary activities in spite of protests from his parents because of his adherence to the secular, revolutionary ideology outlined in this story.[12] Nor, apparently, was Mohammad the only person inspired by the beliefs of Behrangi into political resistance; large pictures of the writer were frequently carried in demonstrations.

5. As revolutionary activity escalated, interest in Islam, in Shiah religious figures, and in the customs and rituals connected with Islam increased. But this upsurge in religiosity and respect for religion and religious figures was visible *only* among people supporting the revolution. There was no change

in the attitudes of Shiites or others who did not support the revolutionary movement.

For women, wearing the veil and exhibiting modest behavior in other ways was a way of demonstrating revolutionary sentiment. Thousands of women who previously had never or rarely worn the veil put it on during participation in demonstrations, and increased their use of it for other occasions as well. In Aliabad, for example, women who supported the revolution began wearing veils, even in their own homes, tying them on to leave their hands free for housework. The Islamic scarf, a very large, solid-colored piece of material, became popular. The scarf was tucked in at the sides to come down over the forehead and cover all strands of hair. Some women sewed *maqnaas* for themselves—pieces of material sewn somewhat like a scarf, but with material under the chin to cover the neck. It covers the whole head and falls half-way to the waist in front and back, leaving only a round hole for the face. During demonstrations, one could see some women going to even greater lengths to modestly cover themselves. Some women wore black gloves to cover their hands; others wore veils over their faces. There were innovations in clothing, too; long tunics, veils with sleeves sewn into them to allow for greater freedom of the hands, and a special Islamic duster for those who didn't wish to wear the more cumbersome veil were among the new styles in women's clothing.

During the fall months of 1978, attendance at mosques increased dramatically. In the village, a much larger group went to the mosque for afternoon prayers, after which a village native or a visitor from Shiraz often gave a religio-political speech. The mosque became a gathering place exclusively for persons holding pro-revolution sentiments, and shah supporters no longer felt welcome there. Village activists went to Shiraz for evening speeches at the mosques and, on Fridays, for gatherings at mosques or shrines followed by long antigovernment marches. One village woman who had moved to Shiraz with her husband happened to live near the main shrine, Shah Cheraq. Every day, she told me, she packed a lunch and went with her children to Shah Cheraq or the nearby mosque to find out the revolutionary program for the day. During the fall and the early winter of 1978, a rally or march took place almost every day. This woman told me, "I don't have a life of my own any more. My life is revolution and Islam."

People bought religious books, listened to tapes of religious speeches, discussed religious matters (including the characteristics and activities of the opposition religious figures), and used Islamic rhetoric and metaphors in discussing the political situation. Many people began praying more regularly, and more often invoking God and the saints in their speech. In the summer of 1978, during Ramadan—the month of religious fasting—Shiites who had become supporters of the revolution were more likely to fast than in past years. There was more interest in and receptivity to an Islamic worldview. People discussed the importance and advantages of the modesty of women and the segregation of the sexes, and the pitfalls of being overly concerned with material goods and temporal power. It is Islamic to lead a simple life as Ayatollah Khomaini does, they contended. Spiritual development and victory over selfishness are more important than success in terms of material gain.

This increased commitment to the Shiah ethos because of its close identification with the revolutionary movement brought with it a resurgence of interest in and respect for religious matters, activities, and leaders, and for religious ritual and belief. A resurgence of interest in Shiism was indeed apparent. But this resurgence was visible *only* among people who were also active in the revolution against the shah's regime. There was no surge of interest in Islamic practices or activities among those not having an antigovernment tilt, nor did people turn to those Shiah religious figures who did not advocate resistance to the government. Rather, people gave allegiance and respect to the Shiah leaders who were calling for struggle against the government.

Shiism provided the unifying ideology and symbolic system of the politically powerless, including both Shiites and non-Shiites, in their struggle against dependency. But this process was initiated by a transformation in Shiism, not by a religious transformation among Iranians.[13] Only because the new emphasis in Shiism — to struggle against tyranny, repression, and imperialism — spoke to ideas and attitudes currently on the rise among Iranians did Shiism enjoy increased respect, loyalty, and devotion among many people during this period. Nevertheless, as Iranians became aware of the added meaning and relevance of this new emphasis of Islam in their lives, their religiosity increased. Many people who had previously lagged in their interest in Islam felt a new devotion and a resurgence of passion toward their religion. And even among those whose faith had never failed them in previous years, a renewed centrality of religion in their lives could be observed. Agnostics, atheists, and leftists from Shiite backgrounds gained a new respect for Shiism as they participated in the familiar rituals, joined in revolutionary activities organized by religious figures, and found the Shiah idiom and ethos of increasing relevance in their lives. Even non-Shiites participating in the revolution held the religion and its leaders in greater regard.

The increased meaningfulness and centrality that Shiism in its new, transformed emphasis gained through speaking to the current political concerns of believers in turn affected the political behavior of Muslims. They demonstrated their devotion to their religion not only by carrying out ritual obligations, but also through following the admonitions of the revolutionary mode of Shiism to throw fear aside and revolt against dependency and repression.

On the other hand, those who did not support the revolution did not show any increased interest in religion. Only after the departure of the shah on 16 January 1979, and especially after the fall of the government on 11 February 1979, did those people who had supported the shah and held the revolution in disfavor begin to show any signs of increased religiosity. For example, Seyyid Yakub Askari, the main representative of the shah's government in Aliabad, did not show any increased interest in religion until after the departure of the shah. Then, as he gradually began to realize that the revolution might succeed and the shah lose power permanently, he hung several pictures of Ayatollah Khomaini in his home. After the fall of the government he began praying more regularly. He and others who had joined with him in the struggle to turn back the revolutionary tide went to the mosque in a group, where they were publicly chastised for their political stance. They apologized. After this, Seyyid Yakub invited the visiting preacher for dinner and presented him with gifts. Other village supporters of the shah also put up pictures of Ayatollah Khomaini in their homes, and over the doorways into their courtyards. Along with Seyyid Yakub they had dutifully pronounced "Death to the shah!" when the fall of the shah seemed imminent. Some even joined in the revolutionary marches in the village.

6. The political nature of the added allegiance to and respect for Islam and Islamic leaders can be further documented by the changes in attitude and behavior of many revolutionary activists after the revolution on 11 February 1979. Shortly after this date, Kurds, leftists, and Shiites who had been religious cynics before the revolutionary movement (or had become secularized) became critical of Ayatollah Khomaini. They had respected Ayatollah Khomaini as a political leader and remained loyal to his leadership only as long as he advocated aims and policies with which they were in agreement. In Aliabad, the "reformed" shah supporters soon saw that their public manifestations of loyalty to Islam and the revolution would not protect them and their property from reprisals for past mistreatment of other villagers. Their increased religiosity and professed loyalty to Ayatollah Khomaini therefore did not last long.

For several months, the villagers accepted the visiting preacher from Qom as a leader in village affairs. He soon became unpopular, however, because of his promotion of policies disagreeable to the village population. Music and dancing at weddings were un-Islamic, he had adamantly declared, and a few weddings in that spring were held without dancing. At least two of these weddings involved families who had had a member active in the revolution and currently a member of the village revolutionary committee. These men were thus anxious to keep up their reputation for religiosity in order to support their legitimacy as political leaders. By May of 1979, however, there were complaints about the rule of no dancing and music at weddings. Although the preacher threatened to leave if the dancing continued, people persisted in this custom. Even extremely devout, pious, and revolutionary women danced at the weddings of relatives.

Soon after the revolution, village residents began agitating to take over the land belonging to the two Askari brothers (as well as land the Askaris had sold to outsiders). The Qom preacher counseled against this action. People were not pleased with his continued attempts to make decisions concerning village affairs. Finally, both because the villagers would not listen to him and because he couldn't work with the village revolutionary committee, he left the area. After his departure, the villagers proceeded to take over land belonging to Seyyid Ibn Ali Askari and farm it for themselves.

The villagers had cooperated with the Qom preacher in working toward the goal that both the preacher and the village activists saw as their own: the removal of the shah. But after this goal had been accomplished, and the preacher — as one supposedly knowledgeable about the rules of Islam — wished to form policy himself, the villagers were no longer willing to work under his direction. Instead, they made decisions themselves about village affairs and their own behavior. They were more concerned with self-determination than following the precepts of Islam as interpreted by the Qom preacher when such precepts advocated behavior contrary to their own wishes.

In the years following the revolution, escalation and waning of overt religiosity continued to roughly parallel support for the regime. Moharram rituals, evening mosque services during the fasting month of Ramadan, and mosque attendance have been boycotted in protest against policies of the Islamic Republic. According to a 1982 "report from an Iranian village," "the peasants publicly express their discontent with the regime and its manipulation of religious symbols by staying away from religious rituals directed by *mullas* from outside the village. . . . There appears to be an erosion of the observance of private rituals as well, because of their association with the Islamic regime."[14] Interviews with visiting Iranians during the summer of 1986 confirmed the declining involvement of previously pious Shiites in religious ritual due to the disapproval of the current government. Whereas such persons fasted during the month of Ramadan and prayed regularly before the revolution, they no longer do so.

7. Further support for viewing the Iranian revolution as a political struggle is the way Iranians themselves saw the conflict. People supporting the shah, those who remained outside of the conflict, and those actively involved in revolutionary activity saw the revolution as a political struggle. Seyyid Yakub Askari considered the revolutionary movement to be a struggle against the political power of the shah and his regime. He explained his defense of the

shah's regime to me thus: "It doesn't matter whether the shah's good or bad —he's the one who has the power." The shah's forces would prevail, he predicted as late as the first week of December 1978: "The shah's not going to go. He doesn't have to go—he has the backing of the U.S."

The peasants of Aliabad, who were not involved in the revolution, tended to look at the struggle as a contention between two politicians for the position as head of the country. One peasant commented, "What difference does it make to us—one shah goes and another comes." After Ayatollah Khomaini's arrival, another peasant stated, "I have lived through four shahs—including the present one" (referring to Ayatollah Khomaini). Even traditionally religious supporters of the revolution tended to see it as a struggle for political power. The revolution would merely result in the removal of the current political figures and the substitution of religious figures, they seemed to feel. They assumed, for example, that the religious forces also had their own "organization"—meaning a security organization like the shah's SAVAK. More educated activists tended to see the conflict as a struggle to change the political system—to obtain freedom, political representation, and self-determination. For example, in early November of 1978 one villager explained to me: "all Iranians of whatever faction have come together under one word—freedom."

Iranians admitted to conscious manipulation of religious symbolism to further the cause of the revolution. As an important organizer in Aliabad confided: "You have to use a language which the people will understand. I felt we needed a revolution, so to get people to join me, I talked in religious terms." This young teacher further explained that "the reason I spoke in the mosque and so on is that you can't go too far in front of the people. They won't understand. Even though Khomaini isn't a very great religious figure, not even as important as Shariatmadari, it was important to have a big person or make a big person to get the people on his side and against the regime. A leftist or someone else could not have mobilized the people like that." This revolutionary leader also admitted to discussing with other activists the money they were supposedly receiving from religious figures in Shiraz for their revolutionary activities, for the benefit of listeners who had not yet decided to become involved—all with the purpose of encouraging more support for the revolution.

8. Another indicator that the revolution is a political phenomenon (even if enveloped in religious symbolism) was the fact that, during the revolution, religious days were used for political purposes. A day or two before Ashura of 1978, Aliabad had seen a bloody conflict between young men who supported the shah and those who opposed him. Both sides had been practicing for the mourning processions of Ashura in the village mosque. This fight was

a political struggle at several different levels, since it marked a difference in national political allegiance and in village-level political allegiance as well. In the pro-shah faction were supporters and relatives of the Askari brothers, whereas the pro-Khomaini faction did not accept the political leadership of the Askaris. The fight was also related to a family quarrel; the leader of the pro-shah faction had mistreated his wife, who was the sister of the pro-Khomaini leader, to the extent that she had finally fled to her father's home. Her family had refused to return her to her husband in spite of his pleading, and because of this refusal, the husband felt great animosity towards Cyrus, his wife's brother.

This incident was one of two responsible for mobilizing the village population in support of the revolution. Heretofore, the majority of the village residents had kept quiet, leaning to neither one side nor the other. But during this violent confrontation just outside the mosque between the two factions, the leader of the pro-shah group knifed Cyrus, his brother-in-law and the leader of the pro-Khomaini faction. Villagers were outraged and angry when Cyrus was left with a very serious wound in his side, since Cyrus was a village favorite who had been orphaned at an early age when his father became a martyr for the village by losing his life in a conflict over water rights with a neighboring settlement. Villagers were shocked and furious that the son of this man who had died for the village could be treated in this fashion. They were outraged by the violent means used by the pro-shah faction to combat the opposition. The reaction to this incident and to the violent behavior of the pro-shah supporters, more than any specifically religious beliefs, was responsible for arousing support for the revolution among previously neutral villagers. As Cyrus himself told me, this incident demonstrated to the people just what shah supporters were like.[15]

Ashura—the "tenth" of the Islamic month of Moharram (11 December 1978)—occurred a few days after this village incident and marked a political struggle both at the national level and at the village level. The great numbers of people participating in the anti-shah demonstration clearly indicated the overwhelming support for Khomaini and the revolution and the lack of support for the shah's regime. In Aliabad, Seyyid Yakub encouraged people to participate in the traditional mourning procession and rituals commemorating the martyrdom of Imam Hosain on the plain of Kerbala (in present-day Iraq) in A.D. 680, but a comparison of the number of people who participated in the village mourning procession (about thirty or forty) with the number of villagers who went to Shiraz and then also marched, shouting anti-shah slogans, in Aliabad—about three or four hundred—provided a clear indication of the political balance of support.[16]

The religious celebrations of the following year, Tasua and Ashura of 1979

—the ninth and tenth of the month of Moharram (corresponding to 29 and 30 November 1979)—also saw political conflict in Aliabad. Seyyid Ibn Ali had been arrested on 6 October 1979 as a result of the great number of complaints sworn out against him for his treatment of Aliabad residents in the years before the revolution. The day before Tasua, however, he had bribed his way out of prison. When the villagers received this news on the morning of Tasua, they forsook the traditional mourning processions of Tasua, the day before the anniversary of the martyrdom of Imam Hosain. Instead, they traveled to Shiraz to demonstrate in front of the homes of religious leaders, urging them to reapprehend Seyyid Ibn Ali.[17] It was more important to bring the village tyrant to justice, villagers argued, than to mourn for Imam Hosain. On the following day, the customary mourning procession of Ashura culminated at the property of Seyyid Ibn Ali, where mourners labored with picks and shovels to tear down the wall surrounding his orchard.

In yet another way the anniversary of Imam Hosain's martyrdom was used for political purposes. The closest supporters of the Askari brothers had fled, and the anti-Askari faction had taken over control of the village. In contrast to previous years, when the Askaris and their allies, as the village political elite, had directed and funded Ashura activities, during Ashura of 1979 the mourning activities were completely under the control of the village opposition. Members of the Askari clan remaining in the village wanted to participate in the mourning processions and rituals. The fact that they were not allowed to do so demonstrated the overwhelming victory of the anti-Askari faction in village politics.

Shiism provided an idiom and symbolic context used in expressing, organizing, and promoting the political struggle not only against the shah and his regime and policies, but also against his representatives at the local level. Political and economic conditions and complaints, as well as the expressed goals of Islam and Islamic leaders, resulted in the increasing use of the language of Shiism and in increased devotion to and respect for religion and those religious leaders who had advocated resistance to the shah's government. Religion was used in an active, self-confirming protest and revolt against subjugation, arrogance, and willfulness to obtain freedom and self-determination. Shiism was instrumental in the political struggle, not only at the local but also at the national and international levels.

Shiism and Cultural Revolution

Shiism is an important part of the cultural heritage that gave Iranians the self-identity, courage, confidence, and impetus to assert themselves and resist

the shah, his government, and his backer, the United States government.[18] The
process of this cultural revolution will be traced in the following paragraphs.

In the last few decades it has been possible to discern in many Iranians
a singular lack of pride and confidence in their nation, culture, other Iranians, and themselves.[19] They have seemed to be ashamed of things Iranian,
while admiring and respecting all things Western and wishing to emulate
the West. There appear to be two main explanations for this attitude. First
of all, many Iranians began to use the standards of the West in judging themselves, their nation, and their culture. The prevalent attitude of many Westerners toward Iran — and toward other, similar "less developed nations" — was
that the country was backward and underindustrialized, and that certain aspects of Iranian culture and social customs prevented its citizens from being
hard-working, independent and dedicated to personal advancement in terms
of profession or career, and from building a modern industrialized nation
along the lines of one of the European countries. Iranians were further judged
to be uncooperative, suspicious to the point of paranoia, and untrustworthy,
and to lack initiative, responsibility, and reliability.[20] The only way Iranians
could become acceptable to Westerners, as individuals and as a nation, would
be to become more like Americans, and for the Iranian nation and economy
to become more "American." Many upper and upper-middle-class Iranians,
including "Westernized" Iranians, shared these attitudes in looking at themselves. As a result, they separated themselves from "traditional" and poorer
Iranians, and showed no interest in learning about Iranian culture and how
ordinary Iranians live.[21] Instead, they were obsessed with all things American,
all aspects of American culture, and all types of American styles. Because the
upper classes tended to distance themselves from Iranian culture and the way
of life of average Iranians and instead imitated Western ways, Iran could be
seen as divided into two cultures.[22]

But Iranians aspiring to Western ways found that somehow they still failed
to become "just like" Americans. They continued to find themselves lacking
when they applied Western standards and prejudices in judging themselves.
Iranians couldn't work together, they believed. Further, they didn't trust each
other, and were incapable of important accomplishments because of their dis-
position to petty quarrels and infighting. In the mid-seventies, I sat in a Washington, D.C. living room, listening in shock (and then arguing) when three
highly educated Iranians, in tones of depression and despair, cited these supposedly "innate" characteristics of Iranians as they sought to analyze why the
Iranian people had not been able to rebel against the shah and his regime.

A second explanation of why many Iranians experienced a lack of pride
and confidence in themselves and their fellows was that they were ashamed
of their acquiescence to control and pressure by political superiors and the
shah's regime in general. One Iranian who had taken part in the Washington

conversation mentioned above described to me his experience during the Shah's visit to the U.S. capital in 1977. Because this person held a relatively important job in the city, he was invited by the Iranian embassy to the reception for the shah at the White House. He didn't want to go, and called the embassy with an excuse. He was then unequivocally told that if he weren't present at the reception, his passport would be revoked. So he went, and—as he described to me later how he had sat at the reception, sick with self-contempt —his self-loathing and despair were still apparent in his voice and eyes.

Another Iranian, while a student in the United States, was invited as the representative of Iranian students attending school in the southern states to come to the shah's coronation, and for other festivities as well. He tried to find excuses, but was persuaded into making such trips on several occasions, partly out of fear and partly to take advantage of the opportunity to see family and friends. Finally, the last time he was asked to come, he refused. He had an American wife, he explained, and would no longer be able to make such trips because of family responsibilities. Furthermore, he had decided to become an American citizen, and would not be returning to Iran any more. Again, his sadness and lack of self-respect because of his earlier behavior was apparent in his face as he related this history to me.

Such Iranians were ashamed of themselves for their lack of courage in the face of pressure, and for allowing themselves to be manipulated through a combination of fear and a desire to keep and improve upon advantaged positions and lifestyles. They felt contempt for their fellow Iranians as well, for the same reason, and for the Iranian nation in general because it was formed of a people that did not resist tyranny but gave in to political oppression out of cowardice and self-interest.[23]

Among some groups, however, resistance to cultural and political control had been kept alive in the form of stubborn adherence to disapproved religio-cultural practices. The shah and his father before him had long attempted to change customs and culture in Iran—to make Iranians less Iranian and more Western. Beginning in 1935, Reza Shah, the father of the late shah, mounted a "campaign to persuade people to dress like Europeans."[24] For example, efforts were made to coerce women to go without veils. Likewise, the performance of passion plays commemorating the martyrdom of Imam Hosain was outlawed in 1932.[25] There were also government efforts to control and limit the mourning processions for Imam Hosain during the month of Moharram, as well as the practice of self-flagellation. However, these practices continued, in defiance of government policy and the wishes of the shahs.

The refusal to give up these "backward, uncivilized, unmodern" customs can be seen as the refusal to part with one's own culture and identity while making oneself over in the form desired by another. Use of the veil and other

Islamic practices became a battle of wills, then—a matter of political contention, much like that Franz Fanon described during the Algerian struggle for independence from France. There, use of the veil and the modesty and segregation of women were "attributed to religious, magical, fanatical behavior" by the colonizers, Fanon states, although it was "in fact the assertion of a distinct identity, concern with keeping intact a few shreds of national existence."[26] Precisely because the colonizers were so intent on removing the veil, the latter became a "mechanism of resistance."[27] The long decades of struggle by the two shahs to persuade Iranian women to forsake their veils was in part responsible for the prevalent use of the veil as a symbol of political opposition during the revolution.

The religious opposition and their bazaar supporters had been using Islamic aspects of Iranian culture in their struggle against the political domination of the shah and his regime for several decades.[28] However, the 1970s seemed to be a period of thoughtfulness and reevaluation by educated middle and upper-middle-class Iranians. Praise and adulation of American culture and society declined, and anti-American sentiment increased. At the same time, Iranians gradually became more interested in and appreciative of their own culture. Iranian handicrafts began to appear in homes, and some people began using *kursis,* (the traditional heating system—a charcoal brazier under a low wooden table, around which people sit with a blanket covering the table and tucked around their waists). Some wealthy people even had "Iran rooms," which contained no furniture except for a beautiful rug on which they sat in accordance with the traditional custom. And greater interest in Islam was a part of this new appreciation for things Iranian. Sharif Arani reports: "the upsurge of the literate public's interest in Islam was reflected in a dramatic rise in the number of religious publications; in 1976–77 these exceeded all secular fields combined."[29] As Amilcar Cabral, in his study of the national liberation movement to free Guinea (Bissau) and the Cape Verde Islands from Portugal, has noted: "the study of the history of national liberation struggle shows that generally these struggles are preceded by an increase in expression of culture, consolidated progressively into a successful or unsuccessful attempt to affirm the cultural personality of the dominated people, as a means of negating the oppressor culture."[30]

In the case of Iran, this restored interest in Iranian culture on the part of educated and upper-class Iranians eventually culminated in a cultural revolution against the political domination of the shah and his U.S. patrons. This use of culture in revolution was successful in large part because of the work of the late Dr. Ali Shariati. Shariati's work transformed Shiite ideology, combining the worldviews, aims, and cultures of the lower-class, less educated, more traditional Iranians with those of the middle and upper-class Iranians who had become somewhat Westernized in outlook; thus he made his revolutionary ideology appealing to both groups, uniting them in a concerted effort against the shah's regime. Under Dr. Shariati's influence, the martyrdom of Imam Hosain—an event with which average Shiite Iranians identified—became an example of the kind of struggle against tyranny and injustice to be followed by "modern" Shiites. Dr. Shariati's ideology of self-reliance, responsibility, anti-imperialism, and humanism appealed also to the educated classes.

The role of Imam Hosain in Dr. Shariati's progressive ideology was similar to Miguel Hidalgo's use of the Brown Virgin (or Our Lady of Guadalupe) in the Mexican revolution of independence in 1810. In this situation, too, "mere imageless concepts such as 'popular sovereignty' could not rouse and then channel the energies of the popular masses."[31] According to the anthropologist Victor Turner, Hidalgo knew "that if he were to wave a religious banner it would have to be one symbolizing the widest possible corporate unity and continuity to be found in Mexico."[32] The Brown Virgin appealed to the Indians, because of her "continuity with the Aztec mother of the gods, Tonantzin,"[33] and to the Criollos, because she was Mexican yet also Christian.[34]

In much the same way, a progressive Shiite ideology of revolution against political oppression brought together the largest number of Iranians possible. The emphasis on Islam and the martyrdom of Imam Hosain, the culture of the traditional Iranians, appealed to the Iranian Shiite masses, while the emphasis on a progressive Islam was attractive to the more educated Shiite, some of whom had become rather secularized.[35] In addition, the advocacy of tolerance, self-determination, and responsibility aroused respect from non-Shiites and leftists. To be sure, a number of different ideologies were preaching the same message of antiimperialism and antityranny, courage, self-determination, and self-sacrifice for the good of society. Shiite ideologies were, however, probably the most important in terms of number of people influenced, since the great majority of Iranians and hence of participants in the revolution were Shiites.

These ideologies encouraged self-assertion, the rejection of dependency and Western hegemony, and an active resistance to political repression. In conjunction with acceptance of these ideologies and their own revolutionary experiences, the views of Iranians toward themselves, toward their fellow Iranians, and toward the Iranian nation as a whole were radically transformed.[36] Dr. Shariati, for example, counseled against imitation of the West.[37] He also taught that one should forget one's own interests to the extent of dying to oneself, and should struggle "for the well-being of the community."[38] Of special importance was his statement: "All people are not only equal, but are siblings."[39] The sense of unity, brotherhood, and empathy for all other Iranians that grew during the process of the revolution was crucial to the escalation of determination to overthrow the shah. Because of this sentiment of closeness, Iranians reacted with outrage and fury upon hearing of the killing of Iranians in other parts of the country—and because of this empathy, Iranians were willing to give their lives for unrelated Iranians, or to act in retaliation for the murder of others as they would previously have done only for close relatives or friends. The family circle thus expanded to include all Iranians in the anti-shah movement.

Self-confidence, pride, and identity were augmented by participation in marches and demonstrations. Violent acts serve as "bridge-burning acts," Gerlach and Hine suggest,[40] for they "symbolize a rejection of the existing social order, and actualize the personal change necessary for participation in a new order."[41] In the case of the Iranian revolution, however, a violent act was not necessary to proclaim such rejection and to actualize personal transformation. Rather, merely participating in demonstrations—especially in the Ashura march of December 1978—seems to have accomplished such changes. Such participation was potentially extremely dangerous, and therefore required great commitment and courage. People who joined in the march felt that they had met a great challenge with success, and experienced a surge of joy, pride, and confidence with their public declaration of political resistance.

Iranians rejected Western culture and refused to use its standards to judge themselves—to try to become acceptable and accepted by becoming more like Westerners. They no longer wished to seek position, recognition, and material gains by acquiescing to those in control of political power. Their attitudes and behavior were similar to those of the Black Power and student movements discussed by Gerlach and Hine: "Both groups demand recognition and respect for themselves *in their present state;* they are not concerned about meeting existing social requirements for recognition and respect. Both demand power to control or to share in the control of institutions, even as they reject socially prescribed methods of gaining such power."[42]

Iranians turned their backs on a life dedicated to fulfilling someone else's definition of what they should become. Rather, they were now determined to define themselves, no longer willing to be politically manipulated through fear and appeals to their self-interest. One woman described her emotions during the Ashura march of December 1978 as follows:

> When I went to the Ashura march I didn't know if there would be soldiers shooting at us or not, or perhaps we might be bombed from the air. But I didn't care. I had given up on my own life. There was no fear in my heart. My heart was filled with hate. I put all the hate in my voice. Hearing the great sound of *Allah-o akbar* ["God is Great"] made me weep. I was full of hate for the shah—It was only three months after the 17 of Shahrivar ["Black Friday," the

massacre at Zhaleh Square in Tehran on 8 September 1978]. When I thought of myself I was but a drop in the sea. I felt smaller and smaller. Sometimes I felt lost among all of those voices. I was very proud of my nationality. On this day I was so proud. Before I had been ashamed that I didn't take part in political resistance. But on this day I was so happy I could take part. On Zand Avenue a woman was standing on a balcony all dressed in black as all of us were. She was holding her child and probably couldn't join us. But she was shouting *marg bar shah* ["Death to the shah"] with such force that the balcony was shaking. Later I told my sisters (who were in the United States at the time), "You missed the best year of your lives."

Conclusion

Shiism enjoyed added prestige, respect, and importance in Iran, not because of any revival of interest in religion per se, but because some Shiite leaders were preaching an ideology of revolution, self-assertion, pride in nation and culture, and resistance to political and cultural domination.[43] From a revolutionary interpretation of Shiism, politically repressed Iranians found the courage, determination, self-confidence, and organizational framework to revolt against the shah's regime, its representatives at the local level, and the American presence in Iran. Through rejecting the shah and his political system and its borrowed Western culture, and finding the courage to affirm themselves in spite of coercion and intimidation on the one hand, and the inducements of material advantages and privileged positions on the other, Iranians rediscovered their dignity and self-pride. Through participation in the anti-shah demonstrations they regained their self-respect and confidence. They felt that, having succeeded in overcoming the fear of possible death and taken part in the march, they were capable of anything. Imbued with a new confidence in their fellows and in the Iranian nation, millions of Iranians had lost their fear, and were cooperating in an anti-shah stance. They looked at the Iranian nation rather as a little David who wasn't afraid to go to battle with a huge and powerful Goliath—the armed forces of the shah and, backing him, the most powerful military force in the world, the United States. The newly united nation of Iran was full of power and strength, they felt, and could be victorious in the struggle. After the Ashura march, Iranians were entirely convinced that, because of their great strength of purpose and their determination, their lack of fear and self-interest, and their overwhelming unity, they were a powerful force that, *dast-e khali* ("empty handed"— weaponless), would prevail against the military might of the shah's regime.

One villager, a *seyyid* who prided himself on his devoutness and piety, looked back on the revolution and explained it to me in the following words:

The shah is a tyrant over us. The very word, shah, means tyrant. All of the resources of the country were taken by a handful of people. The rest of the people of Iran had nothing except toil and poverty. If that same money which the shah took out of the country had been divided up among Iranians, everyone would have had a good standard of living. The shah made plans with the United States so that we would always be dependent. It's like if someone brought you here and kept you and made tea, food and clothes for you, so you wouldn't learn how to do these things, then told you to do everything for yourself. But you wouldn't know how to make tea, because it was always placed prepared in front of you. Wheat and everything was brought from the outside. We weren't allowed to produce for ourselves. The U.S. sent us wheat that otherwise would have been thrown into the sea, but in exchange took money and oil. They didn't let us have factories to produce our own arms. We have oil—but it's crude oil. We weren't allowed to build refineries to produce our own fuel. The shah did all of this. The shah was like the U.S.'s robot. If they told him to put in a new prime minister, he put in a new prime minister. If they told him that today he had to go to London, he went to London, to come to the U.S., he went. They were afraid of Islam, because Islam says all must be at the same level. Islam says we must know about each other's problems and help each other. Islam says for all to become one—just like the people all became one and kicked the shah out—in spite of all of his power and support from the United States. Why did he leave the country? Because of unity and cooperation. Everyone was all together. We all were one and we weren't afraid of anything, not tanks or machine guns or bullets.

Many of the revolutionary slogans used by demonstrators during the revolution, often stated in Islamic idiom, expressed the perceived relationship between Iranian national identity and independence and the elimination of the shah and U.S. domination. The following are examples:

Ta shah kafan nashavad	Till the shah's in his burial shroud
Iran vatan nashavad	Iran won't be a nation.
Shah jenayat mikonad	The shah commits crimes [and]
Carter hemayat mikonad	Carter protects him.
In shah-e amrikai edam boyad shavad	This American shah must be executed.
Jumhuri-yeh islami elam boyad shavad	The Islamic Republic must be announced.
Naft-ra ki bord? amrika	Who took our oil? The United States.
Gaz-ra ki bord? shuravi	Who took our gas? The Soviet Union.
Pulra-ra ki bord? Pahlavi	Who took our money? Pahlavi.
Marg bar in selseleh-yeh Pahlavi	Death to the Pahlavi dynasty.
Marg bar in selseleh-yeh Pahlavi	Death to the Pahlavi dynasty.
Na sharqi na qharbi	Neither East nor West
Jumhuri-yeh islami	Islamic Republic.

Shaheen Dil has argued that "the idea that South Asian politics is being swept by a wave of Islamic resurgence is more myth than reality. . . . What is happening in these countries is not a resurgence of Islamic fervor leading to jihad, or holy war against the infidels, but rather a desperate attempt at self-definition in a world where the powerless are too often defined in terms of the powerful."[44] The same argument can be applied to the Iranian case. The use of Islamic ideology, leaders and language was an attempt to rally a people with the confidence and unity necessary to struggle against political domination and the hegemony of a foreign power when the only weapons available were morale and numbers. Shiism provided the cultural instrument for political assertion and revolution. A politically rebellious people heeded the call of a religion and of religious leaders who were advocating resistance and revolution. Since the revolution, however, increased religiosity or respect for Shiism and Shiah religious figures on the part of Iranians is a function of political adherence and loyalty to the revolution and to the subsequent "Islamic" government. Those persons continuing to support this government will continue in their manifestations of greater religiosity, while those who have become disillusioned no longer have any interest in religious activity and ideology, and may even feel repugnance for Islam.

The resurgence of Islam in Iran before and during the Iranian revolution was a political, as well as a religious, phenomenon. Because political dissidence against local political elites, the shah, and his regime, and the hegemony of his American supporters was organized and expressed mainly through Shiism, the religion and religious figures enjoyed increased power, prestige, and respect. The resurgence of Islam in Iran — the increased meaningfulness, force, and centrality of Islam in the lives of Iranians — was the concomitant of, not the reason for, political dissidence.

Notes

1. A critical difference between Shiah and Sunni interpretations of Islam relates to the Shiah understanding of the imamate, or position of successors to the Prophet Mohammad. According to Shiah belief, the imam is chosen by "divine decree." Imams are therefore without error and sin, and through their inheritance of the "spiritual authority of the Prophet" are able to further reveal and interpret the will of God and to mediate on behalf of believers. The Household of the Prophet is dear to Shiites. Among the twelve imams, three are important: Ali, the first imam and son-in-law of the Prophet, is remembered for his qualities of justice and compassion. His son, Imam Hosain, the third imam, and Hosain's family are central to the Shiah concepts of

martyrdom and "redemptive suffering." Finally, Shiites await the reappearance of the Hidden Imam or Mahdi, the Twelfth Imam, who disappeared into occultation in infancy. See Allamah Sayyid Muhammed Husayn Tabatabai, *Shiite Islam,* trans. Seyyid Hossein Nasr (Albany: SUNY Press, 1975). Two other books are most helpful in providing insight on Shiah Islam: Mahmoud Ayoub, *Redemptive Suffering in Islam: A Study of the Devotional Aspects of Ashura in Twelver Shiism* (The Hague: Mouton Publishers, 1978), and Peter J. Chelkowski, ed., *Taziyeh: Ritual and Drama in Iran* (New York: New York University Press and Soroush Press, 1979).

2. Abner Cohen, *Custom and Politics in Urban Africa: A Study of Hausa Migrants in Yoruba Towns* (Berkeley: University of California Press, 1969), pp. 2, 190.

3. See Richard Cottam, "Revolutionary Iran and the War with Iraq," *Current History* 80, no. 462 (January 1981): 7.

4. During this eighteen months I also spent two weeks in Kurdistan—Mahabad and Sanandaj—and visited Tehran, Tabriz, Bushire, and Yasuj. During these travels and also on frequent visits to Shiraz and villages in the Shiraz area, I spoke with many Iranians from a variety of religious, ethnic, and political backgrounds. Quite a number of these were intimate friends of long standing, and thus frank in presenting their views. Also useful have been four other trips to Iran since 1966, of durations varying from two to twenty-one months, and conversations with numerous Iranians from different socioeconomic levels and walks of life, both during these visits and in the United States. Since the revolution I have maintained contact with many Iranians and have interviewed visitors from Iran and residents of the U.S. returning from trips to Iran. Field research was made possible by a fellowship granted by the Social Science Research Council and the American Council of Learned Societies. The conclusions and opinions in this article are those of the author and not necessarily those of the councils. A great debt is owed many kind and openminded Iranians who offered me friendship and assistance during tense times. Finally, I am grateful to Richard Antoun for providing constructive criticism.

5. See Mary Hegland, "One Village in the Revolution," *MERIP Reports* no. 87 (May 1980): 7–12.

6. The reasons why peasants did not become involved in the revolution are discussed in Mary Hegland, "Peasants and the Process of Revolution: An Iranian Case Study" (Paper presented at the conference on Imperialism, Religion and Revolution in the Middle East sponsored by the Alternative Middle East Studies Seminar, 1980).

7. See Michael Fischer, *Iran: From Religious Dispute to Revolution* (Cambridge: Harvard University Press, 1980), p. 190; Peter Gran, "Political Economy as a Paradigm for the Study of Islamic History," *International Journal of Middle East Studies* 11, no. 4 (July 1980): 516–17; and Richard Hrair Dekmejian, "The Islamic Revival in the Middle East and North Africa," *Current History* 78, no. 456 (April 1980): 171.

8. Farhad Kazemi, *Poverty and Revolution in Iran* (New York: New York University Press, 1980).

9. Janet Bauer, "New Models and Traditional Networks: Migrant Women in South Tehran, Iran," in *Women in the Cities: Female Migration and Urban Adaptation,* (1980); and idem, "Women, the Media and Social Change in Pre-Revolutionary Iran," in *Telecommunications in Transcultural Perspective* (Winnipeg: University of Winnipeg, 1980).

10. See also Cottam, "Revolutionary Iran," p. 6, and Fred Halliday, "Theses on the Iranian Revolution," *Race and Class* 21, no. 1 (Summer 1979): 84, 85.

11. See Samad Behrangi, *The Little Black Fish and Other Modern Persian Stories by Samad Behrangi,* trans. Mary and Eric Hooglund (Washington, D.C.: Three Continents Press, 1976). I am indebted to Eric Hooglund, who was present in the room with Mohammad, for providing me with this information.

12. Samad Behrangi tells the story of the Little Black Fish who broke away from home, and

the belief of the community that their little stream and the pleasures of going for a swim were all there was to the world. In opposition to his mother's wishes and taunted in ridicule and anger, the Little Black Fish left and eventually died to save others and kill a tyrant. The motto of the Little Black Fish was as follows: "If some day I should be forced to face death—as I shall—it doesn't matter. What does matter is the influence that my life will have on the lives of others." Ibid., p. 16.

13. For a more complete description of this transformation in popular Shiite ideology, see Mary Hegland, "Two Images of Husain: Accommodation and Revolution in an Iranian Village," *Shiism from Quietism to Revolution,* ed. Nikki R. Keddie (New Haven: Yale University Press, 1983), pp. 218–35.

14. A special correspondent, "Report from an Iranian Village," *MERIP Reports* 12, no. 3 (March–April 1982): 28. See also "Current Political Attitudes in an Iranian Village," *Iranian Studies* 16, nos. 1–2 (Winter–Spring 1983): 3–29.

15. Such was also the reaction to events of violence elsewhere in the nation.

16. Mary Hegland, "Ritual and Revolution in Iran," *Political Anthropology Yearbook Volume 2: Culture and Political Change,* ed. Myron J. Aronoff (New Brunswick, N.J.: Transaction Books, 1983), pp. 93, 94.

17. See Hegland, "One Village," pp. 11, 12.

18. Robert Dillon, "Laying Bare the Background," *MERIP Reports* no. 80 (June 1980): 28. Dillon has stated: "[The Iranian religious heritage] provided resources to rekindle Iranian courage, sincerity and brotherhood where despotism had previously compelled the protective adaptation of caution, individualism and dissimulation."

19. See Richard W. Cottam, *Nationalism in Iran: Updated through 1979* (Pittsburgh: University of Pittsburgh Press, 1979), pp. 324, 327, 345, 352.

20. See, for example "Message from Iran: Aug. 13, 1979," *New York Times,* 27 January 1981, p. A19.

21. See Amilcar Cabral, *Return to the Source: Selected Speeches by Amilcare Cabral* (New York: Monthly Review Press, 1974), pp. 59–64, for a discussion of the internal cultural divide that tends to develop between the "marginal class" who "aspire to a way of life which is similar if not identical to the foreign minority" and the masses. Cabral's discussions of "National Liberation and Culture" and "Identity and Dignity in the Context of the National Liberation Struggle" can quite profitably be applied to the revolutionary experience in Iran. The framework of the second section of this article owes much to Cabral's analysis of these subjects. Other influences are Luther Gerlach and Virginia Hine, *People, Power, Change: Movements of Social Transformation* (Indianapolis: Bobbs-Merrill Educational Publishing, 1979); Franz Fanon, "On National Culture," in *The Wretched of the Earth* (New York: Grove Press, 1966; idem, *A Dying Colonialism* (New York: Grove Press, 1967); and Victor Turner, "Hidalgo: History as Social Drama"; idem, *Dramas, Fields and Metaphors: Symbolic Action in Human Society* (Ithaca, N.Y.: Cornell University Press, 1978).

22. Nikki Keddie has also made this observation in her "Oil, Economic Policy and Social Conflict in Iran," *Race and Class* (1979): 14. Anne Betteridge has discussed her observations of this phenomenon with me in conversation.

23. Richard Cottam has argued, accurately in my estimation, that, "The Shah . . . survived by a combination of coercion and an ability to satisfy demands of important societal elements for material wealth and influence." Cottam, *Nationalism,* p. 363.

24. Fischer, *Iran,* pp. 97, 98.

25. Ibid., p. 172.

26. Fanon, *Dying Colonialism,* p. 41.

27. Ibid., p. 63.

28. As well as at earlier points in history. See Thaiss, "Religious Symbolism," and Hamid Algar, "Introduction: A Bibliographic Sketch," in Ali Shariati, *On the Sociology of Islam: Lectures by Ali Shariati* (Berkeley, Calif.: Nizan Press, 1979).

29. Sharif Arani, "Iran: From the Shah's Dictatorship to Khomaini's Demagogic Theocracy," *Dissent* 27 (Winter 1980): 13.

30. Cabral, *Return to the Source,* p. 43.

31. Turner, "Hidalgo," p. 106.

32. Ibid.

33. Ibid., p. 151.

34. See June Nash, "The Passion Play in Maya Indian Communities," *Comparative Studies in Society and History* 10, no. 3 (April 1968), and idem, *We Eat the Mines and the Mines Eat Us: Dependency and Exploitation in Bolivian Tin Mines* (New York: Columbia University Press, 1979), for other examples of a combined native-borrowed symbolic complex used as a means of self-identity, self-assertion, and resistance.

35. As Mansour Farhang points out, "Shariati effectively articulated the growing conviction among the Iranian intelligentsia that the ideology of any progressive and lasting change in the degenerate socio-political structure of the country has to be rooted in the native history and values of the society." Mansour Farhang, "Resisting the Pharaohs: Ali Shariati on Oppression," *Race and Class* 21, no. 1 (Summer 1979): 32. See also Nikki R. Keddie, "Iran: Change in Islam/Islam and Change," *International Journal of Middle Eastern Studies* (1968): 535; idem, "Shiism and Revolution," *Religion, Rebellion, Revolution: An Interdisciplinary and Cross-Cultural Collection,* ed. Bruce Lincoln (London: Macmillan, 1985): 157–82; Arani, "Iran," p. 14; and Gerad Chaliand, *Revolution in the Third World* (New York: Penguin Books, 1979), p. 103. Ashraf and Banuazizi have pointed to four variants of Shiah Islam, the adherents of which were all united within the "revolutionary coalition": radical Islam, militant Islam, liberal Islam, and traditionalist Islam. See Ahmad Ashraf and Ali Banuazizi, "The State, Classes, and Modes of Mobilization in the Iranian Revolution," *State, Culture and Society* 1, No. 3 (Spring 1985): 3.

36. See Gerlach and Hine, *People, Power, Change,* for such transformations in other movements.

37. Ali Shariati, "Islam and Human Kind," in *Tell the American People: Perspectives on the Iranian Revolution and Voices of the Revolution,* ed. David H. Albert (Philadelphia: Movement for a New Society, 1980), p. 148.

38. As quoted in Algar, "Introduction," p. 12. See also Ali Shariati, "Reflections of a Concerned Muslim: On the Plight of Oppressed Peoples," *Race and Class* (1979): 39.

39. Shariati, "Islam and Humankind," p. 155.

40. Gerlach and Hine, *People, Power, Change,* p. 143.

41. Ibid., p. 148.

42. Ibid., p. 156.

43. As Ahmad Ashraf and Ali Banuazizi have pointed out, only a minority of the ulama were active in the revolution: "The majority of the ulama maintained their conservative stance through the entire revolutionary course, remaining suspicious of radical youth and of Khomeini, and avoiding direct involvement in the struggle. Nearly all high-ranking members of the clergy, including all the Grand Ayatollahs and most of the theology teachers in religious schools and seminaries, were either opposed to, or else remained silent about, Khomeini's militant interpretation of the role of Islam and of the clergy." Ahmad Ashraf and Ali Banuazizi, "The State, Classes and Modes of Mobilization in the Iranian Revolution," *State, Culture and Society* 1, no. 3 (Spring 1985): 26.

44. Shaheen F. Dil, "The Myth of Islamic Resurgence in South Asia," *Current History* 78, no. 456 (April 1980): 166, 169.

V

OVERVIEW

10

Three Forms of Religious Convergence

NINIAN SMART

E vents in the late seventies and early eighties have impressed many Western observers with the way in which religion has become politically important. We can point to the Islamic resurgence in Iran, the Moral Majority
in the United States, and the Gush Emunim in Israel. It is easy to conclude
that we are witnessing a world revival of conservative forces. From one point
of view these manifestations are indeed conservative, but from another perspective they are radical and innovative movements. They are conservative in
their wish to reestablish elements of a tradition perceived to be under threat,
and because of their mode of arguing from scriptural sources they are often
referred to by Westerners as "fundamentalist." But it is unwise to bring pre-
conceived categories to bear on these phenomena, especially when we are examining a non-Western religious tradition such as Islam.

In the West we are accustomed to a rather sharply drawn line between
religion and politics. Although a distinction between religion and politics
can occur in the Islamic context, it is somewhat misleading. In Islam, part
of the religious tradition is the *Sharia,* the Law, and this law covers both private and public life. In covering elements of public life and implying arrangements that in modern Western thinking would come under the head of legislation, there is no line drawn between religion and the desirable polity in
which Muslims wish to live.

Even in the Western context it is possible to draw the line too sharply. It
is not easy to make an absolute distinction between religious and secular (or
nonreligious) worldviews.[1] For example, the distinction between Marxism as
a worldview and Catholic Christianity is on the surface very great, but the
two may be merged in the form of liberation theology. More than this, secular ideologies may function as norms of social belief and practice: the state
secular ideology in East Germany, for example, is functionally reminiscent
of the old State Lutheranism. If the comparative study of religion had origi-
nated not in the West but in China, it is doubtful whether the definition
of its boundaries would leave out Maoism. (Confucianism itself does not strictly
correspond to the usual idea of a religion in Western terms.) In Western so-

223

cieties, it is convenient to draw a line between religious and political ideologies, a distinction with ramifications in such areas as tax collection, education,
and public ceremony; but it is a culture-bound and controversial distinction.

It is therefore more realistic to see as our task the analysis of worldviews.
Worldviews are often a syncretic blend of themes drawn both from traditional
religion and modern "secular" sources. The form of Christian outlook sponsored by the Moral Majority is one in which both Biblical and patriotic values
are brought together.[2] If it is possible to view the Panama Canal treaties from
a biblical perspective, you can be sure that premises in addition to biblical
ones are being brought to bear. Similarly, Ayatollah Khomaini's conception
of an Islamic Republic is heavily influenced, naturally enough, by the modern idea of the State. If the Gush Emunim are involved in creating Jewish
settlements on the West Bank, this is in the context of the modern, Zionist
state of Israel. "Next year in Jerusalem" for long had a distant eschatological
meaning; actually now it means "in the state of Israel." We have seen both
changes occurring, religious and political, in worldviews that appeal to particular groups of people.

Such modifications take place because a worldview, although put together
somewhat like a collage, has an organic aspect; that is, a change in one part,
or an addition, will affect the meaning of the whole. As we have noted, the
creation of the state of Israel colors the meaning of Jerusalem in the Jewish
imagination. The belief that Jesus was the Son of God changed Christian ideas
about the Creation. Likewise, the context in which a worldview is held has
consequences for its significance. Thus, a biblical literalist in the postcritical
era has consciously opted for a way of interpreting texts that was natural and
virtually inevitable in the preceding era. That is why so-called fundamentalism is a modern phenomenon. Fundamentalists attempt to go back to a sim-
pler tradition, but there is really no going back. With modern worldviews,
the introduction of modern concepts changes the sense of the religious ingredients; the Islamic *Sharia* imposed within the milieu of the modern nation-
state is a different phenomenon from its older embodiments in premodern
Islamic cultures. It is, then, necessary to recognize modern ingredients in religious worldviews, especially when they purport to go back to roots or re-
enact the old.

The context of religious worldviews has in fact been revolutionized over
the last two centuries. The emergence of the Enlightenment coupled with
the Industrial Revolution saw the creation of new sciences and technologies
of great power. At the same time, older political arrangements were dissolv-
ing, mainly under the impact of nationalism. Indeed, the notion of the nation-
state came to dominate not only Europe but, through colonialism, most of
Asia and then Africa. The nation-state concept had an impact upon the Ameri-

cas, though in the case of the United States in particular, nationalism took a far from typical form. In Europe and Asia, particularly, nationalism has been linguistic, cultural,[3] and sometimes religious. In the United States a new culture was in the making, and the whole came to be controlled by a sense of the values incorporated in the Constitution. Theodor Herzl's Zionism was an offshoot of the nineteenth century European nationalist movement. It helped to create a peculiar state — peculiar in that it is heavily migrant in population yet appeals to very ancient roots in the land.

In the Middle East, both pan-Arab and pan-Islamic sentiments have modified the nationalisms of the various states of the region. Here, too, a typical confluence between modernizing forces and nationalism has been apparent: the secular ideology of Ataturk's Turkey, Baath socialism in Syria and Iraq, Nasser's Egyptian nationalism, and the shah's romantic reconstruction of Iran, for instance. All of these represented different ways of combining the national idea with the need for new forms of economics and education after the colonial era faded. We may note the nationalist ideal, then, as one of the Western exports to the non-Western world.

Industrial capitalism and its counterpart, socialism, were also important ingredients in the new order. They threatened or even swept away older forms of rural existence. They depended on the development of science, engineering, and technology, which greatly affected education. Capitalism in particular nourished individualism. Older traditionalist values came to be questioned, not merely because of the Enlightenment perspective underlying much of Western education but also because older authority was questioned by a differently educated younger elite that was beginning to experience a consumerist society. Older religions were forced to cope with various forces and themes: nationalism, capitalism, scientific education, individualism, consumerism. As socialism helped to counter some of these themes, it was attractive to societies feeling the threats of the various powerful new forces.

Ultimately, the problem posed to traditional societies is how to preserve as much of their traditional cultural and religious values as possible while at the same time acquiring the benefits of the new forces. For despite their solvent effects, the new forces have their attractions: industrialization and science provide a national strength against the intrusive outsider, and can promise economic advancement for the masses; capitalism can generate an intriguing consumerism; and individualism ensures certain personal liberties important for a rising middle class. (Socialism, for its part, can promise social solidarity and protection for the poor.) Yet severe problems emerge when wedding some of these elements with older religious beliefs and practices. Urbanization may ruin some of the roots of traditional ritual geared to a rural life; scientific education seems to run counter to some of the beliefs in the scriptures, and undermines the traditional training of priests, ulema, and rabbis; and individualism calls into question older ethical pronouncements. Nevertheless, an accommodation could be attempted, and was first pioneered in the West by liberal Protestantism. Critical scholarship applied to the Bible encouraged liberals to take a step backward from literalism; new interpretations of cosmology and evolutionary theory combined with optimistic progressivism in helping to shape a new Protestant eschatology; and a social gospel combined some of the criticism of naked capitalism with the Sermon on the Mount. It was a powerful new mixture.

But a backlash followed, and "fundamentalist" forms of Christianity became important. Actually, the new fundamentalism was itself a mixture of traditional ethical and religious ideals drawn from biblical Protestantism with the individualism and technology of the capitalist world. Though it involved going "back to the Bible," the new fundamentalism inhabited a very different milieu from that of primitive Christianity. In more recent times, the movement known as the Moral Majority has represented a resurgence of fundamentalist values coming after a period when liberal Christian and other lobbies had enjoyed a strong political entrenchment in Washington. The previous deeply conservative period was during the McCarthy era, when political orthodoxy was demanded. Now, a more explicit mingling of religious and political motifs was apparent. The Moral Majority took a leaf out of liberal Protestantism's book.

As a worldview, however, the new conservatism had built-in tensions. One such tension was between its capitalist individualism (which was in fact undergirded, from a technological point of view, by scientific education) and the exigencies of modern forms of fundamentalism that selectively rejected parts of modern science. How could one be both a Texas oil baron and a biblical literalist? How did geology go with Genesis? In another area of tension: Although patriotism is a strong ingredient in this worldview, so also are such themes as Christianity, censorship, and a model of culture—themes that are in conflict with the U.S. Constitution in guaranteeing the rights of non-Christians, individuals as well as ethnic groups, which could be threatened by the Moral Majority's kind of thinking. Despite these tensions, conservative Christianity seems to be satisfying to the extent that it restores some definiteness; the Bible can be quoted as if its absolute authority were unimpaired, and older values associated with a better way of life under threat from soggy and immoral liberals are reaffirmed. The new conservatism also lends itself to exploitation by the media: the simple biblical message can be conveyed on television more easily than the hesitations and searchings of the liberal.

If one were to characterize the fundamentalist viewpoint in the United States, it can be seen as a blending of Protestantism and patriotism, with an accent on those traditional values threatened by modern scientific education and by some aspects of the individualist ethos arising within modern capitalism. Fundamentalism selectively rejects bits of modern thought, but fundamentalism also has its modern, technical side. It often pioneers new ways of presenting religion through the most up-to-date technological means, such as television, radio, and computerized mailing lists. Its chief ritual is preaching, for which it feels the need of a certainty and an authority flowing from an inerrant Bible. Since interpretation is more easily controlled by taking as much of the text as possible in the most literal way, fundamentalism feels perforce constrained to reject some aspects of modern science. This both restricts and enhances its appeal — restricts it to people with less education, and enhances its appeal in that the "simple" Christian has access to knowledge superior to that of proud intellectuals.

We see, then, a certain rhythm within the fold of the Western world. The ingredients in modern culture sometimes blend easily with traditional Christianity, as in the liberal Protestantism that paved the way for its Catholic equivalent, the Aggiornamento, undertaken by and after Vatican II. But the reaction to this development takes the shape of various forms of the religious right. A third position is the virtual abandonment of Christianity as a dominant worldview for the West, and the substitution of some kind of scientific humanism. More aggressive is the revolt against both Christian and bourgeois values represented by Marxism. But all of these are rhythms that beat, sometimes violently, sometimes softly, within the ambit of the Western world.

These patterns emerged during the colonial era and so were exported in varying ways to the non-Western world, where they began to take on different meanings. Nationalism, in its chauvinist or imperialist form, stimulated countervailing nationalisms with more ambiguous relationships to science, capitalism, and individualism. If these values were threatening to many people of the Protestant and Catholic traditions in the West, they were all the more so to Islam and other religions. It is true that Islam did not have quite the problems presented by the critical-historical treatment of the Bible, but there was enough in Western critical scholarship to provoke both fear and hostility. Yet the new technical forces unlocked by the West seemed desirable, to be used either militarily to throw off Western rule and incursions or as a means of improving the economic lot of citizens. Because the new science and the new economics were borne to the Muslim world by external powers, a further question confronted Muslims that had not the same force for Christians or Jews: How was it that the Islamic world, which once had such a glorious culture — no doubt, the most glorious of the whole human race (in the eyes of Muslims) — had fallen on such bad days?[4] Why had the initiative passed to the Western world, itself scarcely even Christian?

There were various ways of facing these questions. One response was to accept that the superiority of the West was due to its modern, secular, Enlightenment values. Why not, therefore, throw off the dead hand of religion? This was the path chosen by Ataturk: Turkey could in effect join the West and become a Western nation. Another possibility was to embrace a Muslim equivalent to liberal Protestantism. This involved replacement of the *Sharia* by Western-style law within the framework of a modern state, and was a typical pattern — for example, in Egypt. But another and appealing path in the face of the Western challenge was to affirm that the main cause of the relative failure of Islamic civilization in modern times was the faithlessness of so many Muslims; consequently, the greatness of Islam had to be reborn through a resurgence of genuine piety. It is this feeling which helps to refuel some of the most important movements in the contemporary Islamic world, much as the Muslim Brotherhood and Khomaini in Iran. Yet these movements, like their Christian fundamentalist counterparts, are modern in style. They appeal to tradition, but are better viewed as neotraditionalist. That is, they do not go back to tradition as though nothing had happened during the intervening period, but in fact make use of the technology of today's world — if necessary, with technical adaptations to some of the economic arrangements. In banking for example, ingenious alternatives to interest must be worked out. The use of modern weaponry and industrial processes means that Islam is wedded to some of the latest scientific and engineering knowledge. But the framework of values is that of an older Islam; the fighting woman who is learning to fire a submachine gun wears a *chador*,[5] and the sermons of ayatollahs are beamed to distant lands by satellite. Older traditions are revived within a modern framework.

Moreover, the fact that contemporary politics is run on differing principles from those in evidence during earlier phases of Islamic culture imparts a great change to the meaning of the fusion of politics and religion in Islam. Compared with much of the Shia traditions, Ayatollah Khomaini's republicanism is highly innovative. There is no room in his thinking for the older Shia view that politics is corrupt and should be left to rulers. The Ayatollah Khomaini is explicit and bold in his affirmation that political values should be permeated with religious values. For this reason, he has first argued for and then been a main agent in the construction of a constitution for Iran that leaves the directing power in the hands of religious specialists. There is, strictly speaking, no need for legislation, since the *Sharia* stands above society and its guiding interpretation has to be in the hands of those who know the principles of law and of Islamic practice: the ulama and the ayatollahs. The public life of the nation and the private piety of the people are thus blended into a whole. The Islamic Republic is not, of course, a pluralistic government;

it is a form of theocracy. When Islamic values are hitched to the administration of a modern state, the result is powerful. There is restricted consumerism, little individualism, and modified capitalism. To what degree can scientific and technological creativity survive in such an environment? Does one need Karl Popper's open society for science to flower? The answer to this question is a crucial one for the modern world, for it holds the key not only to the evolution of neotraditionalist Islamic societies but of Marxist ones as well.

The general principles of the Iranian constitution are followed in the model constitution drawn up by the Islamic Council.[6] Here we have an independent judiciary, the leadership of an imam, and the overriding principle that all laws must be in accordance with the *Sharia*. The constitution incorporates a variation of the millet system for dealing with non-Muslim minorities. The fact that the ideal of a kind of theocracy is concretized is significant, and although existing Islamic constitutions do not match it, this does not mean that the ideal has no political leverage. The institutionalization of an Islamic constitution in Iran links, moreover, with the pan-Islamic movement and points to the possibility of unified action by the Islamic world, possibly coordinated by the World Organization of the Islamic Conference. This possibility highlights a feature of the Islamic revolution that needs comment.

An Islamic state naturally has universal goals, since Islam is a universal religion. Consequently, in principle the policy of the state will be geared to the realizing of a universal Islamic revival and the establishment of Islamic solidarity. In this respect, an Islamic state cannot be purely nationalist. This is already evident in the way in which Iran presents itself. Iran turned its back on one form of nationalism — namely, Persian nationalism as expressed during the shah's regime. Although the shah did purport to be Muslim in orientation, he was also the exponent of Persian nationalism and the reviver of some of the glories of ancient Persia.

There is an analogy between the shah's ideology and that of Benito Mussolini. The latter kept a reasonable interface with Catholicism, and signed a fateful concordat with the Vatican in 1929. But the revitalized Italy was really the heir to the Roman Empire; the Mediterranean was *mare nostrum,* "our sea." Mussolini modernized Italy in certain respects and acquired strong armed forces (which, however, were internally weak and undermotivated to pursue Mussolini's ambitious war aims). Similarly, the shah drew on ancient tradition to reinforce his claims for Iran as a modern power which, with American support, would come to dominate much of the Middle East. His failure to provide an ideology that could appeal to both the new middle classes and the masses, due to the divisive character of modernization in relation to Islamic traditionalism, opened the way for the momentous events of 1979 when the people turned away from loyalty to the shah. Khomaini and other exponents of Islam had rethought Islam enough to command some allegiance from the middle classes and a great deal of enthusiasm from the masses and the native merchant class. The shah's failure was basically a failure of the ideas and symbols at his command.

The example of Khomaini is stimulating for other Muslims, even if they be non-Shiite. Khomaini succeeded in throwing out Western influence, and that in itself is positive from the perspective of most formerly colonized peoples. He has also shown the possibility of a fully Islamic republic. All this is relevant to a new breed of Islamic intellectual becoming influential in the contemporary world, whose existence it is important to note.[7]

The (mainly younger) breed of new intellectual is disillusioned on a number of fronts. Since he or she has been educated at a modern university, there is little sympathy with the backward-looking religious specialists of traditional society; therefore, one form of tradition has to be set aside. The intellectual is also disillusioned with the older style of modernist who has made too many concessions to purely Western values (or so it is thought). He is disillusioned with the Marxist alternative as well, which at one time had attractions as an antiimperialist worldview with modern goals. The new intellectual is concerned with starting from Islamic premises and reaching a thoroughly modern synthesis that is impressed neither with Marx nor with the West, but borrows freely from either where ideas and techniques are seen to be in accordance with the Islamic worldview. As Ziauddin Sardar, one of the most sophisticated and perceptive Islamic thinkers at the present time, remarks: "The new intellectual can be seen teaching and learning, arguing and discussing at university campuses in Kuala Lumpur and Islamabad, Tehran and Damascus, Cairo and Khartoum, Rabat and Lagos, Aligarh and Ottawa, London and Chicago."[8]

It is to such young people that the Muslim Brotherhood and other relatively radical ways of restructuring Islamic society after the period of Western domination and secular nationalism appeal.[9] Moreover, this group has grown up in a resurgence of pan-Islamic feeling partly because of the ease of modern communication, the accessibility of the Hajj, and the emergence of global thinking. A vital question is whether or not Islamic bonds will turn out to be strong enough to hold the various states together. Nevertheless, it is worth dwelling on the transnational character of much Islamic revivalism; in this transnationalism, Islamic revivalism contrasts with the patriotisms of Christian resurgence, such as those of the American Right, Afrikaner Calvinism, and Romanian Orthodoxy.

The case of Judaism is rather different from either the Christian or the Islamic example. Before we turn to one example of a resurgent movement of the right in that context, let us consider why Israel has become such a potent symbol of Western intrusion for Muslims. Muslims generally think of the successes of Islam as irreversible. At any rate, there is a conception of the House of Islam — the territory in which Islam predominates and outside of which are conducted struggle and warfare for the faith. Israel intrudes into the Islamic sphere and is "unnatural" as well as unjust (because of the deprivation of the rights of the Palestinians). The very existence of Israel is thus symbolically potent. In addition, its continued existence depends on the support of the United States, the headquarters of that capitalism which has done so much to corrupt and undermine traditional Islamic values.[10]

In some ways, the Gush Emunim or Block of the Faithful mirrors these attitudes. The West Bank territory is seen as naturally part of Israel, corresponding to ancient Judea and Samaria. The Gush thus view it as an area for entirely justifiable settlement and conquest. In this, they exhibit a degree of Israeli chauvinism. The Gush have some nonreligious backing that they take pains not to alienate. Their nationalism is, however, of a religious kind and springs from a religious form of Zionism. The controversial character of the Gush Emunim in modern Israel draws our attention to an ideological conflict that has characterized the history of the notion of the Jewish State ever since Herzl. The latter — and many of the others who managed to realize the foundation of the state in 1948 — were, like many other nationalists, both secularists and nationalists. They were under the spell of ideas of progress, modernity, socialism, and democracy. These ideas had sometimes brought conflict elsewhere between nationalist politics and traditional religion — in nineteenth century Italy, for instance, and to some degree in Mussolini's Italy. The definition of Jewishness, however, of necessity was ultimately religious, for it was religion that maintained Jewish culture and identity through the ages. A split therefore existed between national ideology and national definition. This situation cried out for a religious type of nationalism, and various forms have indeed emerged, including the personal position of Menachem Begin. Since Israel is a place of migration, an extra edge to religious commitment is provided by the ability of the Gush to recruit from the United States on behalf of a voluntarily undertaken spiritual path with political goals.

In this selective treatment of various types of religious nationalism I have omitted many examples, such as the many new Christian movements in Africa and Islamic revival in Pakistan, Malaysia, the Sudan, and elsewhere,[11] not to mention Mahdism in northern Nigeria, the group who took the Great Mosque in Mecca,[12] and a variety of Jewish spiritual and political movements. The cases examined all exhibit unresolved conflicts and problems. Proponents of resurgences are usually so sure of themselves that they preclude pluralism. Yet all of the movements have arisen from a multicultural situation in which differing values coexist in the same society. An epistemological problem remains unresolved even by such a sophisticated thinker as Ziauddin Sardar.

Although knowledge may have to be reshaped according to an Islamic pattern, how do we know that even that pattern has truth? By what criteria do we consider the Quran to be divine revelation? Any certainty in these matters will be internal and incommensurable—and such certainty is scarcely worth having. On the other hand, any transcultural criteria will at best turn out to be soft. We need not be relativists, but we do need to be soft nonrelativists. This philosophical comment points to the hard nature of conflict in the religio-political sphere. The cure is perhaps some form of dialogue. The movements we have considered, however, are mainly concerned with problems of cultural identity and pride, and such issues often lead to strife rather than to dialogue.

Notes

1. See Ninian Smart, *Worldviews: Crosscultural Explorations of Human Beliefs* (New York: Macmillan-Scribner's, 1983).

2. A good treatment of this is Richard Quebedeaux, *By Whose Authority* (San Francisco: Harper and Row, 1981), especially pp. 138ff.

3. For a discussion and analysis of varieties of European nationalism, see Jaroslav Krecji, "What is a Nation?" in Peter Merkl and Ninian Smart, eds., *Religion and Politics in the Modern World* (New York: New York University Press, 1983), pp. 29ff.

4. See Yvonne Y. Haddad, *Contemporary Islam and the Challenge of History* (Albany: SUNY Press, 1982), esp. pp. 83ff.

5. A perceptive essay on this theme is that of John Alden Williams, "Veiling in Egypt as a Political and Social Phenomenon," in John L. Esposito, ed., *Islam and Development: Religion and Sociopolitical Change* (Syracuse, N.Y.: University Press, 1980), pp. 71–86.

6. The text is reproduced in Ziauddin Sardar, *Islamic Futures* (New York: Mansell, 1985), pp. 326–45.

7. See Sardar, *Islamic Futures,* ch. 15.

8. Ibid., p. 323.

9. Charles Wendell, ed., *Five Tracts of Hasan Al-Banna (1906–49)* (Berkeley: University of California Press, 1978).

10. See Gil Carl Alroy, *Attitudes towards Jewish Statehood in the Arab World* (New York: American Association for Peace in the Middle East, 1971).

11. See John L. Esposito, *Voices of Resurgent Islam* (New York: Oxford University Press, 1983).

12. James Buchan, [ch. 25] in David Holden and Richard Johns, *The House of Saud* (London: Pan Books, 1981).

II

Conclusion: Religious Resurgence in Today's World —

Refuge from Dislocation and Anomie or Enablement for Change?

MARY ELAINE HEGLAND

With the benefit of the information and perspectives gained through the preceding chapters, we are now in a position to address the questions raised in the introduction and to suggest tentative responses as well as direction for further inquiry and research. World-wide attention has been devoted to the "Islamic revival," and particularly to the resurgence of Shia Islam in Iran. But are the Islamic Revival and the takeover in Iran by Shiite figures and organizations discrete, unique phenomena, or are they related in some way to the resurgence of religion elsewhere? The purpose of this volume is a close examination of manifestations of Islamic resurgence in an effort to uncover underlying contributing factors. Such an examination can then be utilized to form questions for application to other examples of religious resurgence.

The image developing is of a resurgence of religion brought about by people wishing to improve their own lives and the lives of others. Such people may have recently emerged into national or international prominence and activity. Economic transformation and other advantages of "modernization" have freed groups of people from previous constraints and allowed them to participate in national and/or international-level politics and awareness. Other groups and individuals have become disenchanted with such previously captivating ideologies as nationalism. Cynical about the intent of the elites promoting the ideals of nationalism — namely, that all members of the nation are citizens, and equal under the law to participate in policy formation and receive the benefits administered by the nation-state — people have begun to look elsewhere. Participants in religious resurgence seem to have as a main aim the improvement of life here on earth. Although disillusioned with secular nationalism and present political elites, many political actors of today are nevertheless influenced by the now continuing tradition of nationalism and the assumption that the involvement of governments is necessary to bring about improvements in living conditions. Critical of the perceived ineffectiveness of secular ideologies in speaking to their concerns and interests, believers none-theless merge a secular ideology—that of nationalism—with their revived hope in religion as a way of improving their lives. Thus, much of the visibility of the religious resurgence comes from people putting pressure on, dissenting against, overthrowing, or taking over governments.

Religious Resurgence: The Evidence

Not all religious groups are experiencing a resurgence, Wuthnow indicates, and Gaffney points to the variety of activity and intent included within the term *Islamic resurgence.* These articles do demonstrate an upsurge in activity focused around religious themes, but along with other authors of this volume they find such an upsurge to coincide with the demands and interests of particular groups or categories of people. In Iran, for example, the revival of interest in Islam during the 1960s was in part the result of concerted and determined efforts by the clerical establishment to build a wide and devoted political base throughout the population. Disturbed by the secularization of society and the attacks by the government on their influence, the clerical es-tablishment resisted government policy and attempted to build a network of support through educational efforts.[1] They organized assistance and reli-gious activities for urban migrants,[2] and reached out to the rural population by sending large numbers of mullas to villages. Needless to say, the efforts of this group to reestablish their influence in society, using a religious ideol-ogy as an organizing and motivating force, have been highly successful.

Bazaar personnel and traders constitute another group organizing around Islam. Gustav Thaiss's study of the Tehran bazaar, based on fieldwork con-ducted between 1967 and 1969, demonstrated how following the ritual re-quirements of Islam and exhibiting pious behavior testified to a bazaar trad-er's creditworthiness and spoke well of his reputation, both among other traders and with the public. Mutual participation in ritual activities promoted trust within the bazaar community.[3] The bazaar had been under attack by the shah's regime previous to the revolution,[4] so it was natural for *bazaris* to become involved in Islamic resistance. As did the clerical establishment, bazaar traders employed their networks of connection and Shia ideology and ritual to spread dissension against the Pahlavi government. There are indica-tions of a growth in the strength of traders during the 1960s and 1970s in Iran, in terms of both numbers and wealth.[5] Such expanding influence was due in large part to oil revenue, which provided the general population with greater purchasing power, in turn making possible the proliferation of traders and shopkeepers.

Yet another example of a coincidence between a resurgence in Islam and an economic interest group has been documented by the anthropologist, Judith Nagata, in Malaysia. One of the organizations forming the Islamic movement in that country, the Arqam, stresses economic self-sufficiency and urges its members to become involved in business—often the production and selling of religiously pure food items and religious articles. In addition to the economic interests of the Malay ethnic group in general, Arqam lecturers exhort Malays "to treat life as a sort of economic *jihad*,"[6] in order to overcome the economically disadvantaged position of the ethnic group. Earlier struggles on the part of the Malay population to obtain opportunities equal to those of the more successful Indian and Chinese ethnic groups had been mobilized under the movements for Malay rights and the Malay Language Society. After the implementation of the Malay Language Act and the government's suppression of further discussion of the Malay language issue and rights for Malays generally (considering them as being too sensitive), "new modes of expression had to be found. The banner now unfurled is that of Islam" (p. 410). Due in part to the government policy of "uplifting" Malays by providing educational and work opportunities, a large new middle class of Malays has evolved which is now mobilizing its own political strength through the branches of the Islamic movement.[7]

Religion is also commonly found as a marker and organizing system for politically disadvantaged groups mobilizing to gain rights and to influence the political process. Such a course can take place at a variety of levels. Hegland's research in the Iranian village of "Aliabad" demonstrates how the religious symbolism mobilizing Iranians for national-level revolution was also utilized in local-level political struggles. Persons previously active in resistance to the local-level political elite realigned under Shia rhetoric to take over land belonging—unfairly, in the estimate of the activists—to the local-level elite. Village teachers who had formerly supported Prime Minister Mossadeq now rephrased their antigovernment sentiments in Islamic terms.[8]

Shia ideology served to unite the newly expanded urban working class and the new professional middle class in Iran in their attempts to gain a political voice. Elsewhere as well, religion has become a unifying ideology for emerging classes struggling to exert political pressure on unresponsive governments.[9] According to Wuthnow's study, for example, evangelicals in the United States were likely to be from disadvantaged backgrounds, nonwhite, old, poorly educated, and from the rural South—although in some cases recently educated and financially reinforced.[10]

Religion has been important in exerting political pressure and mounting resistance against governments. The articles of Wuthnow, Gaffney, and Hegland provide examples of the involvement of religious figures and groups from particular socioeconomic backgrounds in the pressuring and criticizing of national governments. Christianity has served in many countries as an oppositional ideology—in Poland and the Philippines, for example, and especially in Central America. Finally, as Voll's chapter indicates, religion has promoted the assertion of identity against the influence of a foreign country and even against "the West" as a whole.

At a variety of levels, then, people are presenting religious reasons for why their voices should be heard, and why they too should receive justice and social and economic benefits; further, they are insisting that religion should take them and their interests into account. In the words of the American theologian Harvey Cox, the people from "the edges" and from the "bottom" are insisting on a part in the formation of theology and the relevance of theology to themselves and their situation in life (ibid., p. 261).

The Continuing Tradition: Enabling Factors for Change

The chapters on continuing tradition remind us of the dynamic, fluid, responsive, and syncretic qualities of symbolic systems, ideologies, and worldviews. The change and diversity, the merging and converging, of inherited systems of thought as they are influenced by other systems and by the realities in people's lives are truly amazing. Religious traditions come to us carrying the weight of the past, but they are flexible in taking on new nuances and meanings as they are modified by ideas, events and conditions.

Elements of social organization, traditions of charismatic leadership, and the concept of martyrdom all represent parts of this continuing tradition. In several ways, Dekmejian's chapter on charismatic leadership sheds light on current cases of religious resurgence. In the case of Iran, for example, we are reminded of the relevance of the tradition of charismatic leadership to the revolutionary movement in Shia Islam. Dekmejian's discussion of the "crisis milieu," with its characteristics of crisis in "legitimacy of elites, ideology and institutions," identity confusion, and susceptibility to mass appeals is likewise applicable to many situations of current religious resurgence. The present historical period resembles other periods of religious resurgence in being preceded by a period of transformation and change. At present, rural urban migration, changes in class structure and composition, and the substitution of industrial for agricultural means of subsistance have been taking place at a rapid rate. Large groups of people have suddenly moved out of the range of communities where they were held in check by economic and political elites, and into an arena with the potential for mass political participation. They have become available, then, to the appeals of charismatic leaders.

In addition to the closer convergence between the ideals of martyrdom in Christianity and Shia Islam in recent years, another important parallel development can be discerned in the interpretation of Christianity leading up to liberation theology on the one hand, and the changing interpretation and understanding of the implications of Shiism prevalent during the 1978–79 Iranian revolution on the other.[11] In spite of the often-mentioned "revolutionary" emphasis of Shiism, recent writers have pointed out that, traditionally, Shia doctrine and the Shia establishment actually accommodated the secular state and in fact served to support it.[12] According to Mangol Bayat, in order to maintain some freedom in the areas of theology and jurisprudence, the Shia jurists repressed the revolutionary, millenarian impulses inherent in original Shiism. Shia Islam "emerged as the religion of the quiescent, pious, inner-worldly faithful who, shunning politics, patiently await the return of the *Imam,* their Saviour, which would mark the end of time."[13] Willem Floor also questions the idea that "opposition to tyranny is a fundamental and pervasive characteristic of Shia Islam," finding rather that "the ulama formed part of Iran's traditional power elite."[14]

In local communities as well as at the national level, Shia Islam served to support and protect the interests of the political elites and the upper classes.[15] According to an anonymous observer of an Iranian rural area, the prerevolution mullas had sided with the "exploitative landlords."[16] Even the central rituals of Shiism connected with the death of Imam Husain on Ashura, the tenth of the month of Moharram, which so dramatically displayed revolutionary potential during the Iranian uprising, were utilized to legitimize the status quo, promote solidarity and unity around the existing social structure, and demonstrate the power and wealth of elites (and thereby the utility of maintaining loyalty to those elites). The *taziyeh* performances, commemorating the martyrdom of Imam Hosain, received royal patronage.[17] Researchers have documented a number of examples of the use of the Moharram rituals by local-level elites in provincial towns and villages to demonstrate their power and legitimize their position.[18]

In Christianity as well, of course, the clerical establishment accommodated secular rule and even supported the legitimacy of secular government with religious beliefs. As theologian Harvey Cox points out, the religious establishment in Christianity also agreed to a division of spheres of influence in exchange for relative theological freedom. The doctrine of separation of church and state left the state to proceed without undue criticism from religion; according to Cox, "churches were left with little to do in this world but to comfort, console, and prepare people for the next one" (p. 95). Churches and theologians "usually deferred to the power of the classes that had established the right to govern" (p. 96).

Attempts have of course been made in the past, by both Christians and Shia Muslims, to deviate from adherence to the dominant interpretation of their religion promoted by the elites and upper classes, and to propose an interpretation more appropriate to resistance. In recent years, however, a sustained and significant cooperative effort has been apparent, in both Christianity and Shiism, between theologians and clerics on the one hand and the body of believers on the other, to radically modify the implications of the respective faiths for this world activity. In Bayat's view, the Iranian ulama purposefully ended its repressions of Shia millenarianism and resurrected an earlier Shia tradition—the original Shiism—in order to encourage revolt against the shah's modernizing regime, which was cutting down on the influence of the ulama.[19] In order to mobilize support and reassert their influence, Shia clergy needed to listen to their followers and speak to their perceived needs, and Ayatollah Khomaini publicly proclaimed his respect for and confidence in the masses. The clergy also needed to find a way to interest the youth who had been moving away from Islam. To do so, the clerical establishment professed dedication to such concerns of youth as democracy, freedom, and the rights of the masses. Even after the revolution, an anonymous observer found that rural clergy were forced to espouse liberal values in order to maintain status among the youth.[20]

In areas under the influence of the Catholic Church as well, the clerical establishment was forced to listen to followers in order to maintain influence. From his study of "The Political Transformation of the Brazilian Catholic Church," Thomas Bruneau concludes: "The Church intentionally attempted to shift the nature of its power from maintaining the *status quo* to supporting social change *in order to continue to exercise religious influence.*"[21] Liberation theology attempted to draw upon the experience of believers in contemporary Latin America in forming an understanding of the meaning of Christianity.[22] In this effort, the formation of "base communities" that stressed leadership of lay individuals, a new look at the Scriptures, and political and social activism was central.[23] From the interaction between theologians and clerics of both Christianity and Shiism with the body of believers who were concerned about social justice and freedom from repression emerged a transformed understanding of the implication of belief, a transformed interpretation of the means to redemption, and a changed perception about the central figure in the religion—Christ in Christianity and Imam Hosain in Shiism.

Christians have begun to reexamine Christ in the historical context of the repression of the Jewish population by both the Roman domination and the local Jewish ruling elite. Christology has become the focus of important debate relevant both to theology and to church politics. From this debate (and related historical and theological research) has emerged an alternative view of the meaning of Christ. For both faiths, the view of the central figure changed from that of an intercessor whose suffering should be imitated to a revolutionary model whose example of struggle against unjust temporal power should be followed in the movement to transform the world. In the words of theologian Rosemary Ruether, "The poor learn not to be afraid of those in power and to begin to take their destiny into their own hands. . . . This is the real meaning of redemptive suffering, of Jesus and of Christians, not passive or masochistic self-sacrifice."[24] Political attitudes of Latin American Christians have changed "from acquiescence to anger, from accepting systemic poverty to fighting against it."[25] Just so, Iranian attitudes changed from seeking connections with the powerful to revolting against tyranny during the Iranian revolution.[26] The requirements for redemption changed from suffering to actively struggling against the manifestations of evil.

Proponents of this modified interpretation in Christianity and Islam obviously are no longer content with a theoretical or real separation of religion from politics. Christian theologians have criticized the modern church's stance on separation between church and state, and are advocating an activist role for believers in politics and the public sphere.[27] Many Muslim clerics are also intent on a more active role for religion in politics. Reacting to the current revitalization of religion in criticizing governments, those governments have often reacted themselves by emphasizing the religiosity of their officials and the piety of their programs. Muslim leaders have publicized their beliefs and their adherence to ritual requirements and changed policies to reflect religious expectations. Christian leaders have emphasized their religious credentials, as in the case of the American presidential campaign of 1984.

Governments have, of course, long used religion to support their legitimacy. As has long been recognized, religion can be used by either dissident groups or by governments.[28] In Shiism, the symbolic system connected with the martyrdom of Imam Hosain has been used both by political and economic elites and by groups resisting those elites and government policies.[29] Christianity likewise has witnessed a struggle for control over the meaning of rituals surrounding the passion of Christ and the symbolism of the Brown Virgin, Our Lady of Guadalupe.[30]

In Shiism, there is even a conscious recognition among some believers of a double, complementary potential for meaning of religious myths, depending on the appropriate stance for Muslims at any given historical period. In the words of the scholar, Mahmoud Ayoub, written before the Iranian Revolution:

The death of Husayn, however, has meant different things at different periods for the Muslim community. . . . In whatever way the death of Husayn has been understood, it has not lost its aspect of redemption. Redemption may be seen as direct intercession or direct example. In the second case it redeems, so to speak, the community and its ideal by continuing to provide a living example of self-sacrifice. . . . The lesson derived from this modern emphasis is more concrete and relevant to our problems now than the earlier emphasis on abstract sufferings and hope.[31]

It is the multivocality of theological and religious symbolism that allows for the various interpretations advocated by competing political forces.[32] Religious symbolic systems are capable of being imbued with meanings from a variety of sources, and of changing over time in response to a variety of influences. In his study of the relevance of the Brown Virgin, Our Lady of Guadalupe, to the revolt of the educated criollo priest Hidalgo (which led to the Mexican revolution of independence), Victor Turner states:

Our Lady of Guadalupe I would regard not only as an Indian symbol but also as a joint criollo-Indian symbol, which incorporated into its system of significance not only ideas about the earth, motherhood, indigeneous powers, and so on, but also criollo notions of liberty, fraternity, and equality, some of which were borrowed from the atheistical French thinkers of the revolutionary period.[33]

Catholic theologian Rosemary Ruether likewise points out that liberation theology arises from a merging of two heritages. "Liberation theology arises in Latin America from people who know that they are heirs of their Spanish father and not merely their Indian mothers; from peoples whose Catholic Christianity and European languages are a heritage to be claimed and transformed, not merely repudiated" (p. 24). The interpretation of Shia Islam dominant during the Iranian revolution was likewise a synthesis of the heritages of two worlds—Iranian Shiism and Western ideology. It was only after this synthesis and the resulting transformation of Shiism that the religion gained such devotion, and Iranians became so determined to make their religious beliefs relevant to their lives and to change their society to bring it into greater conformity with religious expectations. Before dissemination of this transformed understanding of Shiism, the majority of the youth, who were later to be such a significant force in the revolution, were not much interested in their religion.[34]

Ever moving, ever dynamic, the religious legacies from the past evolve through interaction with the present. The chapters by Davis and Smart emphasize the strong influence of the modern concept of nationalism on religious traditions. The impact of the concept of nation-state and the perception of government as the responsible and reforming agent is so pervasive that even Shia Islam—according to many, the traditionally antigovernment, outside-of-government, watcher-of-government religion—has become the government religion. The *umma* (religious community) has become merged with the nation-state, and the nation-state is now expected to be a community of believers as well. The whole discussion in this section of liberation theology in Catholic Christianity and symbolic "multivocality" in Shia Islam in relation to the omnipresent nation-state emphasizes that the continuing tradition (here, religion) is also an enabling factor for change.

Catalysts of the Current Resurgence

Continuing religious traditions, blending with modern ideas and modified in reaction to existing realities, provide a means of inspiring, organizing, legitimizing, and unifying religious movements. But why have such movements developed at present, rather than at some other point in history? What are the causes or catalysts of the current religious resurgence? Have people turned to religion for comfort in the face of dislocation and anomie resulting from major economic transformation?

Behind the religious resurgence seem to be groups of people enabled by such factors as improved economic status, education, greater integration into society, and increased numbers. These groups are growing increasingly dissatisfied with a previously dominant ideology, and are turning hopefully to an alternative ideology. The chapters by Davis and Voll provide case studies of such processes. According to Davis, both Arab nationalism in Egypt and Zionism in Israel were based on the middle and lower middle classes. In both countries, persons in these classes have become disillusioned with the unresponsiveness of the political elites and their ideologies and are turning to religious nationalism—the Muslim Brethren in Egypt, the Gush Emunim in Israel—as an alternative. Voll's chapter treats a similar phenomenon at the international level: Muslims turning to alternatives arising from the Muslim tradition itself, as a result of their perception of the failure of the West and Western ideologies.

One of the most significant social categories supporting the Islamic resurgence has been the burgeoning urban working class or lower middle class, whose numbers have greatly increased in recent years due to extraordinary rural-urban migration, including villagers who commute to work in urban areas—either daily or, for those who live further away, less frequently.[35] Sharing many of the attitudes and attributes of these urban migrants are those, also working-class, who have remained in villages and smaller towns to work, as well as persons who migrate for labor to foreign countries. Noting the new environment with exposure to a different style of life, the "disruption of traditional bonds," and the often less than adequate living conditions of urban migrants, some analysts have assumed that a related disorientation, anomie, and dislocation are prompting the urban working class into participating in the Islamic resurgence. The evidence for such a conclusion is insufficient, however, and remains to be questioned along the following lines:

1. Assumptions of anomie and social isolation in urban settings appear to be exaggerated. In their 1970–71 study of migrants and native women of Isfahan (Iran), John and Margaret Gulick found an even higher percentage of native women reporting very frequent contact with relatives (79.7%) than did migrant women (76.5%). According to the data gathered by the Gulicks, contact among relatives increases with the number of generations a family lived in Isfahan. The researchers conclude that "city living, far from bringing about less association with relatives, is compatible with it and may even reinforce and encourage it."[36]

Material conditions for the people forming the relatively new lower middle class or proletariat seem to have improved considerably since the onset of the oil boom and the expanded availability of migrant labor opportunities, both within and outside the oil-producing countries. Reinhold Loeffler has provided dramatic documentation of the great expansion in economic opportunities in the Boir Ahmad region of Iran before the revolution, for example. The rapid construction of urban-style homes in smaller towns and villages, such as in Boir Ahmad, a testimony to the improvement in economic conditions, was paralleled by a similar development in the area around Shiraz, where Hegland conducted research in 1978 and 1979. Many urban dwellers enjoyed similar convenient living standards. For those who were less advantaged, it is doubtful that their situation was any worse than it had been in their home villages. Similar classes elsewhere in the Middle East seemed also to be enjoying an improvement in their material well-being.[37]

2. The lower middle classes were not marginal or alienated from society, but, on the contrary, were experiencing increased incorporation into society —and perhaps most important, they were receiving an education. Most researchers on Islamic movements note the involvement in education of members, even the more traditional or lower-class participants. Lately, it has not been unusual for persons from a lower class background, even from rural areas, to attend a university or teacher-training institution. A village might even boast of a son attending school abroad. Education, in turn, made additional

opportunities of employment, access to institutions, contact, networks, and new ideologies available to this class. Due to their urban setting, access to education, and interaction with many others of a similar or varying background, members of this class were less isolated and more exposed to a great variety of influences and contacts.[38]

3. Inadequate evidence is available to support assumptions of anomie, disorientation, uprootedness, and social isolation supposedly suffered by urban migrants. Quite to the contrary, Farhad Kazemi, in his study of the migrant poor of Tehran, discovered that migrants had extensive contact with friends and relatives, both in the home village and the city; did not feel lonely; assisted each other; and found their incomes to have met or exceeded their expectations.[39]

4. Research among leaders and members of religious movements has not found socially isolated, deprived, or anomic individuals. Rather, participants are upwardly mobile, educated, normal, socially engaged persons, who enjoy much better than average opportunity in life. Ibrahim, for example, found members of militant Islamic groups to be "model young Egyptians."[40]

5. Some analysts blame the "disruption of social bonds" and the destruction of the social fabric caused by migration and recent social change for the alienation and anomie that have supposedly led victims to return to the comfort and security of religion. However, such "traditional social bonds" have not always affected individuals positively, and could in fact have resulted in social isolation and deprivation through forced acquiescence to an economic, political, and ideological structure that did not serve the individuals' best interests. Indications suggest that such conditions were often the case in the home villages of recent urban migrants. Hegland's research in an Iranian village provides an example of a situation where government-supported local-level elites successfully controlled the economic, political, and even religious behavior of dependent villagers.[41] Hamied Ansari's research in Egypt documents the use by central authorities of rural elites to maintain control over rural residents there as well (p. 134). Such control probably occurred before the oil boom and labor migration resulted in a dramatic increase of job opportunities. During this earlier period, villagers had little choice but to remain quiescent; opportunities for earning a livelihood other than farming the land administered by such elites (or other work under their control) were almost nonexistent. With the advent of the great expansion in economic opportunities, however, formerly bound individuals—and even more so, their offspring—could escape the constraints of these repressive bonds. They were no longer politically captive, or forced to accept the dominant interpretation of religion and ritual. Aspects of the old structure *did* break down, but the result for affected individuals was not anomie or social isolation, but rather

the freedom to engage in political struggle on their own and to use religious symbolism in resistance to the system and in presenting their own grievances — or to be available to the political manipulation of persons and groups outside of the village.[42] The new economic opportunities thus appeared to disrupt repressive vertical bonds while allowing horizontal bonds of mutual assistance and support to continue.

The new-found strength, resources, and freedom from constraint of the rural migrants and commuters to urban areas and urban working classes is paralleled by the situation of another, overlapping group: the youth. The latter have also experienced a recent tremendous expansion both in relative numbers and in the resources available to them. They have also broken free from traditional bonds and constraints. The jobs and educational opportunities available to young people at present mean that they are no longer beholden to their elders for financial resources and economic opportunities. Above and beyond the very real and practical advantages of education, their possession of a secular, Western education (whether earned abroad or in the native country) confers prestige on them in the eyes of their families, relatives, and friends, who respect and admire education.[43] The exposure of young people to new information, contacts, foreign ideas, travel, and concentration in universities and other institutions, together with their relatively greater independence from family, has given rise to many student movements in the last two decades. The involvement of the young, because of their great numbers and their virtual monopoly over the eagerly sought after modern education, has lent great force to the religious resurgence in recent years.[44]

Another important group in the current religious revival (and, again, one that overlaps with youth) is the expanded middle class. Individuals in this group shared a concern with the lower middle class for turning their new-found power in terms of numbers, education, economic position, access to information and ideologies (from both home and abroad), and opportunities for interaction and organization into political influence.[45]

The argument of this essay, then, is that it was enabled groups, rather than deprived groups, that both formed Islamic movements, and contributed the majority of the participants. The middle and lower middle classes are now finding the resources with which to organize and express their discontent. One could even argue that the clerical and bazaar or trading groups who have been promoters of the Islamic resurgence, although reacting defensively against government attacks, were proceeding with the benefit of additional resources. The numbers of traders and their prosperity had increased due to the improved purchasing power of the population, a result of the oil boom and new opportunities for migrant labor. The expanding support of this group, traditionally allied with the clergy, would in turn serve to provide the ulama with greater organizing and promotional ability. Also providing substantial new resources to the clerical group were donations from other followers, and a dramatically expanded constituency: the thousands of rural people migrating to cities, still using a religious idiom to express themselves and viewing the world from a religious perspective as well as the educated middle classes, turning to their religious culture and heritage as an alternative to the rejected Western supremacy. Likewise, "the oil-boom of the early 1970s brought prosperity to the seminaries and thereby increased the ranks of the lower clergy."[46]

The new enabling factors available to the lower middle and middle classes, providing them with the resources and freedom to participate in religious movements, can be divided into two kinds: ideological and material. Ideologically, movement participants of the lower middle and middle classes had available to them, through education and information networks, such Western ideologies as enlightened liberalism and Marxism, both of which proclaim the right of all to justice and socioeconomic well-being. Such values (and the influence of Western education) are very apparent in the rhetoric, terminology, type of discourse, and demands of the various movements, and even in their theology and the transformed emphasis and meaning of religion. For example, the fundamentalist Tabligh organization in Malaysia organized retreat sessions providing "the opportunity for the intellectual analysis, questioning and exegesis so alien to traditional Malay religious instruction, and so appealing to modern youth."[47] Another group in Malaysia, the Islamic Youth Movement, appeals to "the urban, 'sophisticated' audience, for whom they can pepper their speeches with English and social science concepts, and references to interracial harmony, thus creating an image of enlightened liberalism" (p. 427). Ali Shariati, an Iranian religious reformer, likewise used French terms, referred to Western thinkers, and utilized Western concepts and ideologies in his forging of the transformed Shiism which was so appealing to educated Iranians.[48] Ayatollah Khomaini also spoke of freedom and democracy. Such Islamic movements as the Mojahedin have been strongly influenced by Marxism, as, of course, has been the liberation theology of Latin America.

In the demands of the various Islamic movements, the voice of Western ideologies is apparent. Almost without exception, the movements demand greater socioeconomic equality and the right of meaningful political participation.[49] A striking demonstration of the pervasiveness and hold of liberal and leftist ideology has been presented by a social scientist who conducted research in a rather remote Iranian village in 1980 and 1981. After the Iranian revolution, two-thirds of the educated youth in the village were liberal in political outlook while another thirteen percent were leftist.[50] It is partly because the concepts of justice, freedom, and socioeconomic equality have become so widespread in today's world that religions espousing these values receive such a warm response.

Both the middle and the lower middle classes, then, were enabled by new ideologies, either of a liberal or leftist Western form or of transformed Islamic ideologies influenced by these same Western ideologies. Most people active in Islamic movements were probably touched by both the secular and the religious forms of these ideologies to one degree or another. Moved by these ideologies, Iranians and other third worlders have begun to expect justice, political participation, and greater socioeconomic equality. However, without a breakdown of repressive structures and bonds, persons are not free to act upon their impulses. The second area of enabling factors, the social structural, economic, and demographic, provided the freedom from previous political and economic constraints necessary to demand improvements.[51]

To the questions raised at the beginning of this section, the following answers can be suggested. Transformations in interpretations of religious belief and ritual took place as a result of interaction between clerics who were willing to reinstitute "latent revolutionary tendencies" in religion partly to retain or regain their own influence, and believers holding values of justice, freedom, and social equality—inculcated by a secular, modern education—and wishing to exert an influence in society. Believers were able to respond to the call to intensify their religious commitment, empowered by the expectations taught by the revised ideologies and by the freedom from political and economic constraint brought about by transformations in economic structures and related social structural changes.

The Religious Resurgence and Political Systems

If supporters of the religious resurgence have as a principal aim the improvement of temporal life, influenced by the ideas of this day and age, they also believe governments to be the appropriate and/or effective agents of bringing about such improvements. The religious revival is highly visible in interaction between proponents of revival and governments. Most supporters of religious resurgence seem to hope for and expect a transformation of society that will bring social reality more into congruence with their beliefs. Some groups are more willing than others to work through existing political structures in bringing about such transformations. Christian fundamentalist groups in the United States, for example, seem to work mainly within the political system. Sharing many goals with the Israeli government, the Gush Emunim often work with the government, although engaging in acts of civil disobedience when these seem necessary to exert additional pressure. Proponents of liberation theology often find themselves not only at odds with governments, but also often do not accept the legitimacy of these governments. Supporters of liberation Shiism were against the Pahlavi government, for example, and at present those Shiites living outside of Iran who still support Ayatollah Khomaini are often dissidents wishing for a new form of government.

Governments have dealt with the resurgence of religious opposition in a variety of ways. Some leaders, such as Reza Shah Pahlvai, Anwar Sadat, Sadam Hosain, and Ja'far Numayri, have sought to emphasize their own religiosity. Governments have often attempted to take over and control religious organizations and activities. Realizing that "the only sure way to challenge Islam is with more Islam," the government party in Malaysia organized its own network of *dakwah* conferences, lecturers, and programs; it also centralized religious instruction, and gave verbal support to Islamic ideals.[52] For Islam, the divergence in the interpretations of religion espoused by opposition groups and that promoted by governments and elites is so notable that scholars in discussing these different interpretations have taken to using such dichotomies as "government Islam" and "people's Islam"; "the Islam to which rulers and dominant elites appeal, and the Islam of the masses (and potentially of revolution)"; and "Islam from above" and "Islam from below."[53] With the more active involvement in the political process of religious ideals, figures, and groups, striking modifications in religious ideology and organization prompted by political conditions and modifications in political structure have become apparent.

The section on political systems concentrates on the Gush Emunim and Shiism, two religious movements whose current resurgence is closely connected with economic and political factors. Schnall's chapter is a thorough treatment of the involvement of an Israeli religious movement, Gush Emunim, in politics. Schnall traces the political history of the group through early pressure for the annexation of conquered territories and settlement through demonstrations promoting settlement, to actual settlement, participation of Gush members in Israeli politics, the formation of a political party to promote settlement, the creation of an alliance of settlements, and the incorporation of Gush goals and attitudes into government policies. According to Schnall, the main aim of the Gush Emunim is "Jewish settlement and renewal," and government institutions are utilized to the extent that they promote and assist this Zionist goal. If they clash, however, "then Zionism and the pioneering spirit must prevail."[54]

Hegland's article likewise points to the practical political aims, at least in one Iranian village, of adherence to a religious movement. Movement followers were those who were complaining about their economic and living conditions and lack of justice, and about political dissatisfaction with local-level politicians, national government officials, and the political influence of the United States. Here, too, participation in the religious resurgence included the aim of very practical political and economic improvements.

Summary

Several characteristics seem to be shared by the current resurgent movements in Christianity, Islam, and Judaism. For all three, the movements are rooted in religious tradition but with an ideology synthesized with other ideological influences and modified to fit more appropriately into present circumstances. The movements are activist in nature, with a belief that redemption is attained through activity in this world, and with the goal of bringing about changes in that world. All of them aim at establishment on this earth of a community of believers.[55] All have political as well as religious aims, and seek either to transform the existing political system or to exert pressure upon it to bring political process more into conformity with movement ideals.[56] Movement participants do not accept the concept of the separation of religion and politics, but believe that political activity should be informed by religious beliefs and values. Movement participants cooperate to one extent or another with persons having more purely secular goals toward ends important for both groups. In several cases, it is apparent that movement ideology bears the mark of secular and political requirements of less religiously motivated pressure groups.

In all cases, the religious movements are related to an assertion of identity—an effort on the part of previously intimidated or relatively politically passive or inactive persons, groups, or nations to make their voices heard over against formerly dominant ideologies, rulers, groups, nations, or international groupings. Even those Islamic regimes that respond to religious opposition groups by using Islam to legitimize their own rule are at the same time making a statement against Western interference through promotion of the indigenous transnational ideology of Islam.

Participants in the resurgent movements of the three faiths seem to have in common a recent improvement in such resources as education, improved financial well-being and economic opportunity, and a change from relative isolation or encapsulation to greater incorporation into the society in general, with improved opportunity for access to information, ideologies, contacts, and organization and support, generally in an urban setting. Movement participants appear to be enabled rather than deprived.

Before the Iranian Revolution, Western observers discerned a secularizing trend in the Middle East and elsewhere; now, a reemphasis on the relevance of religion in today's world is apparent. However, warned by our surprise at the reemergence of religious ideals, motivation, and organization, we should be aware that trends do not necessarily continue indefinitely. What indications are available to assist our speculation on the longevity of the current religious resurgence?

If educated persons holding values of justice, political freedom, and socio-economic equality joined the religious resurgence partly because organizers catered to such values, the continued commitment of such individuals will be partially contingent upon the continued adherence of religious leaders and organizations to these values. In the case of Iran, of course, many persons holding such liberal values no longer have any real loyalty to the Islamic regime. Rather, they have either left the country or are part of the (for the most part silent) opposition, for many of the same reasons that led them to oppose the shah's regime. They generally find the present government even more repugnant, due to escalated repression, the senseless and tragic war with Iraq, and the inability of the government to maintain living standards and economic opportunities at previous levels. Travelers report that, even among people who took religion seriously before the escalation of the revolutionary movement, religiosity has declined. An anonymous researcher found villagers to be deeply resentful of the regime of mullas, even as early as 1980–81, and turning against Islam itself (pp. 6–8, 24, 25). This same researcher noted a decline in the conventional religiosity of the younger generation in such areas as prayer, fasting, and pilgrimage, compared with their fathers—a decline that the revolution did not reverse. Such youth did not hold with the union of religion and politics. In comparing beliefs of village fathers and sons, this social scientist concluded as follows:

> The emerging overall process of religious evolution moves clearly in the direction of increasingly rationalist, secular, and politicized world views. Since this process is evidently a function of modern education, it can be expected to continue as education spreads and improves. This suggests that fundamentalist, revivalist, and reform movements, as they may emerge, must be considered episodes, sidelines or—like the Mojahedin ideology—intermediate steps, but not the main trends in the long-range evolution of religion in Iran (p. 20).

The strikingly large percentage of young people holding liberal and leftist beliefs, even within a remote village, is an indication of the pervasiveness of the influence of a secular education accomplished within a short time span.

But might not this trend be reversed with the institution of Islamic education? What will be the effect of a sizable number of young people attending foreign universities while their peers are socialized at home in the Islamic institutions? Will the combination of efforts to impose cultural hegemony through education and inculcation of "Islamic values," the lack of a viable competing ideology, the mosque system of controlling access to resources and economic opportunity and enforcing adherence to Islamic behavior standards, and brutal repression succeed in changing the direction of this "religious evolution" and containing political opposition? If so, for how long?

Other research has found indications that religiosity increases among migrants to urban areas.[57] But after such migrants have resided in an urban area for some time, receiving the same educational and economic benefits that have influenced others to adopt secular attitudes, will such a large constituency still be available for religious organizers?

The population explosion in the Middle East and elsewhere has provided another large category, overlapping with the migrants, for the religious resurgence: the youth. What will the attitudes of these young people be as they grow older? If part of the incentive for their participation in religious movements has been rebellion against the older generation, how will the succeeding generation express its independence? Great changes can take place in the attitudes of the young people, even in less than one generation, as Americans are well aware.

The religious resurgence has taken place at present, partly due to the successful synthesizing and adaptation of religious ideologies to fit them to the needs of today's world. What would be the competing ideologies that would succeed in a challenge to these religious ideologies? Given the continued lack of socioeconomic equality and justice, and the dearth of other organizing and motivating ideologies to address these concerns, it seems that religions will have a central role for some time to come. It seems likely, too, as Smart suggests, that religions will play a part in continued international conflicts. Likewise, in those countries where no other forms of oppositional political organization or ideology are permitted, religion will likely continue to give meaning to people struggling to keep courage and hope, and to provide a voice for condemning injustice and describing what should be in its place.

However, if religious forces succeed in gaining power as in Iran, populations might react to subsequent disappointments by turning away from religion. Many Iranians have reported a declining commitment to Islam and decreased involvement in religious ritual, blaming their attitudes on their unhappiness with the Islamic Republic. If this trend of turning away from religion continues, dissatisfied citizens may once again rally around a competing ideology in the hope of constructing a better society. Disillusioned with the bankruptcy of religious ideology, forever hopeful humans might again turn to secular ideology in the continuing search for a means of making a better world.

Notes

1. See Azar Tabari, "The Role of the Clergy in Modern Iranian Politics," in Nikki R. Keddie, ed., *Religion and Politics in Iran: Shi'ism from Quietism to Revolution* (New Haven: Yale University Press, 1983), pp. 47–72; Willem M. Floor, "The Revolutionary Character of the Ulama: Wishful Thinking or Reality?" in Keddie, *Religion and Politics,* pp. 73–97; Ervand Abrahamian, "Structural Causes of the Iranian Revolution," *MERIP Reports* no. 86 (March/April 1980): 3–15; and Mangol Bayat, "Islam in Pahlavi and Post-Pahlavi Iran: A Cultural Revolution?" in John L. Esposito, ed., *Islam and Development: Religion and Sociopolitical Change* (Syracuse, N.Y.: Syracuse University Press, 1980), pp. 87–106.

2. See Farhad Kazemi, *Poverty and Revolution in Iran: The Migrant Poor, Urban Marginality and Politics* (New York: New York University Press, 1980), pp. 63, 91–94.

3. Gustav Thaiss, "Religious Symbolism and Social Change: The Drama of Husein" (Ph.D. diss., Washington University, St. Louis, Mo., 1973), p. 427. See also Howard J. Rotblat, "Social Organization and Development in an Iranian Provincial Bazaar," *Economic Development and Cultural Change* 23, no. 2 (January 1975): 292–305.

4. See Abrahamian, "Structural Causes," p. 25.

5. See Farah Azari, "The Economic Base for the Revival of Islam in Iran," in Farah Azari, ed., *Women of Iran: The Conflict with Fundamentalist Islam* (London: Ithaca Press, 1983), pp. 72–90.

6. Judith Nagata, "Religious Ideology and Social Change: The Islamic Revival in Malaysia," *Pacific Affairs 53,* no. 3 (Fall 1980): 405–39.

7. This exchange of symbolic systems on the part of an interest group is similar to the process studied by Abner Cohen, whereby Hausa traders in Nigeria began organizing by means of adherence to the Tijaniyya order when tribal identification was no longer appropriate; or his later study of change from Creole identity to Masonic Lodge organization by the Americo-Liberian elite of Sierra Leone. Abner Cohen, *Custom and Politics in Urban Africa: A Study of Hausa Migrants in Yoruba Towns* (Berkeley: University of California Press, 1969), and idem, *The Politics of Elite Culture: Explorations in the Dramaturgy of Power in a Modern African Society* (Berkeley: University of California Press, 1981).

8. See also Mary Hooglund (Hegland), "One Village in the Revolution," *MERIP Reports* no. 87 (May 1980): 7–13. Some comments by James Scott appear to have some relevance here: "It is by no means clear that all or even most of the participants in vast popular movements share the ideas which motivate their erstwhile leaders. There is, in fact, good reason to believe that within most popular rebellions which link a radical intelligentsia to a peasantry one will find both the ideas which may justify the label 'nationalist' or 'communist' and a popular revolt with quite divergent visions of order and justice which threatens to usurp the rebellion for its parochial ends." James Scott, "Revolution in the Revolution: Peasants and Commissars," *Theory and Society* 7, nos. 1, 2 (January/March 1979): 97–134.

9. For example, see Hanna Batatu, "Iraq's Underground Shi'i Movements," *MERIP Reports* no. 102 (January 1982): 3–9; idem, "The Muslim Brethren," *MERIP Reports* no. 110 (November–December 1982): 12–20; and Saad Eddin Ibrahim, "Egypt's Islamic Militants," *MERIP Reports* no. 12, no. 2 (February 1982): 5–17.

10. Harvey Cox reaches the same conclusion regarding the American fundamentalists: "Fundamentalism . . . interprets and defends the perceived life interests of an identifiable social group . . . the small town and rural poor." Harvey Cox, *Religion in the Secular City: Toward a Postmodern Theology* (New York: Simon and Schuster, 1984), p. 6.

11. Many sources of information on liberation theology and the changing understanding and interpretation of Shia Islam are now available to the American public; the following are only a small sample: Gustavo Gutierrez, trans. Robert R. Barr, *The Power of the Poor in History* (Maryknoll, New York: Orbis Books, 1983); Gustavo Gutierrez, trans. and eds. Sister Caridad Inda and John Eagleston, *A Theology of Liberation: History, Politics and Salvation* (Maryknoll, New York: Orbis Books, 1973); Leonardo Boff, *Jesus Christ Liberator* (Maryknoll, New York: Orbis Books, 1978); Trevor Beeson and Jenny Pearce, *A Vision of Hope: The Churches and Change in Latin America* (Philadelphia: Fortress Press, 1984); and Martin Lange and Reinhold Iblacker, eds., *Witnesses of Hope: The Persecution of Christians in Latin America* (Maryknoll, New York: Orbis Books, 1981). Some references on Ali Shariati include Ali Shariati, trans. Hamid Algar, *On the Sociology of Islam* (Berkeley, Calif.: Mizan Press, 1979); idem, trans. R. Campbell, *Marxism and Other Western Fallacies* (Berkeley, Calif.: Mizan Press, 1980); idem, trans. Ali A. Behzadnia and Najla Denny, *Hajj* (Houston, Tex.: Free Islamic Literatures, 1980); Ervand Abrahamian, "Shari'ati and the Iranian Revolution," *MERIP Reports* no. 102 (January 1982): 24–28; Shahrough Akhavi, "Shariati's Social Thought," in Nikki R. Keddie, ed., *Religion and Politics in Iran: Shi'ism from Quietism to Revolution* (New Haven: Yale University Press, 1983), pp. 125–44; and Abdulaziz Sachedina, "Ali Shariati: Ideologue of the Iranian Revolution," in John L. Esposito, ed., *Voices of Resurgent Islam* (Oxford: Oxford University Press, 1982), pp. 297–307.

12. See Mangol Bayat, "Islam in Pahlavi," pp. 87–106; idem, "The Iranian Revolution of 1978–79: Fundamentalist or Modern?" *The Middle East Journal* 37, no. 1 (Winter 1983): 30–42; and Nikki R. Keddie and Juan R. I. Cole, "Introduction," in Juan R. I. Cole and Nikki R. Keddie, eds., *Shi'ism and Social Protest* (New Haven: Yale University Press, 1986), pp. 1–29.

13. Bayat, "Islam in Pahlavi," p. 91.

14. Willem M. Floor, "Revolutionary Character," p. 93.

15. Nagata notes the cooperation between secular elites and the ulama in Malaysian rural areas, providing the ulama with financial benefits and the elites with "prestige, legitimacy and blessing." Judith Nagata, "Islamic Revival and the Problem of Legitimacy among Rural Religious Elites in Malaysia," *Man* 17, no. 1 (March 1982): 46, 47.

16. Anon., "Current Political Attitudes in an Iranian Village," *Iranian Studies* 16, nos. 1, 2 (Winter–Spring 1983): 6.

17. Peter Chelkowski, "Dramatic and Literary Aspects of Ta'zieh-Khani-Iranian Passion Play," *Review of National Literatures* 2, no. 1 (Spring 1971): 129. See also L. Bogdanov, "Moharram in Persia," *Visra-Bharati Quarterly* 1 (1923): 118–27, and J. M. Unvala, "The Moharram Festival in Persia," *Studi e Materiale de Storia Delle Relegioni* 3 (1927): 82–96.

18. See Richard Antoun, "The Gentry of a Traditional Peasant Community Undergoing Rapid Technological Change: An Iranian Case Study," *Iranian Studies* 9, no. 1 (Winter 1976): 2–21; Mary-Jo DelVecchio Good, "Social Hierarchy in Provincial Iran: The Case of Qajar Maragheh," *Iranian Studies* 10, no. 3 (Summer 1977): 129–63; Robert A. Fernea, *Shaykh and Effendi: Changing Patterns of Authority Among the el Shabana of Southern Iraq* (Cambridge: Harvard University Press, 1970); Mary Hegland, "Ritual and Revolution in Iran," in Myron J. Aronoff, ed., *Political Anthropology*, vol. 2, *Cultural and Political Change* (New Brunswick: Transaction Books,

1983), 75–100; and Emrys Peters, "A Muslim Passion Play: Key to a Lebanese Village," *The Atlantic Monthly* 198 (1956): 176–80.

19. Mangol Bayat, "Islam in Pahlavi," p. 97; idem, "Tradition and Change in Iranian Socio-Religious Thought," in Michael E. Bonine and Nikki Keddie, eds., *Continuity and Change in Modern Iran* (Albany: SUNY Press, 1981), p. 55; and idem, "Iranian Revolution," p. 35.

20. Anon., "Current Political Attitudes," p. 20.

21. Thomas Bruneau, *The Political Transformation of the Brazilian Catholic Church* (London: Cambridge University Press, 1974), p. 72.

22. Daniel H. Levine, *Religion and Politics in Latin America: The Catholic Church in Venezuela and Colombia* (Princeton, N.J.: Princeton University Press), p. 43.

23. Cox, *Religion in the Secular City*, p. 119.

24. Rosemary Radford Ruether, *To Change the World: Christology and Cultural Criticism* (New York: Crossroad, 1983), p. 28.

25. Cox, *Religion*, p. 140.

26. Mary Hegland, "Two Images of Hussain: Accommodation and Revolution in an Iranian Village," in Nikki R. Keddie, ed., *Religion and Politics in Iran: Shi'ism from Quietism to Revolution* (New Haven: Yale University Press, 1983), pp. 227, 228.

27. Cox, *Religion in the Secular City*, pp. 16, 17, 62.

28. See Albert Hourani, "Conclusion," in James Piscatori, ed., *Islam in the Political Process* (Cambridge: Cambridge University Press, 1983), p. 299; Bassam Tibi, "The Renewed Role of Islam in the Political and Social Development of the Middle East," *The Middle East Journal* 37, no. 1 (Winter 1983): 11; John L. Esposito, "Introduction: Islam and Muslim Politics," in John L. Esposito, *Voices of Resurgent Islam* (New York: Oxford University Press, 1970), p. 11; John Obert Voll, *Islam, Continuity and Change in the Modern World* (Boulder, Colo.: Westview Press, 1982), p. 115; Guenter Levy, *Religion and Revolution* (New York: Oxford University Press, 1974), p. 584; and George Wilbur Braswell, Jr., "A Mosaic of Mullahs and Mosques: Religion and Politics in Iranian Shi'ah Islam" (Ph.D. diss., University of North Carolina, Chapel Hill, 1975).

29. Ervand Abrahamian, "The Causes of the Constitutional Revolution in Iran," *International Journal of Middle East Studies* 10, no. 3 (August 1979): 404, 405, 413; Hanna Batatu, "Iraq's Underground," p. 6; Mary Hegland, "Ritual and Revolution in Iran"; Mary Hooglund (Hegland), "Religious Ritual and Political Struggle in an Iranian Village," *MERIP Reports* 12, no. 1 (January 1982): 10–23; and Chandra Jayawardena, "Ideology and Conflict in Lower Class Communities," *Comparative Studies in Society and History* 10, no. 4 (1968): 413–46. During the Moharram processions of October 1984 in South Lebanon, large pictures of young Shiites killed in the conflict with Israel were displayed. The commemorations of the martyrdom of Imam Hosain were thereby incorporated into the protest against Israeli occupation. Bradley Graham, "Islamic Fundamentalism Rises: W. Beirut Dons the Chador," *Washington Post*, 5 October 1984, pp. A1, A26. See also Salim Nasr, "Roots of the Shi'i Movement," *MERIP Reports*, no. 133 (June 1985): 10–16; Augustus Richard Norton, "Harakat amal [The movement of hope]," in Myron J. Aronoff, ed., *Political Anthropology* vol. 3, *Religion* (New Brunswick, N.J.: Transaction Books, 1984), 3:105–32; and chapters in Juan R. I. Cole and Nikki R. Keddie, *Shi'ism and Social Protest* (New Haven: Yale University Press, 1986).

30. June Nash, "The Passion Play in Maya Indian Communities," *Comparative Studies in Society and History* 10, no. 3 (April 1968): 318–27, Victor Turner, "Hidalgo: History as Social Drama," in Victor Turner, ed., *Dramas, Fields, and Metaphors: Symbolic Action in Human Society* (Ithaca, N.Y.: Cornell University Press, 1978), pp. 98–155; and Cox, *Religion in the Secular City*, pp. 243–61.

31. Ayoub, *Redemptive Suffering in Islam*, p. 19. See also Thaiss, "Religious Symbolism," pp. 264, 324, 325, 400–2, on the intertwining of passive and active, suffering and resistance,

in Shiism, and "The Latent Revolutionary Tendencies of the Shi'a," pp. 239–47, and Mary Hegland on "Accommodation and Revolution: Symbiotic Ideologies," in "Two Images of Husain: Accommodation and Revolution in an Iranian Village," in Nikki R. Keddie, ed., *Religion and Politics in Iran* (New Haven: Yale University Press, 1983), pp. 230–32.

32. In the words of Anthony Wallace, "A given symbol, of course, need not have the same meaning for all; the meaning, indeed, resides in the perceiver rather than in the symbol itself. Thus, the meaning of a symbol may change over time, and of course, differ from person to person and group to group." Anthony Wallace, *Culture and Personality* (New York: Random House, 1970), p. 93. See also Abner Cohen: "One of the major characteristics of symbolic formations is their multiplicity of meaning. . . . A symbol will not do its work if it did not have this ambiguity and flexibility. Indeed it is this very flexibility that ensures a measure of continuity of social organization. . . . Symbols are continuously interpreted and reinterpreted." Abner Cohen, *Two-Dimensional Man: An Essay on the Anthropology of Power and Symbolism in Complex Society* (Berkeley: University of California Press, 1976), pp. 36, 37.

33. Turner, "Hidalgo," p. 153. See also Cox, *Religion in the Secular City,* pp. 244–48, 260.

34. See Thaiss, "Religious Symbolism," pp. 96, 384.

35. Ali Dessouki, *Islamic Resurgence in the Arab World* (New York: Praeger, 1982); Hanna Batatu, "Iraq's Underground Shi'i Movements," p. 3; Saad Eddin Ibrahim, "Anatomy of Egypt's Militant Islamic Groups: Methodological Notes and Preliminary Findings," *International Journal of Middle East Studies* 12, no. 4 (December 1980): 11, 13; Hamid Ansari, "The Islamic Militants in Egyptian Politics," *International Journal of Middle East Studies* 16, no. 1 (March 1984): 123–44; Said Amir Arjomand, "Religion and Revolution in Iran," *Contemporary Sociology* 11, no. 4 (July 1982): 393; and Nikki R. Keddie, *Roots of Revolution: An Interpretive History of Modern Iran* (New Haven: Yale University Press, 1981), p. 246.

36. John H. and Margaret Gulick, "The Domestic Social Environment of Women and Girls in Isfahan, Iran," in Lois Beck and Nikki R. Keddie, eds., *Women in the Muslim World* (Cambridge, Harvard University Press, 1978), p. 512. See also Janet Bauer, "Poor Women and Social Consciousness in Revolutionary Iran," in Guity Nashat, ed., *Women and Revolution in Iran* (Boulder, Colo.: Westview Press, 1983), pp. 141–69; Janet Abu-Lughod, "Migrant Adjustment to City Life: The Egyptian Case," *The American Journal of Sociology* 67, no. 1 (July 1961): 22–32; and Andrea B. Rugh, *Family in Contemporary Egypt* (Syracuse, N.Y.: Syracuse University Press, 1984).

37. See Unni Wikan, "Living Conditions Among Cairo's Poor: A View from Below," *The Middle East Journal* 39, no. 1 (Winter 1985): 7–26; Shahid Javed Burki, "International Migration: Implications for Labor Exporting Countries," *The Middle East Journal* 38, no. 4 (Autumn 1984), 668–84; and David W. Skully, "Lower Oil Prices Have Mixed Meaning for Region's Agricultural Imports," *Middle East and North Africa Situation and Outlook Report,* United States Department of Agriculture (April 1986): 35–39.

38. See Ansari, "Islamic Militants," and Batatu, "Iraq's Underground" and "Muslim Brethren," for example.

39. Farhad Kazemi, *Poverty and Revolution,* pp. 60–62, 64, 83. See also Janet Abu-Lughod and Richard Hay, Jr., eds., *Third World Urbanization* (Chicago: Maaroufa Press, 1977); Ned Levine, "Old Culture–New Culture: A Study of Migrants in Ankara, Turkey," *Social Forces* 51 (March 1973): 355–68; Henry Munson, Jr., *The House of Si Abd Allah: The Oral History of a Moroccan Family* (New Haven: Yale University Press, 1984); Henry Munson, Jr., "Migration and Islamic Militancy: Challenging the Conventional Wisdom" (Paper presented to the Middle East Studies Association Annual Meeting, November 1986); Joan M. Nelson, *Access to Power: Politics and the Urban Poor in Developing Nations* (Princeton, N.J.: Princeton University Press, 1979); Janice E. Perlman, *The Myth of Marginality: Urban Poverty and Politics in Rio De Janeiro* (Berkeley: University of California Press, 1976); Julian Y. Kramer, *Self Help in Soweto: Mutual Aid Societies*

in a South African City (New York: Lilian Barber Press, 1974); and Helen Icken Safa, *The Urban Poor of Puerto Rico: A Study in Development and Inequality* (New York: Holt, Rinehart and Winston, 1974). In her chapter on community solidarity and extracommunity relationships, Safa is very clear about the social integration of the shantytown under study: "The shantytown is a very cohesive community. . . . The cohesion of the shantytown community clearly distinguishes it from the anomie normally thought to characterize urban neighborhoods" (p. 61).

40. Ibrahim, "Anatomy of Egypt," p. 440. See also Henry Munson, Jr., "The Social Base of Islamic Militancy in Morocco," *Middle East Journal*, 40, no. 2 (Spring 1986): 267–84.

41. Mary Elaine Hegland, "Imam Khomaini's Village: Recruitment to Revolution" (Ph.D. diss., SUNY Binghamton, 1986).

42. Vatikiotis also notes: "It is modernization which in the last thirty years produced the new urban masses that now express their economic and political grievances in Islamic terms." P. J. Vatikiotis, "Islamic Resurgence: A Critical View," in Alexander S. Cudsi and Ali E. Hillal Dessouki, eds., *Islam and Power* (Baltimore: The Johns Hopkins University Press, 1981), p. 175. John Voll states: "The potential for mass mobilization that has resulted from modernization has played a significant role in the transformation of radicalism in the Islamic World." Voll, *Islam, Continuity and Change* . . . p. 279.

43. Hegland found this to be the case in her own research in an Iranian village. Villagers respected education and admired and listened to the young people who traveled to Shiraz (or even further away) for schooling. Several villagers commented that it was the educated young who had helped them to see the light about the shah — that they themselves were illiterate and so hadn't understood. Nagata found this to be the case in Malaysia, where educated young people used this advantage to reinforce their authority for revivalist activities. Both rural and urban Malays were in awe of university degrees. Nagata, "Islamic Revival," p. 51.

44. A fragment of a life history from Antoun's field research illustrates the contribution of educated youth with rural backgrounds to Islamic resurgence. A young Jordanian villager, the son of a lower-echelon local civil court clerk from a tribal background, after receiving an undergraduate degree at Cairo University in the 1970s, went to England. There he earned his own way by working (after being cut off financially by his father), saved money, registered at Leeds University, and earned a Ph.D. in Linguistics. His dissertation was on the Arabic dialects of the Jordan valley. Upon his return to Jordan in the early 1980s he became a professor of linguistics at Yarmouk University in northern Jordan, not far from his native village. While in northern England, he had become involved with a small group of Muslims who met regularly to study the works of the famous fundamentalist Pakistani scholar Abu al-A'la Mawdudi. At one and the same time, this son-of-the-village, product of an economic backwater in Jordan, gained eminence and respect as a result of his Western education and became involved in Islamic resurgence while still in the West, an involvement that continued in a university setting on his return to Jordan. This highly educated young man has become an exemplar for other villagers in two respects, simultaneously: as a successful middle-class professional and as a leader of Islamic resurgence. His is a personal odyssey dramatizing the point that modernization and Islamic resurgence are not only quite reconcilable but complementary. On this point, see also Munson, "Social Base . . ."; Ibrahim, "Anatomy of Egypt," p. 446; Batatu, "Iraq's Underground Shi'i Movements," p. 3; idem, "Muslim Brethren," p. 20; Ervand Abrahamian, "The Guerrilla Movement in Iran, 1963–1977," *MERIP Reports* no. 86 (March/April 1980): 4; and, Bayat, "Islam in Pahlavi . . . ," p. 100.

45. According to Nagata, most leaders and many of the members of the three main organizations of the *dakwah* movement in Malaysia were drawn "from the ranks of the young, middle classes and highly educated professional Malays." Nagata, "Islamic Revival . . .", p. 51.

46. Ervand Abrahamian, "Iran in Revolution: The Oppositional Forces," *MERIP Reports* 9, nos. 2, 3 (March/April 1979): 8.

47. Nagata, "Religious Ideology . . ." p. 422.

48. Ervand Abrahamian, "Shari'ati and the Iranian Revolution," *MERIP Reports* no. 102 (January 1982): 24–30.

49. See anon., "Current Political Attitudes," p. 7. Regarding the Muslim Brethren in Syria, for example, Batatu notes that their demands for "political emancipation" and "freedom" are "obviously drawn from the moral armories of classical liberalism." Batatu, "Muslim Brethren," p. 13. Vatikiotis states that "their [the new urban masses'] demands are modern, while their formulation remains traditionally Islamic." Vatikiotis, "Islamic Resurgence," p. 175. According to Mangol Bayat, "Three-quarters of a century of modernizing reforms [in Iran] were not fruitless. Perhaps one of the most important accomplishments has been the creation of sizable middle and lower middle classes. Members of these classes are modern in outlook by virtue of their education and professional occupations. They are the carriers of change and, through them, modern values and benefits have 'trickled down' to the lower classes." Mangol Bayat, review of *Roots of Revolution: an Interpretive History of Modern Iran,* by Nikkie R. Keddie, *The Middle East Journal* 37, no. 1 (Winter 1983): 102.

50. Anon., "Current Political Attitudes," pp. 13, 14.

51. For further discussion in this area see Hegland, "Khomaini's Village," especially ch. 9, "Peasants and Commuters in the Revolutionary Process: Economic Alternatives," pp. 519–81.

52. Nagata, "Religious Ideology . . .", pp. 427, 428.

53. Richard Antoun, review of *The Politics of Islamic Reassertion,* ed. Mohammed Ayoub, *American-Arab Affairs,* no. 4 (Spring 1983): 149; Hourani, "Conclusion" p. 229; and Dessouki, "Islamic Resurgence . . ."

54. For several other sources on the Gush Emunim, see David Newman, *The Impact of Gush Emunim: Politics and Settlement in the West Bank* (New York: St. Martin's Press, 1985); Kevin A. Avruch, "Traditionalizing Israeli Nationalism: The Development of Gush Emunim," *Political Psychology, Journal of the International Society of Political Psychology* 1, no. 1 (Spring 1979): 47–57; Lilly Weissbrod, "Gush Emunim Ideology—From Religious Doctrine to Political Action," *Middle Eastern Studies* 18, no. 3 (1982): 265–75; David J. Biale, "Mysticism and Politics in Modern Israel: The Messianic Ideology of Araham Isaac Ha-Cohen Kook," in Peter Merkl and Ninian Smart, eds., *Religion and Politics in the Modern World* (New York: New York University Press, 1983); Arthur Hertzberg, "The Religious Right in the State of Israel," *The Annals of the American Academy of Political and Social Science-Religion and the State: The Struggle for Legitimacy and Power* 483 (January 1986): 84–92; and Myron J. Aronoff, "Gush Emunim: The Institutionalization of a Charismatic, Messianic, Religious-Political Revitalization Movement in Israel," Myron J. Aronoff, ed., *Political Anthropology Volume III–Religion and Politics* (New Brunswick, N.J.: Transaction Books, 1984): 63–84.

55. Said Arjomand has argued that even this emphasis on community, the ummah, in the thinking of Ali Shariati derives from his study of the French sociologist, Emile Durkheim, again demonstrating the pervasive influence of Western thinking in Shariati's theology. Said Amir Arjomand, "*A La Recherche de la Conscience Collective:* Durkheim's Ideological Impact in Turkey and Iran," *The American Sociologist* 17, no. 2 (May 1982): 94–102.

56. See also Cox's comments on the similarities in aim of the Christian fundamentalists and the liberation theologians. Cox, *Religion in the Secular City,* pp. 60–62.

57. Oscar Lewis, "Some Perspectives on Urbanization with Special Reference to Mexico City," in Aidan Southall, ed., *Urban Anthropology: Cross-Cultural Studies of Urbanization* (New York: Oxford University Press, 1973), p. 131.

GLOSSARY

Amana
: alliance formed among the Jewish settlements in the West Bank

anomie
: feeling of alienation or isolation from society or social structures

Ashkenazic
: European Jewish

ayatollah
: high-level Shiah cleric

the Azhar
: Islamic university in Cairo, in operation for centuries

bazaar
: market area of an Iranian city or town, dominated by shops; or, the social and political groups of merchants and shopkeepers

charismatic
: having extraordinary personal characteristics that facilitate leadership

dakwah
: "renewed commitment to the Faith"—the Islamic resurgence in Malaysia

development
: economic growth and technological innovation and their social organizational correlates

evangelical
: Christian who believes in the literal interpretation of the Bible and claims to have been "born again"

fundamentalism
: religious attitude stressing fundamental or basic principles of a faith, often through adherence to the literal statements of the most important scripture, such as the Bible or Quran

gharbzadegi
: Persian term meaning "struck" (or contaminated) by the West

guru (sing. & pl.)
: religious teacher(s) in Malaysia

Gush Emunim
: religious movement in Israel that has as its main aim the permanent Jewish settlement of the occupied Palestinian territories

hadith
: Tradition of the Prophet

Hassan al-Banna
: founder of the Muslim Brethren

imam
: in Shiah Islam, one of the twelve lineal successors to the Prophet Mohammad; or, more generally, a leader of a Shiah religious community

Imam Hosain	Shiah leader martyred on the Plains of Kerbala in A.D. 680
jihad	a striving or struggling against evil
kampung	Malaysian village
kibbutz/im	Jewish collective settement/s in Israel
Knesset	Israeli parliament
liberation theology	form of Christianity modified by Latin and South Americans, emphasizing political activity to improve conditions for oppressed peoples
liberation Shiism	Shiism as modified by Ali Shariati and others, teaching that Shiahs should resist tyranny and injustice
martyr	person who prefers death to giving up religious principles
Moharram	Shiah month of mourning for the martyrdom of Imam Husain
mosque	building used for worship and religious gatherings by Muslims, corresponding to church and temple
mulla	Iranian Muslim preacher
Muslim Brethren	religious organization founded in the 1920s in Egypt, which advocated social and political reform
nationalism	awareness of, loyalty to, and identification with a country and its government, along with the latter-day assumption that all citizens are able to participate in policy formation and receive benefits distributed by the government
Peace Now	Israeli organization pressuring for compromise over the captured territories and improved relations with neighboring Arab countries
populist	relying upon and catering to the support of the masses
religious nationalism	the modified nationalism found in some contemporary countries wherein national loyalty and identity are based on a religious ideology
religious resurgence	rising importance and visibility of religion; increased impact of religion in political life
secular	nonreligious; temporal; based on nonreligious ideology
secularization	the trend of decreasing relevance and visibility of religious leaders, organizations, activities, beliefs, structures and publications
shahid	"witness" or martyr in the Muslim faith

shaykh	Egyptian preacher
Shiism	branch of Islam that rejected election of the successors to the Prophet Mohammad and insisted on the lineal succession to the Prophet, Muhammad, through his daughter, Fatma, and his son-in-law, Ali, and on the mediation of the imams and their descendants
Shiite	a follower of Shiism
shirk	term for polytheism in Islam
Sunni	the majority branch of Islam who acknowledge the first four caliphs, honor the six "authentic" books of tradition, and belong to any of the four accepted schools of jurisprudence
tajdid	renewal
tawhid	the oneness and unity of God
ulama	Islamic scholars or specialists
usrah	religious group or cell, often based at a university, formed by persons involved with the Malaysian Islamic resurgence
yishuv	the Jewish community in Palestine/Israel in all of its aspects (social, political, economic, etc.)
West Bank	area west of the Jordan River wrested by the Israelis from Jordanian control in the 1967 war; remains in contention between Israelis and Arabs
Zionism	Jewish ideology that teaches the necessity and religious importance of Jews returning to "Eretz Israel" (the land of Israel) or geographical Palestine, establishing a Jewish state, and maintaining political control of the area

INDEX

Mitchell, Richard, 140

Mobilization, political: of evangelicals in U.S., 27–30; for revolution by knifing in Aliabad (Iran), 207

Modernity: economic, in Islam, 141; nonwestern, 138–39

Modernization, 135–36

Modesty: in the Iranian Revolution, 202–3

Moral Majority, 223–24, 226; lack of influence of, 30–32; and political mobilization, 27–29

Mosques: in Egypt, 4; government, 45–46; in Minya (Egypt), 47; number of, in Egypt, 63n.29; organization of, 45–49; popular, 46–47; and preachers, 43–44; as pulpits for political communication, 40, 42; and revolutionary activity in Aliabad, Iran, 202; of Shaykh Abu Bakr, 48–49; of Shaykh Ali, 56–57

Mossadeq (Iranian prime minister), 200, 235

Movement, Islamic: Sadat represses press coverage of, 37

Movements, religious, 2, 3, 78–79; and change, 3; charismatic, 5; and class struggle, 151; cycles of, 109; in Egypt, 145–66; explanations for, 2–3, 146–47; and ideology, 147–49; in Israel, 145–46; Mizrahi, 152; and religious texts, 148; similarities in, 248

Movements, social: and change, 3; explanations for, 2–3

Mubarak, President: and Islamic activists, 40

Muhammad, Prophet, 70–72, 96, 98, 112

Muhammad Ahmad. See Mahdi, the

Mujahidin: and *tawhid*, 137–38

Mulla (in Aliabad, Iran from Qom): disagreements with, 204–5; organizing dissent in Aliabad, 199–200. See also Clerics; Preachers; *Ulama*

Muslims: and "failure of the West," 7, 127–42; liberated by failure of the West, 133–34; in Malaysia, 6; and martyrdom, 5; new partner in dialogue for Muslim scholars, 134–35; and shift away from secularism, 137;

Muslims (*cont.*)
and the West in 18th century, 128–29; and the West in 19th century, 129; and the West by 20th century, 129–30

Muslim Brotherhood, 140, 148–50, 230; and defeat in Six Day War, 36; in Egypt, 36, 139, 161–64; social bases of, 160–61; in the Sudan, 139, 146, 150; suppressed by Nasser, 36

Mussolini, Benito, 229, 231

Nagata, Judith, 5–6, 235

Nasser, Gamal Abdul, 39, 56, 81, 131, 157; charisma shaken by Six Day War, 36–37; and control of Islamic institutions by state, 35–37; manipulation of Egyptians by, 37; support of, by Shaykh Abu Bakr, 48; suppresses the Muslim Brothers, 36

Nathan of Gaza, 101–3

National Religious Party (of Israel), 169–71, 185–87; and generational conflict, 170

Nationalism, 10, 135, 224–25, 227; Arab, 146–47, 150–51, 157; corporate Arab, 162; decline of secular, populist, and religious resurgence, 7; Jewish, 9; Persian, 229; religious, 8; religious in Egypt, 145–66; religious in Israel, 145–66; religious in the West, 166n.33; secular, 8, 156–57

Neighborhoods: in Malaysia, 112

Neotraditionalist, 228

Networks: of *bazaris* in Iranian religious dissent, 234; of *dakwah* cadres in Malaysia, 122; and fundamentalism, 118–19, 121–23; of Malaysian students, 118; and resurgence in Malaysia, 6. See also Groups, face-to-face; Groups, peer

Oil boom, 132; and freedom from traditional social bonds, 243–46; and improved resources for traders and clerics, 244–45; and improvement in material conditions, 242; and job opportuni-

RELIGIOUS RESURGENCE

was composed in 10 on 12 Garamond on Digital Compugraphic equipment
by Metricomp;
printed by sheet-fed offset on 50-pound, acid-free Glatfelter Antique Cream,
Smyth sewn and bound over binder's boards in Joanna Arrestox B,
by Maple-Vail Book Manufacturing Group, Inc.;
with dust jackets printed in two colors
by Niles and Phipps Lithographers;
designed by Will Underwood;
and published by

SYRACUSE UNIVERSITY PRESS
SYRACUSE, NEW YORK 13244-5160